Solutions Manual

LARRY NYHOFF

C++
AN INTRODUCTION TO COMPUTING
SECOND EDITION

JOEL ADAMS   SANFORD LEESTMA   LARRY NYHOFF

PRENTICE HALL, Upper Saddle River, NJ 07458

Publisher: Alan Apt
Production Editor: Shea Oakley
Supplement Cover Designer: Liz Nemeth
Special Projects Manager: Barbara A. Murray
Supplement Cover Manager: Paul Gourhan
Manufacturing Buyer: Donna Sullivan
Editorial Assistant: Kate Kaibni
Acquisitions Editor: Laura Steele

Printed in the United States of America

10 9 8 7 6 5 4 3 2 1

ISBN 0-13-775511-2

Prentice-Hall International (UK) Limited, *London*
Prentice-Hall of Australia Pty. Limited, *Sydney*
Prentice-Hall Canada, Inc., *London*
Prentice-Hall Hispanoamericana, S.A., *Mexico*
Prentice-Hall of India Private Limited, *New Delhi*
Prentice-Hall of Japan, Inc., *Tokyo*
Simon & Schuster Asia Pte. Ltd., *Singapore*
Editora Prentice-Hall do Brazil, Ltda., *Rio de Janeiro*

INTRODUCTION

Answers to all of the written exercises of the text *C++: An Introduction to Computing* 2e are included in this manual. Answers to most of the programming problems are also given. For the others, some indication is given of the degree of difficulty and/or what language features are used; algorithms, functions, program segments, and hints are given in some cases.

The solutions given for programming problems are intended to indicate to you, the instructor, what a problem requires for its solutions and some techniques that can be used in solving it. If you choose to present some of them as examples in class, you should rewrite them according to your programming style and preferences.

Comments and corrections about the solutions or the text should be sent to any of the authors:

Joel Adams (616-957-9562, adams@calvin.edu)
Sanford Leestma (616-957-6350, lees@calvin.edu)
Larry Nyhoff (616-957-6351, nyhl@calvin.edu)

Department of Computer Science
Calvin College
3201 Burton SE
Grand Rapids, MI 49546

My thanks to students Ted Pohler and Jon Fife for helping with some of the solutions. My sincere thanks also to former student Ed Ball for the superb job he did in preparing the solutions for the first edition of this text, many of which were picked up and modified in varying degrees for this edition.

Larry Nyhoff

CONTENTS

Chapter 0: Beginning Snapshots

Exercises — Part of the Picture: The History of Computing

1. The mechanization of arithmetic and the stored program concept.

2. D, E, T, U, Q, W, R, G, F, M, S, C, P, L, N, O, V, B, A, H, J, K, I.

3. Al-Khowarizm: Developed some of the first step-by-step procedures for doing computations. The word *algorithm* is derived from his name.

4. William Oughtred: Invented a circular slide rule. Slide rules were used be scientists and engineers until the computer made them obsolete.

5. Charles Babbage: Invented the Difference Engine and the Analytical Engine. He has been called the *Father of Computing*.

6. Blaise Pascal: French mathematician who invented one of the first mechanical calculators, called the Pascaline.

7. John von Neumann: Credited with the development of the stored program concept.

8. Herman Hollerith: Designed a system for processing information stored on punch cards. These systems were used to compile the 1890 U.S. census statistics.

9. Joseph Jaquard: Invented an early automated machine called the Jaquard Loom, which was programmed with punch cards.

10. Gottfired Willhelm von Liebniz: Invented an improved adding machine that could also do all four basic operations and was more accurate than Pascal's.

11. John Atanasoff: The first to develop a fully electronic computer (in 1939).

12. Steven Jobs and Steve Wozniak: tFounded the Apple Computer Company, which produced the popular Apple II out of a production facility located in a garage.

13. Robert Noyce: a pioneer in the development of transistors and a cofounder of the Intel Corporation.

14. J. P. Eckert: He and J. W. Mauchly constructed the ENIAC and went on to build the UNIVAC (in 1946).

15. John Backus: He and a team of 13 other programmers developed FORTRAN, one of the first high-level languages to gain widespread acceptance.

16. Alan Turing: Developed the universal machine concept, which formed the basis of computability theory.

17. Konrad Zuse: A German engineer who developed a series of computers that used binary arithmetic.

18. Grace Mary Hopper: A programmer for the Mark I and led the development of COBOL. She also discovered the first computer bug, which is still preserved in the Smithsonian Institution.

19. Ken Thompson: Developed the UNIX operating system.

20. Dennis Ritchie: Developed the C programming language

21. Bjarne Stroustrup: Developed the language C with Classes, adding object-oriented and other features to C, which soon developed into C++.

22. ENIAC: Electronic Numerical Integrator And Computer, the best known of the early electronic computers.

23. Analytical Engine: A sophisticated machine designed by Charles Babbage whose design had many of the same components as modern-day computers.

24. Jacquard loom: Early use of a "program" to control a mechanical device.

25. UNIVAC: The first commercially available electronic computer, sold to the U.S. census bureau in 1951.

26. Mark I: An early electromechanical computer, built in the United States in 1944.

27. MITS Altair 8800: The first computer to use a microprocessor. It was made from a hobby kit.

28. Apple II: The PC that led to the development of Apple Computer. It came assembled and complete with monitor and keyboard.

29. Cray I: The first supercomputer.

30. DOS: Microsoft's first operating system.

31. Java: A modern C++-based object-oriented programming language in which applications can be compiled for any platform with no modification. It is popular in web-based applets because different platforms can all use them.

32. First generation: Early computers that used vacuum tubes; e.g. ENIAC, UNIVAC.
    Second generation: Vacuum tubes replaced by transistors, making the machines smaller, less expensive, and more reliable.
    Third generation: Used integrated circuits and began implementing multiprogramming and timesharing schemes.
    Fourth generation: Use very-large-scale integrated circuits, making computers even smaller and faster.

Exercises — Part of the Picture: Introduction to Computer Organization

1. B, D, E, F, G, H, I, C, D, A

2. stored program concept: The concept of storing a program in the memory of the computer rather than on some external media such as punched cards.

3. FORTRAN: FORmula TRANslation, one of the first high-level programming languages. It is still widely used for scientific programming.

4. ALU: That part of the central processing unit that performs basic arithmetic and logical operations.

5. CPU: Controls the operation of the entire computer system, performs arithmetic/logic operations, stores and retrieves instructions and data.

6. peripheral devices: Hardware devices such as terminals, printers, disk drives, and tape drives that are not part of the central processing unit.

7.   bit: A digit, 0 or 1, in the binary number system.

8.   byte: A group of bits, usually eight.

9.   word: A basic storage unit consisting of a machine-dependent number of bits (commonly 16 or 32) whose contents are directly accessible by means of its address.

10. K: $2^{10} = 1024$, a common unit used in counting bytes of memory.

11. Megabyte (MB): 1024 K. [1 gigabyte (GB) = 1024 MB and 1 terabyte (TB) = 1024 GB.]

12. source program: A program written in a high-level language such as C++.

13. object program: A machine language program produced by a compiler.

14. machine language: A language used directly by a particular computer in all of its calculations and processing.

15. assembly language: A programming language similar to machine language which used mnemonics in place of opcodes and variable names in place of numeric addresses.

16. An assembler translates assembly language programs into machine language programs.

17. A compiler translates source programs into object programs.

18. A linker connects items that are outside the object file o produce the executable program.

Exercises — Part of the Picture: Ethics and Computing

1.   ACM: Association for Computer Machinery, a professional organization for computer science.

2.   chain mail: Messages that request each recipient to forward the message (often accompanied with something) to several other user.

3.   copyright: The right of an author to print and publish work, exclusively of all other persons.

4.   fair use: Legal use of a (small) portion of a copyrighted work and attributing it to the author

5.   firewall: Systems that monitor traffic between networks to ensure that all network traffic is legitimate.

6.   hacker: Today it means a computer criminal. It used to refer to people who wrote poor programs and later to a person who liked computers.

7.   IEEE: Institute of Electrical and Electronics Engineers

8.   patent: A document that secures the rights to an invention

9.   piracy: Duplicating software without paying for it.

10. rogue software: Software designed with malicious intent. Viruses and Worms are examples of this kind of software.

11. RSI: Repetitive stress injury

12. site license: A license that allows software to be installed on a network

13. telecommuting: Working for an employer from a computer-equipped office in one's home

14. Trojan horse: Rogue software that appears to have a useful purpose, but may or may not actually be useful and carries out malicious activity on the system.

15. virus: A program that infects computers and usually does something harmful as well.

16. worm: A program that replicates itself until it overwhelms a computer's resources.

Chapter 1: Problem Solving and Software Engineering

Exercises 1.3

1. Behavior: A prompt for the length of the side of a square should appear on the screen. The user should enter this length at the keyb oard. The perimeter and the area of the square should be computed and appear on the screen.

    Objects: *length*, a double variable to store the side length
    perimeter, a double variable to store the calculated perimeter
    area, a double variable to store the calculated area

    Operations: i. Output a prompt for the length of a side of the square
    ii. Input a real value from cin and store it in in *length*
    iii. Compute *perimeter* and *area*
    Multiply real values
    perimeter = 4 * *length*)
    area = *length* * *length*

    iv. Output *perimeter* and *area* to cout

    Algorithm: 1. Output a prompt for the length of a side of the square to cout.
    2. Input a real value from cin and store it in *length*.
    3. Compute p*erimeter* = 4 * *length*.
    4. Compute *area* = *length* * *length*.
    5. Output *perimeter* and *area* to cout.

2. Behavior: A prompt for a temperature on the Celsius scale should appear on the screen. The user should enter this temperature at the keyb oard. The corresponding temperature on the Fahrenheit should be computed and appear on the screen.

    Objects: *tempCelsius*, a double variable to store the Celsius temperature
    tempFahrenheit , a double variable to store the Fahrenheit temperature
    9, 5, and 32, real constants in the conversion formula

    Operations: i. Output a prompt for the temperature on the Celsius scale
    ii. Input a real value from cin and store it in in *tempCelsius*
    iii. Compute *tempFahrenheit*
    Multiply and add real values
    tempFahrenheit = 9 / 5 * *tempCelsiu* + 32
    iv. Output *tempFahrenheit* to cout

    Algorithm: 1. Output a prompt for the temperature on the Celsius scale to cout.
    2. Input a real value from cin and store it in *tempCelsius*.
    3. Compute *tempFahrenheit* = 9 / 5 * *tempCelsiu* + 32.
    4. Output *tempFahrenheit* to cout.

3. Read the documentation of your compiler for information on entering and executing a C++ program.

4.

```
/* This program adds and subtracts the values of variables Alpha and Beta.
 * Output (screen): The values alpha + beta and alpha - beta
 ********************************************************************/

#include <iostream.h>              // cout, cin, <<, >>

int main()
{
    int alpha = 1723,              // the first value
        beta = 2057,               // the second value
        difference = alpha - beta, // find their difference
        sum = alpha + beta;        // find their sum

    // output the resulting value
    cout << "\nThe sum of " << alpha << " and " << beta
         << " is " << sum << ".\n";
    cout << "\nThe difference of " << alpha << " and " << beta
         << " is " << difference << ".\n";

    return 0;
}
```

5.

```
/* This program calculates the perimeter and area of a square with
 * a given side.
 *
 * Input (keyboard):  The length of the side of a square
 * Output (screen):   The perimeter and area of the square
 ********************************************************************/

#include <iostream.h>              // cout, cin, <<, >>

int main()
{
    double  length;               // length of a side

    cout << "\nPlease enter the length of a side of the square: ";

    cin >> length;

    double perimeter = 4.0 * length,
           area = length * length;

    cout << "\nThe perimeter of the square is " << perimeter << ".\n"
         << "\nThe area of the square is " << area << ".\n";

    return 0;
}
```

6.
```
/* This program converts a temperature on the Celsius scale to the
   corresponding Fahrenheit temperature.

   Input  (keyboard):  A temperature on the Celsius scale
   Output (screen):    The corresponding Fahrenheit temperature
-----------------------------------------------------------------*/

#include <iostream.h>            // cout, cin, <<, >>

int main()
{
    double tempCelsius;                // the Celsius temperature

    cout << "\nPlease enter a temperature in Celsius : ";
    cin >> tempCelsius;

    double tempFahrenheit = Celcius * 9 / 5 + 32;

    cout << "\nThe corresponding Fahrenheit temperature is "
         << tempFahrenheit << ".\n";

    return 0;
}
```

Chapter 2: Types and Expressions

Exercises 2.2

1. valid
2. invalid; - is not a legal character in an identifier
3. valid
4. valid
5. invalid; identifiers cannot begin with a number
6. valid
7. invalid; . is not a legal character in an identifier
8. valid
9. invalid; identifiers cannot begin with a number
10. invalid; / is not a legal character in an identifier
11. invalid; $ is not a legal character in an identifier
12. valid
13. valid
14. valid
15. valid
16. invalid; identifiers cannot contain spaces

17. integer	18. real	19. real	20. neither
21. neither	22. real	23. neither	24. neither
25. integer	26. neither	27. real	28. real
29. neither	30. neither	31. neither	32. real
33. neither	34. neither	35. real	36. neither

37. valid	38. valid	39. invalid	40. valid
41. valid	42. valid	43. valid	44. valid
45. valid	46. valid	47. valid	48. invalid

49.
```
const double RATE = 1.25;
```

50.
```
const double REGULAR_HOURS = 40.0, OVERTIME_FACTOR = 1.5;
```

51.
```
const int YEAR = 1776;
const char FEMALE = 'F',
          BLANK = ' ';
```

52.
```
const int ZERO = 0;
const char ASTERISK = '*',
APOSTROPHE = '\'';
```

53.
```
double item, number, job;
```

54.
```
int shoeSize;
```

55.
```
double mileage;
unsigned cost, distance;
```

```
long alpha, beta;
char code;
double root;
```

```
57.   int numberOfDeposits = 0,
          numberOfChecks = 0;
      double totalDeposits = 0.0,
             totalChecks = 0.0,
             serviceCharge = 0.25;

58.   char symbol_1 = ë í, symbol_2 = ë;í, debug = ëTí;

59.   const int YEAR = 1997;
      const double MAXIMUM_SALARY = 99999.99;
      int prime, number;
      char initial;
```

Exercises 2.3

1. 1   2.   0

3. 0.9   4.   0

5. 0.5   6.   1

7. 2   8.   2

9. 1   10. 2

11. 12   12. 12.5

13. 0   14. –15.0

15. –15.0   16. 1 8

17. 3   18. 1

19. 3   20. 4.0

21. 4.0   22. ERROR; `sqrt(-4.0)` is undefined

23. 2   24. 1

25. 8.0   26. 2

27. 2.66666 . . .   28. 20.0

29. 5.1   30. 4.0

31. 6.25   32. 3.0

33. `10 + 5 * B - 4 * A * C`

34. `(3 * (4 - n)) / (2 * (m * m + n * n))`

35. `sqrt(a + 3 * b * b)`

36. `sqrt((m + n) / 2)`

37. `abs(A / (m + n))`

38. `exp(x * log(a))`

39. `double(int(amount * 100.0 + 0.5)) / 100.0`

40. **(a)** `double(int(12.342 * 100.0 + 0.5)) / 100.0`
       `= double(int(1234.7)) / 100.0 = 1234.0 / 100.0 = 12.34`

(b) `double(int(12.348 * 100.0 + 0.5)) / 100.0`
    `= double(int(1235.3)) / 100.0 = 1235.0 / 100.0 = 12.35`

(c) `double(int(12.345 * 100.0 + 0.5)) / 100.0`
    `= double(int(1235.0)) / 100.0 = 1235.0 / 100.0 = 12.35`

(d) `double(int(12.340 * 100.0 + 0.5)) / 100.0`
    `= double(int(1234.5)) / 100.0 = 1234.0 / 100.0 = 12.34`

(e) `double(int(13.0 * 100.0 + 0.5)) / 100.0`
    `= double(int(1300.5)) / 100.0 = 1300.0 / 100.0 = 13`

41. `Cost = double(int(Cost * 10.0 + 0.5)) / 10.0;`

42. `Cost = double(int(Cost * 1000.0 + 0.5)) / 1000.0;`

Exercises 2.4

1. true   2. false   3. false   4. true   5. true

6. false   7. false   8. false   9. false   10. true

11-13.

a	b	a || !b	!(a && b)	!a || !b
false	false	true	true	true
false	true	false	true	true
true	false	true	true	true
true	true	true	false	false

14-16.

a	b	c	(a && b) || c	a && (b || c)	(a && b) || (a && c)
false	false	false	false	false	false
false	false	true	true	false	false
false	true	false	false	false	false
false	true	true	true	false	false
true	false	false	false	false	false
true	false	true	true	true	true
true	true	false	true	true	true
true	true	true	true	true	true

17. `x > 3`

18. `(2 < y) && (y < 5)`

19. `(r < 0) && (z > 0)`

20. `(Alpha > 0) && (Beta > 0)`

21. `Alpha * Beta > 0`

22. `(-5 < x) && (x < 5)`

23. `(a < 6) || (a > 10)`

24. `(p == q) && (q == r)`

25. `((x < 3) && !(y < 3)) || (!(x < 3) && (y < 3))`

26. `a && b && !c`

27. `a && (b || c)`

28. `(a && !b) || (!a && b)`

Exercises 2.6

1. valid

2. invalid; left side must be a variable

3. invalid; `char` variables can contain only one character

4. valid

5. valid

6. invalid (unless A is a variable variable)

7. invalid; left side must be a single variable

8. valid, but not useful and not recommended

9. valid

10. valid

11. invalid (unless A is a variable name)

12. valid, but not usually recommended

13. valid

14. valid

15. valid

16. invalid; ++ is defined only for integers

17. 15

18. 7

19. 6

20. 6

21. 0.390625

22. 0

23. (the ASCII character 4; not very useful)

24. '2'

25. '4'

26. (the ASCII character 4; not very useful)

27. 2

28. 50 (the ASCII value of '2'; not very useful)

29. 50 (the ASCII value of '2'; not very useful)

30. 10

31. 51 (the ASCII value of '3'; not very useful)

32. 3

33. true

34. true

35. true: `1 < int1 < 20` is evaluated as `(1 < int1) < 20; 1 < int1` produced `true` which is represented as 1, so the expression becomes `1 < 20` which is true.

36. true

37. `number += 77;`

38. `number -= 3;`

39. `number += 2 * number;`

40. `number += number % 10;`

41. `number -= int(x);`

42. `distance = rate * time;`

43. `xCoord += deltaX;`

44. `resistance = 1 / ((1 / res1) + (1 / res2) + (1 / res3));`

45. `area = 0.5 * b * h;`

46. `price = double(stocknumber % 1000) / 100.0;`

47. `tax = double(int(tax + 0.5))`

Answers will vary for 48-50.

48. $a = 2, b = 3, c = 2; 2 * (3 / 2) = 2 * 1 = 2$, but $(2 * 3) / 2 = 6 / 2 = 3$

49. $a = 4, b = 2; 4 / 2 = 2$, but $4 * (1 / 2) = 4 * 0 = 0$

50. $a = 2, b = 3, c = 4; (2 + 3) / 4 = 5 / 4 = 1$, but $(2 / 4) + (3 / 4) = 0 + 0 = 0$

Exercises 2.8

Answes for 1-14 may vary slightly, depending on your compiler. Note that _ denotes a blank.

1.
   ```
   436437438
   ```

2.
   ```
   alpha =_____-567
   ____0.0004
   _0.0004
   ```

3.
   ```

   ___-6e+02
   __436
   Tolerance:__0.0004
   ```

4.
   ```

   alpha =_____-567.39
   beta =0.0004
   rho =___436
   -----------127
   ```

5.
   ```
   Tolerance =0.0004436-567
   ```

6.
   ```
   ___-6e+03__-6e+03___16____2
   ```

7.
   ```
   rho =_____436*****
   ```

8.
   ```
   ___-5.7e+02____0.0004
   ```

9.
   ```
   ___-5.7e+02____0.0004new balance =2.6e+03 c_____8
   ```

10.
   ```
   i =-------------15j =_____8
   ------15 --------------8
   ```

For 11-14 it may be necessary with some older versions of C++ to add the statement

```
cout << setiosflags(ios::fixed | ios::showpoint);
```

before the given output statements:

11. ```
    cout << setw(8) << setprecision(4) << r1
         << "    " << c
         << setw(5) << n1 << '\n'
         << n2 << "PDQ"
         << setprecision(5) << r2;
    ```

12. ```
    cout << setw(8) << setprecision(3) << r1
         << setw(11) << setprecision(4) << r2
         << "***" << n1 << "   " << c << '\n'
         << setw(9) << setprecision(2) << r1
         << setw(4) << n1 << n2;
    ```

13. ```
    cout << "Roots are " << setw(7) << setprecision(3) << r1
         << " and " << setw(8) << setprecision(5) << r2;
    ```

14. ```
    cout << "Approximate angles: "
         << setw(5) << setprecision(1) << r1
         << " and " << setprecision(1) << r2
         << ".0\nMagnitudes are "
         << setw(6) << n1 << " and " << setw(5) << -n2;
    ```

15. a = 1; b = 2; c = 3; x = 4.0; y = 5.5; z = 6.6

16. a = 1; b = 2; c = 3; x = 4.0; y = 5.0; z = 6.0

17. a = 1; b = 3; c = 5; x = 2.2; y = 4.4; z = 6.6

18. Error: real values cannot be read into integer variables

19. a = 1; b = 2; c = 3; x = 4.0; y = 5.5; z = 6.6

20. a = 1; b = 2; c = 3; x = 4.0; y = 5.5; z = 6.6

21. a = 1; b = 2; c = 3; x = 4.0; y = 5.5; z = 6.6

Programming Problems

1.

```
/* prog2-1.cpp reads two three-digit integers and then calculates and
 * prints their product and the quotient and remainder that result
 * when the first is divided by the second, with ASCII graphics.
 *
 * Input:  two three-digit integers
 * Output: the product, quotient, and remainder
 **********************************************************************/

#include <iostream.h>              // cin, cout, >>, <<
#include <iomanip.h>               // setw

int main()
{
   int integer1,                   // first integer
       integer2;                   // second integer

   cout << "Please enter two three-digit integers: ";
   cin >> integer1 >> integer2;

   int product = integer1 * integer2,
       quotient = integer1 / integer2,
       remainder = integer1 % integer2;

   cout << "\n    " << setw(3) << integer1
        << "\n  x " << setw(3) << integer2
        << "\n  -----"
        << '\n' << setw(7) << product << endl;

   cout << "\n      " << setw(3) << quotient
        << " R " << remainder
        << "\n      -----"
        << "\n " << setw(3) << integer2
        << " ) " << setw(3) << integer1 << endl;

   return 0;
}
```

2.

```
/* prog2-2.cpp reads the lengths of the two legs of a right triangle and
 * calculates and prints the area of the triangle and the length of
 * the hypotenuse.
 *
 * Input:  lengths of two legs of a right triangle
 * Output: the area of the triangle, and
 *         the length of the hypotenuse
 **********************************************************************/

#include <iostream.h>                    // cin, cout, >>, <<
#include <math.h>                        // sqrt()

int main()
{
   double leg1,                          // one leg
          leg2;                          // the other leg
```

```
   cout << "Please enter the lengths of the "
        << "two legs of a right triangle: ";

   cin >> leg1 >> leg2;

   double area = 0.5 * leg1 * leg2,
          hypotenuse = sqrt(leg1 * leg1 + leg2 * leg2);

   cout << "\nArea of the triangle: " << area
        << "\nLength of the hypotenuse: " << hypotenuse << endl;

   return 0;
}
```

3.

```
/* prog2-3.cpp program reads values for the coefficients a, b, and c of
 * a quadratic equation and finds the two roots of the equation using
 * the quadratic formula.
 *
 * Input:  coefficients a, b, and c
 * Output: the two roots of the quadratic equation
 ********************************************************************/

#include <iostream.h>              // cin, cout, >>, <<
#include <math.h>                  // sqrt()

int main()
{
   double  a,                      // x squared coefficient
           b,                      // x coefficient
           c;                      // constant coefficient

   cout << "Please enter the coefficients a, b, and c "
        << "of the quadratic equation:\n";

   cin >> a >> b >> c;

   double sqrtDisc = sqrt(b*b - 4*a*c),
          root1 = (- b + sqrtDisc) / (2*a),
          root2 = (- b - sqrtDisc) / (2*a);

   cout << "\nThe roots of this quadratic equation are:\n"
        << root1 << " and " << root2 << endl;

   return 0;
}
```

4.
```cpp
/* This program converts a measurement given in feet to the
 * equivalent number of yards, inches, centimeters, and meters.
 *
 * Input:  feet
 * Output: yards, inches, centimeters, meters
 *****************************************************************/

#include <iostream.h>              // cin, cout, >>, <<

int main()
{
   double feet;                    // measurement in feet

   cout << "Please enter a length in feet: ";

   cin >> feet;

   double
      yards = feet / 3.0,
      inches = feet * 12.0,
      centimeters = inches * 2.54,
      meters = centimeters / 100.0;

   cout << '\n' << feet << " ft. = " << yards << " yd."
        << '\n' << feet << " ft. = " << inches << " in."
        << '\n' << feet << " ft. = " << centimeters << " cm"
        << '\n' << feet << " ft. = " << meters << " m"
        << endl;

   return 0;
}
```

5.
```cpp
/* prog2-5.cpp reads a student's number, his or her old GPA, and
 * the number of old course credits, and then prints these
 * with appropriate labels.  It then reads the course credit and
 * grade for each of four courses, calculates current GPA and
 * cumulative GPA, and prints them with appropriate labels.
 *
 * Input:  the student number, old GPA, old course credits, and
 *         course and grade for four courses
 * Output: student number, old GPA, old course credits,
 *         current GPA, and cumulative GPA
 *****************************************************************/

#include <iostream.h>              // cin, cout, >>, <<

int main()
{
   int studentNumber;                  // student's number
   double oldGPA,                      // old Grade Point Average
          oldCourseCredits;            // old course credits
```

```
    cout << "Please enter student number, old GPA,"
         << "\n   and number of old course credits:\n";

    cin >> studentNumber >> oldGPA >> oldCourseCredits;

    cout << "\nStudent #" << studentNumber
         << "\nOld GPA: " << oldGPA
         << "\nOld Course Credits: " << oldCourseCredits;

    double course1, grade1,              // credit and grade for course 1
           course2, grade2,              // credit and grade for course 2
           course3, grade3,              // credit and grade for course 3
           course4, grade4;              // credit and grade for course 4

    cout << "\n\nPlease enter course credit and grade for course 1: ";
    cin >> course1 >> grade1;

    cout << "Please enter course credit and grade for course 2: ";
    cin >> course2 >> grade2;

    cout << "Please enter course credit and grade for course 3: ";
    cin >> course3 >> grade3;

    cout << "Please enter course credit and grade for course 4: ";
    cin >> course4 >> grade4;

    double oldHonorPoints = oldCourseCredits * oldGPA,
           newHonorPoints = course1 * grade1 + course2 * grade2 +
                            course3 * grade3 + course4 * grade4,
           newCourseCredits = course1 + course2 + course3 + course4,
           currentGPA = newHonorPoints / newCourseCredits;

    cout << "\nCurrent GPA: " << currentGPA;

    double cumulativeGPA = (oldHonorPoints + newHonorPoints) /
                           (oldCourseCredits + newCourseCredits);

    cout << "\nCumulative GPA: " << cumulativeGPA << endl;

    return 0;
}



6.
/* prog2-6.cpp reads the number of dooflingies to be shipped and prints the
 * number of huge, large, medium, and small containers needed to send the
 * shipment in the minimum number of containers and with the miniumum
 * amountof wasted space.
 *
 * Input:  the number of dooflingies to ship
 * Output: the number of the various containers required
 *******************************************************************/

#include <iostream.h>                    // cin, cout, >>, <<
#include <iomanip.h>                     // setw()

int main()
{
    const int HUGE_MAX = 50,             // size of huge container
              LARGE_MAX = 20,            // size of large container
              MEDIUM_MAX = 5;            // size of medium container
```

```
    int dooflingies;                           // dooflingies to ship

    cout << "\nPlease enter the number of dooflingies to ship: ";

    cin >> dooflingies;

    int hugeNum = dooflingies / HUGE_MAX;       // number of huge containers
    dooflingies %= HUGE_MAX;

    int largeNum = dooflingies / LARGE_MAX;     // number of large containers
    dooflingies %= LARGE_MAX;

    int mediumNum = dooflingies / MEDIUM_MAX; // number of medium containers
    dooflingies %= MEDIUM_MAX;

    int smallNum = dooflingies;                 // number of small containers

    cout << "\nContainer      Number"
         << "\n=========      ======"
         << "\n  Huge         " << setw(4) << hugeNum
         << "\n  Large        " << setw(4) << largeNum
         << "\n  Medium       " << setw(4) << mediumNum
         << "\n  Small        " << setw(4) << smallNum << endl;

    return 0;
}
```

7.

```
/* prog2-7.cpp reads the amount of a purchase and the amount received
 * in payment and then computes the change in dollars, half dollars,
 * quarters, dimes, nickels, and pennies.
 *
 * Input:  amount of purchase and amount received
 * Output: amount of change in coins
 *********************************************************************/

#include <iostream.h>                // cin, cout, >>, <<

int main()
{
    int amountOfPurchase,            // amount of the purchase in cents
        amountReceived;              // amount received in cents

    cout << "Please enter the amount of purchase (in cents): ";
    cin >> amountOfPurchase;

    cout << "Please enter the amount received (in cents): ";
    cin >> amountReceived;

    int centsChange = amountReceived - amountOfPurchase;
                                     // amount of change in cents

    int dollars = centsChange / 100;    // dollars of change
    centsChange %= 100;

    int halfDollars = centsChange / 50; // half dollars of change
    centsChange %= 50;

    int quarters = centsChange / 25;    // quarters of change
    centsChange %= 25;
```

```
    int dimes = centsChange / 10;        // dimes of change
    centsChange %= 10;

    int nickels = centsChange / 5;       // nickels of change
    centsChange %= 5;

    int pennies = centsChange;           // pennies of change

    cout << "\nChange:\n\t"
         << dollars << " dollar(s),\n\t"
         << halfDollars << " half-dollar(s),\n\t"
         << quarters << " quarter(s),\n\t"
         << dimes << " dime(s),\n\t"
         << nickels << " nickel(s), and\n\t"
         << pennies << " pennies.\n";

    return 0;
}
```

8.

```
/* prog2-8.cpp reads two angular measurements given in degrees, minutes,
 * and seconds and then calculates and prints their sum.
 *
 * Input:  two angular measurments in degrees, minutes, seconds
 * Output: the sum of the measurements
 ************************************************************************/

#include <iostream.h>                    // cin, cout, >>, <<

int main()
{
    int degrees1, minutes1, seconds1,    // first angular measurement
        degrees2, minutes2, seconds2;    // second angular measurement

    cout << "Please enter an angle (in degrees minutes seconds): ";
    cin >> degrees1 >> minutes1 >> seconds1;

    cout << "Please enter another angle: ";
    cin >> degrees2 >> minutes2 >> seconds2;

    int secondsTotal = (seconds1 + seconds2) % 60;
    int minutesCarry = (seconds1 + seconds2) / 60;
    int minutesTotal = (minutes1 + minutes2 + minutesCarry) % 60;
    int degreesCarry = (minutes1 + minutes2 + minutesCarry) / 60;

    int degreesTotal = (degrees1 + degrees2 + degreesCarry) % 360;

    cout << "\nThe sum of the two angles: "
         << degreesTotal << " degrees, "
         << minutesTotal << " minutes, "
         << secondsTotal << " seconds.\n";

    return 0;
}
```

9.
```
/* prog2-9.cpp reads two three-digit integers and then prints their
 * product in "long" format.
 *
 * Input:  two three-digit integers
 * Output: long multiplication of the two integers
 ***********************************************************************/

#include <iostream.h>              // cin, cout, >>, <<
#include <iomanip.h>               // setw()

int main()
{
    int integer1,                  // the first integer
        integer2;                  // the second integer

    cout << "\nPlease enter two three-digit integers: ";
    cin >> integer1 >> integer2;

    int hundreds = integer2 / 100,      // hundreds digit of second integer
        tens = (integer2 / 10) % 10,    // tens digit of second integer
        ones = integer2 % 10;           // ones digit of second integer

    int line1 = integer1 * ones,        // line 1
        line2 = integer1 * tens,        // line 2
        line3 = integer1 * hundreds,    // line 3
        product = integer1 * integer2;  // actual product

    cout << "\n    " << setw(4) << integer1
         << "\n x  " << setw(4) << integer2
         << "\n -------"
         << '\n' << setw(8) << line1
         << '\n' << setw(7) << line2
         << '\n' << setw(6) << line3
         << "\n -------"
         << '\n' << setw(8) << product << '\n';

    return 0;
}
```

10.
```
/* prog2-10.cpp determines if weather conditions will allow pesticide
 * spraying:     temperature >= 70 degrees F and
 *               relativeHumidity is between 15% and 25% and
 *               windSpeed <= 10 mph
 *
 * Input:  temperature, relative humidity, and wind speed
 * Output: true (1) if it's OK to spray and false (0) otherwise
 ***********************************************************************/

#include <iostream.h>                   // cin, cout, >>, <<

int main()
{
    double temperature,  relativeHumidity, windSpeed;

    cout << "Please enter the temperature (degrees Fahrenheit): ";
    cin >> temperature;

    cout << "Please enter the relative humidity (percent): ";
    cin >> relativeHumidity;
```

```cpp
    cout << "Please enter the wind speed (miles per hour): ";
    cin >> windSpeed;

    bool OkToSpray =
             (temperature >= 70) &&
             (15 <= relativeHumidity) && (relativeHumidity <= 35) &&
             (windSpeed <= 10);

    cout << "OK to spray? " << OkToSpray << endl;

    return 0;
}
```

11.

```cpp
/* prog2-11.cpp determines if a loan should be approved:
 *          income >= $25,000 or assets >= $100,000
 *      and    liabilities < $50,000
 *
 * Input:  income, assets, and liabilities
 * Output: true (1) if loan is approved and false (0) otherwise
 ***********************************************************************/

#include <iostream.h>                    // cin, cout, >>, <<

int main()
{
    double income, assets, liabilities;

    cout << "Please enter income: ";
    cin >> income;

    cout << "Please enter assets: ";
    cin >> assets;

    cout << "Please enter liabilities: ";
    cin >> liabilities;

    bool creditOK =
             ( (income >= 70.0) || (assets >= 100000) )
           && (liabilities < 50000);

    cout << "Loan approved? " << creditOK << endl;

    return 0;
}
```

12.
```
/* prog2-12.cpp reads three real numbers, determines if they can be the
 * three sides of a triangle, and if so, if the triangle is equilateral,
 * isosceles, or scalene.
 *

 * Input:  side1, side2, side3
 * Output: triangle, equilateral, isosceles, scalene
 ********************************************************************/

#include <iostream.h>                        // cin, cout, >>, <<

int main()
{
   double side1, side2, side3;

   cout << "Please enter the three sides of a triangle: ";
   cin >> side1 >> side2 >> side3;

   bool triangle = (side1 + side2 > side3) &&
                   (side2 + side3 > side1) &&
                   (side1 + side3 > side2),
        equilateral = triangle &&
                      (side1 == side2) &&
                      (side2 == side3),
        isosceles = triangle &&
                    ( (side1 == side2) ||
                      (side2 == side3) ||
                      (side1 == side3) ),
        scalene = triangle && !isosceles;

   cout << "\nTriangle? "  << triangle
        << "\nEquilateral? " << equilateral
        << "\nIsosceles? " << isosceles
        << "\nScalene? "  << scalene << endl;

   return 0;
}
```

Chapter 3: Functions

Exercises 3.2

1.
```
/* CelsiusToFahr receives a temperature in Celsius and converts it
 * into a Fahrenheit temperature.
 *
 * Receive:  tempCelsius, a temperature in degrees Celsius
 * Return:   the equivalent number of degrees Fahrenheit
 *************************************************************************/

double CelsiusToFahr(double tempCelsius)
{
   return tempCelsius * 1.8 + 32;
}
```

2.
```
/* USToCanadian receives a number of US dollars and the US-to-Canadian
 * exchange rate and returns the equivalent number of Canadian dollars.
 *
 * Receive: USDollars, a number of US dollars
 *          USCanExchangeRate, the number of Canadian dollars equal to
 *             one US dollar
 * Return:  the equivalent number of Canadian dollars
 *************************************************************************/

double USToCanadian(double USDollars, double USCanExchangeRate)
{
   return USDollars * USCanExchangeRate;
}
```

3.
```
/* CanadianToUS receives a number of Canadian dollars and the US-to-Canadian
 * exchange rate and returns the equivalent number of U.S. dollars.
 *
 * Receive: CanadianDollars, a number of Canadian dollars
 *          USCanExchangeRate, the number of Canadian dollars equal to
 *             one US dollar
 * Return:  the equivalent number of US dollars
 *************************************************************************/

double CanadianToUS(double CanadianDollars, double USCanExchangeRate)
{
   return CanadianDollars / USCanExchangeRate;
}
```

4.
```
/* Range receives two integers and returns the range between them.
 *
 * Receive: int1, int2, two integers
 * Return:  the range between int1 and int2
 *************************************************************************/

#include <stdlib.h>          // abs

int Range(int int1, int int2)
{
   return abs(int1 - int2);
}
```

5.

```
/* Wages calculates wages earned given hours worked and hourly pay rate.
 *
 * Receive: hoursWorked, the hours worked
 *          hourlyPayRate, the hourly pay rate
 * Return:  the wages earned
 *************************************************************************/

double Wages(double hoursWorked, double hourlyPayRate)
{
    return hoursWorked * hourlyPayRate;
}
```

6.

```
/* CircleCircumference returns the circumference of a circle of
 *given radius.
 *
 * Receive: radius, the radius of a circle
 * Return:  the circumference of the circle
 *************************************************************************/

double CircleCircumference(double radius)
{

    const double PI = 3.14159265358979323846;

    return 2.0 * PI * radius;
}
```

7.

```
/* CircleArea returns the area of a circle of given radius.
 *
 * Receive: radius, the radius of a circle
 * Return:  the area of the circle
 *************************************************************************/

double CircleArea(double radius)
{

    const double PI = 3.14159265358979323846;

    return PI * radius * radius;
}
```

8.

```
/* RectanglePerimeter returns the perimeter of a rectangle of given height
 * and width.
 *
 * Receive: height, width, the dimensions of a rectangle
 * Return:  the perimeter of the rectangle
 *************************************************************************/

double RectanglePerimeter(double height, double width)
{
    return 2.0 * (height + width);
}
```

9.
```
/* SquareArea returns the area of a square with a given side length.
 *
 * Receive: side, the side of a square
 * Return:  the area of the square
 ***********************************************************************/

double SquareArea(double side)
{
   return side * side;
}
```

10.
```
/* TrianglePerimeter returns the perimeter of a triangle of given
 * side lengths.
 *
 * Receive: side1, side2, side3, the side lenghts of a triangle
 * Return:  the perimeter of the triangle
 ***********************************************************************/

double TrianglePerimeter(double side1, double side2, double side3)
{
   return side1 + side2 + side3;
}
```

11.
```
/* TriangleArea returns the area of a triangle of given side lengths.
 *
 * Receive: side1, side2, side3, the side lenghts of a triangle
 * Return:  the area of the triangle
 ***********************************************************************/

#include <math.h>          // sqrt

double TriangleArea(double side1, double side2, double side3)
{
   double s = (side1 + side2 + side3) / 2.0;

   return sqrt(s * (s - side1) * (s - side2) * (s - side3));
}
```

12.
```
/* BacteriaPopulation returns the population of a colony of bacteria,
 * given the initial population, the time elapsed, and the constant of
 * growth of the colony.
 *
 * Receive: initialPop, the initial population of the colony
 *          time, the time elapsed
 *          k, the rate constant for the growth of the colony
 * Return:  populatio of the colony of bacteria
 ********************************************************************/

#include <math.h>          // exp

long int BacteriaPopulation(long int initialPop, double time, double k)
{
   return long(initialPop * exp(time * k));
}
```

13.
```
/* SecondsToMinutes converts Seconds to Minutes.
 *
 *    Receive: seconds
 *    Return:  minutes
 **********************************************/

long int SecondsToMinutes(long int seconds)
{
   return seconds / 60;
}
```

14.
```
/* MinutesToHours converts Minutes to Hours.
 *
 * Receive: minutes
 * Return:  hours
 **********************************************/

long int MinutesToHours(long int minutes)
{
   return minutes / 60;
}
```

15.
```
/* HoursToDays converts Hours to Days.
 *
 * Receive: hours
 * Return:  days
 **********************************************/

double HoursToDays(long int hours)
{
   return hours / 24.0;
}
```

16.
```
/* SecondsToDays converts Seconds to Days.
 *
 * Receive: seconds
 * Return:  days
 **********************************************/

double SecondsToDays(long int seconds)
{
   return HoursToDays( MinutesToHours( SecondsToMinutes(seconds) ) );
}
```

17.
```
/* PhoneDisplay receives a 7-digit number and displays it as a phone
 * number should appear (###-####)
 *
 * Receive: sevenDigits, an int 7 digits long.
 * Output:  the same number in phone number format.
 ***********************************************************************/

void PhoneDisplay(long int sevenDigits)
{
   int lastFour = sevenDigits % 10000,
       firstThree = sevenDigits / 10000;

   cout << firstThree << '-' << lastFour;
}
```

18.
```
/* HeatIndex will calculate and return the heat index for a given
 *temperature in degrees Fahrenheit and relative humidity.
 *
 * Receive: t, a temperature in degrees Fahrenheit,
 *          r, a relative humidity
 * Return: the heat index for these values.
 ***********************************************************************/

double HeatIndex(double t, double r)
{
   return -42.379 + 2.04901523 * t  +  10.14333127 * r
          - 0.22475541 * t * r      -  (6.83783e-3) * t * t
          - (5.481717e-2) * r * r   +  (1.22874e-3) * t * t * r
          + (8.5282e-4) * t * r * r - (1.99e-6) * t * t * r * r;
}
```

19.
```
/* PrintZero displays the "stick number" 0.
 *
 * Output:  the stick figure for zero
 *****************************************************************/

void PrintZero()
{
   cout << " --- \n"
           "|   |\n"
           "|   |\n"
           "|   |\n"
           " --- \n";
}
```

```
/* PrintOne displays the "stick number" 1.
 *
 * Output:  the stick figure for one
 ****************************************************************/

void PrintOne()
{
   cout << "  |  \n"
           "  |  \n"
           "  |  \n"
           "  |  \n"
           "  |  \n";
}

/* PrintTwo displays the "stick number" 2.
 *
 * Output:  the stick figure for two
 ****************************************************************/

void PrintTwo()
{
   cout << " --- \n"
           "    |\n"
           " --- \n"
           "|    \n"
           " --- \n";
}

/* PrintThree displays the "stick number" 3.
 *
 * Output:  the stick figure for three
 ****************************************************************/

void PrintThree()
{
   cout << " --- \n"
           "    |\n"
           " --- \n"
           "    |\n"
           " --- \n";
}
```

Exercises 3.3

1. yes

2. no

3. yes

4. yes

5. 5

6. out of range

7. 0

8. ```
if (taxCode == 'T')
    price += (taxRate * price);
```

9. ```
if (taxCode == 1)
  {
    cin >> x >> y;
    cout << (x + y);
  }
```

10. ```
if ((0 < a) && (a < 5))
    b = 1 / (a * a);
  else
    b = a * a;
```

11.
```
double Cost(int distance)
{
   if (distance >= 1000)
      return 12.00;
   else if (distance > 500)
      return 10.00;
   else if (distance > 100)
      return 8.00;
   else
      return 5.00;
}
```

12.
```
/* RootsAreReal returns true if a quadratic function has real roots and
 * false if not. This is based on the coefficients A, B, and C.
 *
 * Receive: A, B, and C, the coefficients of a quadratic equation
 * Return: true if the roots are real, false if not
 ---*/

bool RootsAreReal(double A, double B, double C)
{
   return (B * B - 4 * A * C >= 0);
}
```
```

13.
```
/* PrintPollutionClass outputs a string corresponding to the given
 * pollution index.
 *
 * Receive:  index, a pollution index
 * Output:   the pollution class
-------------------------------------------------------------------*/

void PrintPollutionClass(double index)
{
   if (index < 35.0)
      cout << "Pleasant\n";
   else if (index > 60.0)
      cout << "Hazardous\n";
   else
      cout << "Unpleasant\n";
}
```

14.
```
/* ClassifyWindChill will classify wind chill's effect on a person.
 *
 * Receive: chillTemp, the value of a wind chill.
 * Output:  the classification of the wind chill.
-------------------------------------------------------------------*/

void ClassifyWindChill(double windChill)
{
   if (windChill >= 10)
      cout << "Not dangerous or unpleasant\n";
   else if (windChill >= -10)
      cout << "Unpleasant\n";
   else if (windChill >= -30)
      cout << "Frostbite is possible\n";
   else if (windChill >= -70)
      cout << "Dangerous: Frostbite likely\n";
   else
      cout << "Instant Ice Cube: Frostbite in 30 seconds\n";
}
```

Exercises 3.4

1.  ```
    -2 squared = 4
    -1 squared = 1
    0 squared = 0
    1 squared = 1
    2 squared = 4
    3 squared = 9
    ```
    ```

2. 1
    1
    2
    2
    1
    3
    3
    2
    1
    4
    4
    3
    2
    1
    5
    5
    4
    3
    2
    1

3. 3
    0
    1
    2
    3
    4

4. 111
    121
    122
    131
    132
    133
    211
    221
    222
    231
    232
    233
    311
    321
    322
    331
    332
    333

5. 111

    121
    122

    131
    132
    133

    222

    232
    233

    333

6. 000
    112
    228
    18

7. 000
    112
    228
    18

8. 5123###
    31###
    1***

9, 10, 11
(a) `limit = 10`

Pretest loop	
number	sum
0	0
1	1
2	3
3	6
4	10
5	15

Posttest loop	
number	sum
0	0
1	1
2	3
3	6
4	10
5	15

Test-in-the-middle loop	
number	sum
0	0
1	1
2	3
3	6
4	10
5	15
6	15

(b) `limit = 1`

Pretest loop	
number	sum
0	0
1	1
2	3

Posttest loop	
number	sum
0	0
1	1
2	3

Test-in-the-middle loop	
number	sum
0	0
1	1
2	3
3	3

(c) `limit = 0`

Pretest loop	
number	sum
0	0
1	1

Posttest loop	
number	sum
0	0
1	1

Test-in-the-middle loop	
number	sum
0	0
1	1
2	1

12.

```
/* SumToN computes the sum 1 + 2 + ... + n.
 *
 * Receive: n, an integer value
 * Return:  the value of the sum 1 + 2 + ... + n
 ******************************************************/

int SumToN(int n)
{
   int sum = 0;

   for (int i = 1; i <= n; i++)
      sum += i;

   return sum;
}
```

13.

```
/* SumMToN computes the sum of the integers from m to n.
 *
 * Receive: m and n, two integers
 * Return:  the value of the sum of m to n
 ********************************************************/

int SumMToN (int m, int n)
{
   if (m > n) return 0;          // no integers between m and n

   int sum = 0;                  // compute sum = m + (m + 1) + ... + n
```

```
    for (int i = m; i <= n; i++)
        sum += i;

    return sum;
}
```

14.
```
    for (int n = 1; n <= 100; n++)
        cout << n * n << endl;
```

15.
```
    for (int n = 50; n > 0; n--)
        cout << n * n * n << endl;
```

16.
```
    for (int i = 1; i <= 49; i += 2)
        cout << sqrt(double(i)) << endl;
```

17.
```
    for (double x = -2.0; x <= 2.0; x += 0.1)
        cout << '(' << x << ','
             << (x * x * x - 3 * x + 1) << ")\n";
```

18.
```
    for (;;)
    {
        cout << x << endl;
        x -= 0.5;
        if (x <= 0) break;
    }
```

19.
```
    for (;;)
    {
        cin >> a >> b >> c;
        cout << (a + b + c) << endl;
        if ( (a < 0) || (b < 0) || (c < 0) ) break;
    }
```

20.
```
    i = 1;
    for (;;
    {
        cout << i * i << endl;
        if ( i * i - (i-1)*(i-1) > 50) break;
        i++;
    }
```

Programming Problems

1.

```
/* prog3-1.cpp is a driver program to test the function
 * CelsiusToFahr() from Exercise 1.
 *
 * Input:  A temperature in Celsius
 * Output: equivalent temperature in Fahrenheit
 ************************************************************/

#include <iostream.h>              // cin, cout, >>, <<

double CelsiusToFahr(double tempCelsius);

int main()
{
   double tempC;

   cout << "Please enter a temperature (degrees Celsius): ";
   cin >> tempC;

   cout << "Equivalent Fahrenheit temperature = " << CelsiusToFahr(tempC) << endl;

   return 0;
}

/* Insert definition of CelsiusToFahr() from Exercise 1 here */
```

2.

```
/* prog3-2.cpp is a driver program to test the functions
 * US_to_Canadian() and Canadian_to_US from Exercises 2 & 3.
 *
 * Input:  US-to-Canadian exchange rate
 *         an amount in U.S. currency and
 *         an amount in Canadian currency
 * Output: equivalent amount in Canadian / U.S. currency
 ************************************************************/

#include <iostream.h>              // cin, cout, >>, <<

double USToCanadian(double USDollars, double USCanExchangeRate);
double CanadianToUS(double CanadianDollars, double USCanExchangeRate);

int main()
{
   double exchRate,
          amountUS,
          amountCanadian;

   cout << "Please enter the US-to-Canadian exchange rate: ";
   cin >> exchRate;

   cout << "\nPlease enter an amount in US currency: $";
   cin >> amountUS;
   cout << "Equivalent amount in Canadian currency = $"
        << USToCanadian(amountUS, exchRate) << endl;
```

```
      cout << "\nPlease enter an amount in Canadian currency: $";
      cin >> amountUS;
      cout << "Equivalent amount in US currency = $"
           << CanadianToUS(amountUS, exchRate) << endl;

      return 0;
}

/* Insert definitions of functions USToCanadian() and
   CanadianToUS() from Exercises 2 and 3 here */
```

3.
```
/* prog3-3.cpp is a driver program to test the function
 * Range() from Exercise 4.
 *
 * Input:  two integers
 * Output: the range of the two numbers
 ****************************************************************/

#include <iostream.h>                  // cin, cout, >>, <<

int Range(int int1, int int2);

int main()
{
    int num1, num2;

    cout << "Please enter two integers: ";
    cin >> num1 >> num2;

    cout << "Range of these numbers is " << Range(num1, num2) << endl;

    return 0;
}

/* Insert definition of Range() from Exercise 4 here */
```

4.
```
/* prog3-4.cpp is a driver program to test the function
 * Wages() from Exercise 5.
 *
 * Input:  hours worked and hourly rage
 * Output: wages earned
 ****************************************************************/

#include <iostream.h>                  // cin, cout, >>, <<

double Wages(double hoursWorked, double hourlyPayRate);

int main()
{
    double hours, rate;

    cout << "Please enter hours worked and hourly rate: ";
    cin >> hours >> rate;
```

```
   cout << "Wages earned = $" << Wages(hours, rate) << endl;

   return 0;
}

/* Insert definition of Wages() from Exercise 5 here */
```

5.
```
/* prog3-5.cpp is a driver program to test the circle-
 * processing functions from Exercises 6 & 7.
 *
 * Input:  radius of a circle
 * Output: circumference and area of the circle
 ****************************************************************/

#include <iostream.h>                 // cin, cout, >>, <<

double CircleCircumference(double radius);
double CircleArea(double radius);

int main()
{
   double radius;

   cout << "Please enter the radius of a circle: ";
   cin >> radius;

   cout << "Circumference of circle is " << CircleCircumference(radius) << endl;

   cout << "Area of circle is " << CircleArea(radius) << endl;

   return 0;
}

/* Insert definitions of functions CircleCircumference() and
   CircleArea() from Exercises 6 and 7 here */
```

6.
```
/* prog3-6.cpp is a driver program to test the rectangle-
 * processing functions from Exercises 8 and 9.
 *
 * Input:  sides of a rectangle
 *         side of a square
 * Output: perimeter of the rectangle
 *         area of the square
 ****************************************************************/

#include <iostream.h>                 // cin, cout, >>, <<

double RectanglePerimeter(double height, double width);
double SquareArea(double side);

int main()
{
   double side1, side2;

   cout << "Please enter the length and width of a rectangle: ";
   cin >> side1 >> side2;
```

```
    cout << "Perimeter of rectangle is " << RectanglePerimeter(side1, side2) << endl;

    cout << "Please enter the side of a square: ";
    cin >> side1;
    cout << "Area of circie is " << SquareArea(side1) << endl;

    return 0;
}

/* Insert definitions of functions RectanglePerimeter() and
   SquareArea() from Exercises 8 and 9 here */
```

7.
```
/* prog3-6.cpp is a driver program to test the triangle-
 * processing functions from Exercises 10 and 11.
 *
 * Input:  sides of a triangle
 * Output: perimeter and area of the triangle
 **************************************************************/

#include <iostream.h>                // cin, cout, >>, <<

double TrianglePerimeter(double side1, double side2, double side3);
double TriangleArea(double side1, double side2, double side3);

int main()
{
    double side1, side2, side3;

    cout << "Please enter the 3 sides of a triangle: ";
    cin >> side1 >> side2 >> side3;

    cout << "Perimeter of triangle is "
         << TrianglePerimeter(side1, side2, side3) << endl;

    cout << "Area of triangle is "
         << TriangleArea(side1, side2, side3) << endl;

    return 0;
}

/* Insert definitions of functions TrianglePerimeter() and
   TriangleArea() from Exercises 10 and 11 here */
```

8.
```
/* prog3-8.cpp is a driver program to test the function
 * BacteriaPopulation() from Exercise 12.
 *
 * Input:  initial population, time elapsed, and grown rate
 * Output: current population
 **************************************************************/

#include <iostream.h>                // cin, cout, >>, <<

long int BacteriaPopulation(long int initialPop, double time, double k);

int main()
{
    long int initPop;
    double time, rate;
```

```
    cout << "Please enter initial population: ";
    cin >> initPop;
    cout << "Please enter a time elapsed and grown rate: ";
    cin >> time >> rate;

    cout << "Current population = "
         << BacteriaPopulation(initPop, time, rate) << endl;

    return 0;
}

/* Insert definition of function BacteriaPopulation()
   from Exercise 12 here */
```

9.

```
/* prog3-9.cpp is a driver program to test the time-converson
 * functions of Exercises 13-16.
 *
 * Input:  seconds
 * Output: equivalent minutes, hours, and days
 ***************************************************************/

#include <iostream.h>                 // cin, cout, >>, <<

long int SecondsToMinutes(long int seconds);
long int MinutesToHours(long int minutes);
double HoursToDays(long int hours);
double SecondsToDays(long int seconds);

int main()
{
    long int seconds, minutes, hours;
    double days;

    cout << "Please enter number of seconds: ";
    cin >> seconds;

    minutes = SecondsToMinutes(seconds);
    hours = MinutesToHours(minutes);
    days = HoursToDays(hours);
    cout << "In minutes this is " << minutes << endl
         << "which in hours is  " << hours << endl
         << "which in days is   " << days << endl;

    cout << "\nComputing days directly from seconds using SecondsToDays() gives "
         << SecondsToDays(seconds) << " days" << endl;

    return 0;
}

/* Insert definitions of functions SecondsToMinutes(),
   MinutesToHours(), HoursToDays(), and SecondsToDays()
   from Exercises 13-16 here */
```

10.

```
/* prog3-10.cpp is a driver program to test the function
 * PhoneDisplay() from Exercise 17.
 *
 * Input:  a 7-digit phone number
```

```
 * Output: phone number in the format ###-####
 ******************************************************************/

#include <iostream.h>                  // cin, cout, >>, <<

void PhoneDisplay(long int sevenDigits);

int main()
{
    long int phoneNumber;

    cout << "Please enter a 7-digit phone number: ";
    cin >> phoneNumber;

    PhoneDisplay(phoneNumber);

    return 0;
}

/* Insert definition of function PhoneDisplay()
   from Exercise 17 here */
```

11.
```
/* prog3-11.cpp is a driver program to test the function
 * HeatIndex() from Exercise 18.
 *
 * Input:  temperature and relative humidity
 * Output: heat index
 ******************************************************************/

#include <iostream.h>                  // cin, cout, >>, <<

double HeatIndex(double t, double r);

int main()
{
    double temp, relHumidity;

    cout << "Please enter the temperature (Fahrenheit) and relative humidity: ";
    cin >> temp >> relHumidity;

    cout << "Head index is " << HeatIndex(temp, relHumidity) << endl;

    return 0;
}

/* Insert definition of function HeatIndex()
   from Exercise 18 here */
```

12.
```
/* prog3-12.cpp is a driver program to test the stick-number
 * functions from Exercise 19.
 *
 * Input:  none
 * Output: stick number representations of 0, 1, 2, 3
 ******************************************************************/

#include <iostream.h>                  // cin, cout, >>, <<
```

```
int main()
{
    PrintZero();
    PrintOne();
    PrintTwo();
    PrintThree();

    return 0;
}

/* Insert definitions of the functions
   from Exercise 19 here */
```

13. The other functions are much like those for 0, 1, 2, and 3.

Section 3.3

14.
```
/* prog3-14.cpp is a driver program to test the function
 * Cost() from Exercise 11.
 *
 * Input:  a distance
 * Output: cost for that distance
 ****************************************************************/

#include <iostream.h>                    // cin, cout, >>, <<

double Cost(int distance);

int main()
{
    int distance;

    cout << "Please enter a distance: ";
    cin >> distance;

    cout << "Cost is " << Cost(distance) << endl;

    return 0;
}

/* Insert definition of function Cost()
   from Exercise 11 here */
```

15.
```
/* prog3-15.cpp is a driver program to test the function
 * RootsAreReal() from Exercise 12.
 *
 * Input:  coefficients of a quadratic equation
 * Output: indication of whether the equation has real roots
 ****************************************************************/

#include <iostream.h>                    // cin, cout, >>, <<
bool RootsAreReal(double A, double B, double C);

int main()
{
    double a, b, c;
```

```
   cout << "Please enter the 3 coeffients of a quadratic equation.\n"
           "coeff. of x^2 first, then coeff of x, and the constant: ";
   cin >> a >> b >> c;

   cout << "Quadratic has real roots (0 = no, 1 = yes)? "
        << RootsAreReal(a, b, c) << endl;

   return 0;
}

/* Insert definition of function RootsAreReal() from Exercise 12 here */
```

16.

```
/* prog3-16.cpp is a driver program to test the function KindOfRoots().
 *
 * Input:   coefficients of a quadratic equation
 * Output:  indication of what kind of roots the equation has
 *******************************************************************/

#include <iostream.h>                  // cin, cout, >>, <<

short int KindOfRoots(double A, double B, double C);

int main()
{
   double a, b, c;

   cout << "Please enter the 3 coeffients of a quadratic equation.\n"
           "coeff. of x^2 first, then coeff of x, and the constant: ";
   cin >> a >> b >> c;

   cout << "This equation has ";
   short int roots = KindOfRoots(a, b, c);
   if (roots == 0)
      cout << "no real roots\n";
   else if (roots == 1)
      cout << "repeated roots\n";
   else
      cout << "distinct real roots\n";

   return 0;
}
```

```
/* KindOfRoots returns true if a quadratic function has real roots and
 * false if not.  This is based on the coefficients A, B, and C.
 *
 * Receive: A, B, and C, the coefficients of a quadratic equation
 * Return:  true if the roots are real, false if not
---------------------------------------------------------------------*/

short int KindOfRoots(double A, double B, double C)
{
   double discriminant = B * B - 4 * A * C;
   if (discriminant < 0)
      return 0;
   else if (discriminant > 0)
      return 2;
   else
      return 1;
}
```

17.

```
/* prog3-17.cpp is a driver program to test the function
 * SumToN () from Exercise 13.
 *
 * Input:  pollution index
 * Output: classification of the pollution index
 ****************************************************************/

#include <iostream.h>              // cin, cout, >>, <<

void PrintPollutionClass(double index);

int main()
{
   double index;

   cout << "Please enter a pollution index: ";
   cin >> index;

   cout << "Pollution classification:";
   PrintPollutionClass(index);

   return 0;
}

/* Insert definition of the function PrintPollutionClass() from Exercise 13 here */
```

18.

```
/* prog3-18.cpp is a driver program to test the function
 * ClassifyWindChill() from Exercise 14.
 *
 * Input:  wind chill
 * Output: classification of the wind chill
 ****************************************************************/

#include <iostream.h>              // cin, cout, >>, <<

void ClassifyWindChill(double windChill);
```

```
int main()
{
   double windChill;

   cout << "Please enter the wind chill: ";
   cin >> windChill;

   cout << "Wind-chill classification: ";
   ClassifyWindChill(windChill);

   return 0;
}

/* Insert definition of the function ClassifyWindChill() from Exercise 14 here */
```

19.

```
/* prog3-19.cpp reads an employee's number, hours worked, and hourly rate
 * and then calculates his or her wages.
 *
 * Input:  empNum, hoursWorked, hourlyRate
 * Output: wages
 ****************************************************************************/

#include <iostream.h>                  // cin, cout, >>, <<
#include <iomanip.h>                   // setprecision(), setiosflags()

double Wages(double hours, double rate);

int main()
{
   long int empNum;                    // employee number
   double hoursWorked,                 // hours worked
          hourlyRate;                  // hourly rate

   cout << "Please enter employee number: ";
   cin >> empNum;

   cout << "Enter hours worked: ";
   cin >> hoursWorked;

   cout << "Enter hourly rate: ";
   cin >> hourlyRate;

   cout << "\nWages for employee #" << empNum
        << setprecision(2) << setiosflags(ios::fixed | ios::showpoint)
        << ": $" << Wages(hoursWorked, hourlyRate) << endl;

   return 0;
}

/* Wages computes an employee's wages.   Hours over 40 are paid
 * at 1.5 times the regular hourly rate.
 *
 * Receive: hours worked and hourly rate
 * Output:  wages.
 ************************************************************/
```

```
double Wages(double hours, double rate)
{
    if (hours <= 40.0)
       return hours * rate;
    else
       return hours * rate + ((hours - 40) * (rate * 0.5));
}
```

20.

```
/* prog3-20.cpp reads an employee's number and displays his/her wages
 * based on his/her annual salary or his/her hours worked and hourly wage.
 *
 * Receive: the employee number and
 *          annual salary or hours worked and hourly wage
 * Return:  wages for the week
 *********************************************************************/

#include <iostream.h>                    // cin, cout, >>, <<
#include <iomanip.h>                     // setprecision(), setiosflags()

double Wages(long int empNumber);

int main()
{
    long int empNum;                     // employee number

    cout << "Please enter employee number: ";
    cin >> empNum;

    double weeklyWages = Wages(empNum);
    cout << "\nWages for employee #" << empNum
         << setprecision(2) << setiosflags(ios::fixed | ios::showpoint)
         << ": $" << Wages(empNum) << endl;

    return 0;
}

/* Wages computes an employee's wages.  If the employee number is
 * 1000 or above, weekly pay is the employee's salary divided by 52.
 * Others the employee is paid on an hourly basis with hours over 40
 * paid at 1.5 times the regular hourly rate.
 *
 * Receive: employee's number
 * Input:   annual salary or hours worked and hourly rate
 * Return:  wages for the week
 *****************************************************************/

double Wages(long int empNumber)

    if (EmpNum >= 1000)
    {
       double annualSalary;

       cout << "Enter annual salary: $";
       cin >> annualSalary;

       return AnnualSalary / 52.0;
    }
```

```
   else
   {
      double hours, rate;

      cout << "Enter hours worked and hourly rate: ";
      cin >> hours >> rate;

   if (hours <= 40.0)
      return hours * rate;
   else
      return hours * rate + ((hours - 40) * (rate * 0.5));
   }
}
```

Section 3.5

21.
```
/* prog3-21.cpp is a driver program to test the function
 * SumToN() from Exercise 12.
 *
 * Input:  a nonnegative integer
 * Output: the sum 1 + 2 + . . . + n
 ********************************************************/

#include <iostream.h>                   // cin, cout, >>, <<

int SumToN(int n);

int main()
{
   int n;

   cout << "Program computes 1 + 2 + ... + n.  Enter n: ";
   cin >> n;

   cout << "Sum = " << SumToN(n) << endl;

   return 0;
}

/* Insert definition of the function SumToN()
   from Exercise 12 here */
```

22.
```
/* prog3-22.cpp is a driver program to test the function
 * SumMToN () from Exercise 13.
 *
 * Input:  nonnegative integers m and n
 * Output: the sum m + (m+1) + . . . + n
 ********************************************************/

#include <iostream.h>                   // cin, cout, >>, <<

int SumMToN (int m, int n);
```

```
int main()
{
    int m, n;

    cout << "Program computes m + (m+1) + ... + n.  Enter m and n: ";
    cin >> m >> n;

    cout << "Sum = " << SumMToN(m, n) << endl;

    return 0;
}

/* Insert definition of the function SumMToN ()
   from Exercise 13 here */
```

23.
```
/* prog3-23.cpp computes Fibonacci numbers.
 *
 * Input:  a nonnegative integer
 * Output: the first n Fibonacci numbers
 **************************************************/

#include <iostream.h>                // cin, cout, >>, <<

int main()
{
    int n;

    cout << "Program computes the first n Fibonacci numbers.  Enter n: ";
    cin >> n;
    if (n <= 0)
       return 0;

    cout << "\nFirst " << n << " Fibonacci numbers are:\n";
    cout << 1 << endl;
    int fib1 = 1,
        fib2 = 1,
        fib3;
    for (int i = 2; i <= n; i++)
    {
        cout << fib2 << endl;

        fib3 = fib1 + fib2;
        fib1 = fib2;
        fib2 = fib3;
    }

    return 0;
}
```

24.
```
/* prog3-24.cpp computes Fibonacci numbers and ratios of consecutive ones.
 *
 * Input:  a nonnegative integer
 * Output: the first n Fibonacci numbers and ratios of consecutive ones
 ************************************************************************/

#include <iostream.h>                // cin, cout, >>, <<
#include <iomanip.h>                 // setw()
int main()
{
    int n;
```

```
        cout << "Program computes the first n Fibonacci numbers and ratios of "
                "consecutive ones\n.  Enter n: ";
        cin >> n;
        if (n <= 0)
           return 0;

        cout << "Fibonacci\n"
                " number          Ratio\n"
                "=======================|n";
        cout << setw(7) << 1 << endl;
        int fib1 = 1,
            fib2 = 1,
            fib3;
        for (int i = 2; i <= n; i++)
        {
           cout << setw(7) << fib2 << "         "
                << double(fib1) / double(fib2) << endl;
           fib3 = fib1 + fib2;
           fib1 = fib2;
           fib2 = fib3;
        }

        return 0;
}
```

25.
```
/* prog3-25.cpp reads values for UnitPrice and TotalNumber and then
 * produces a table showing the total price of from 1 through
 * totalNumber units.
 *
 * Input:  unitPrice, totalNumber
 * Output: the table
 ********************************************************************/

#include <iostream.h>          // cin, cout, >>, <<
#include <iomanip.h>           // setiosflags(), setprecision(), setw()

int main()
{
   double unitPrice;
   int totalNumber;

   cout << "Please enter the unit price: ";
   cin >> unitPrice;

   cout << "Please enter the total number of units: ";
   cin >> totalNumber;

   cout << "\nNumber of Units   Total Price"
           "\n===============   ===========\n";

   for (int i = 1; i <= totalNumber; i++)
   {
      cout << setiosflags(ios::showpoint | ios::fixed)
           << setprecision(2)
           << setw(8) << i << "            $"
           << setw(5) << i * unitPrice << endl;
   }

   return 0;
}
```

26.

```
/* prog3-26.cpp calculates and prints the generation number and the
 * proportions of AA, AB, and BB under appropriate headings for
 * numGen generations, according to the formulas in the text.
 *
 * Output:  table
 **********************************************************************/

#include <iostream.h>          // cin, cout, >>, <<
#include <iomanip.h>           // setiosflags(), setprecision(), setw()

int main()
{
   int numGen;

   cout << "Enter number of generations: ";
   cin >> numGen;

   double AA = 0.25,
          AB = 0.5,
          BB = 0.25,
          prob = (AB / (AB + BB)) / 2.0;

   cout << "\nGeneration      AA        AB        BB"
           "\n==========   ======== ======== ========\n";

   for (int i = 1; i <= numGen; i++)
   {
      cout << setiosflags(ios::showpoint | ios::fixed)
           << setprecision(4)
           << setw(6) << i
           << setw(14) << AA
           << setw(9) << AB
           << setw(9) << BB << '\n';

      AA = prob * prob;
      AB = 2.0 * prob * (1 - prob);
      BB = (1 - prob) * (1 - prob);
      prob = (AB / (AB + BB)) / 2.0;
   }

   return 0;
}
```

27.

```
/* prog3-27.cpp uses a sentinel-controlled forever loop to read data
 *  values as given in the text, calculates the miles per gallon in
 * each case, and displays the values with appropriate labels.
 *
 * Input:  miles traveled and gallons of gasoline used
 * Output: miles per gallon
 **********************************************************************/

#include <iostream.h>          // cin, cout, >>, <<

int main()
{
   const double SENTINEL = -1;

   double miles,
```

```
              gallons,
              milesPerGallon;

      for (;;)
      {
          cout << "\nPlease enter the miles traveled ("
               << SENTINEL << " to quit): ";
          cin >> miles;

          if (miles == SENTINEL) break;

          cout << "Please enter the gallons of gasoline used: ";
          cin >> gallons;

          milesPerGallon = miles / gallons;

          cout << "\nMiles per gallon: " << milesPerGallon << endl;
      }

      return 0;
}
```

28.
```
/* prog3-28.cpp uses a sentinel-controlled forever loop to read several values
 * representing miles, converts miles to kilometers, and displays all values
 * with appropriate labels.
 *
 * Input:  miles
 * Output: kilometers
 *********************************************************************/

#include <iostream.h>          // cin, cout, >>, <<

int main()
{
      const double SENTINEL = -1;
      const double KILOMETERS_PER_MILE = 1.60935;

      double miles,
             kilometers;

      for (;;)
      {
          cout << "Please enter a number of miles ("
               << SENTINEL << " to quit): ";
          cin >> miles;

          if (miles == SENTINEL) break;

          kilometers = miles * KILOMETERS_PER_MILE;

          cout << "\nThe number of kilometers: " << kilometers << endl;
      }

      return 0;
}
```

29.
```
/* prog3-29.cpp reads a set of numbers, counts them, and calculates and
 * displays the mean, variance, and standard deviation of the set of
 * numbers.
 *
 * Input:  a set of numbers
 * Output: the mean, variance, and standard deviation
 *******************************************************************/

#include <iostream.h>          // cin, cout, >>, <<
#include <math.h>              // sqrt

int main()
{
    const char END_DATA = '^Z^';  // end-od-data signal
    int n = 0;                     // total number of numbers entered
    double number,                 // number just entered
           sum = 0.0,              // the sum of all the numbers
           squaresSum = 0.0;       // the sum of the squares of all the numbers

    cout << "Please enter a set of numbers followed by " << END_DATA << endl;

    for (;;)
    {
        cin >> number;

        if (cin.eof()) break;

        n++;

        sum += number;
        squaresSum += number * number;
    }

    if (n == 0)
    {
        cout << "\nNo values entered!\n";
        return 1;
    }

    double mean = sum / double(n),
           variance = (squaresSum - (sum * sum) / (double(n) * double(n))),
           stdDeviation = sqrt(variance);

    cout << "\nMean: " << mean
         << "\nVariance: " << variance
         << "\nStandard Deviation: " << stdDeviation << '\n';

    return 0;
}
```

30.
```
/* Exchange.h provides an interface for a library of
 * monetary-conversion functions.
 *****************************************************/

double USToCanadian(double USDollars, double USCanExchangeRate);

double CanadianToUS(double CanadianDollars, double USCanExchangeRate);
```

```
/* Exchange.cpp provides the function implementations for Heat,
 * a library of monetary-conversion functions.
 ****************************************************************/

#include "Exchange.h"

//---------------------------------------------

double USToCanadian(double USDollars, double USCanExchangeRate)
{
   return USDollars * USCanExchangeRate;
}

//---------------------------------------------

double CanadianToUS(double CanadianDollars, double USCanExchangeRate)
{
   return CanadianDollars / USCanExchangeRate;
}


/* Exchange.doc provides the documentation for Exchange,
 * a library of monetary-conversion functions.
 ********************************************************************/

/* USToCanadian receives a number of US dollars and the US-to-Canadian
 * exchange rate and returns the equivalent number of Canadian dollars.
 *
 * Receive: USDollars, a number of US dollars
 *          USCanExchangeRate, the number of Canadian dollars equal to
 *             one US dollar
 * Return:  the equivalent number of Canadian dollars
 ********************************************************************/

double USToCanadian(double USDollars, double USCanExchangeRate);

/* CanadianToUS receives a number of Canadian dollars and the US-to-Canadian
 * exchange rate and returns the equivalent number of U.S. dollars.
 *
 * Receive: CanadianDollars, a number of Canadian dollars
 *          USCanExchangeRate, the number of Canadian dollars equal to
 *             one US dollar
 * Return:  the equivalent number of US dollars
 ********************************************************************/

double CanadianToUS(double CanadianDollars, double USCanExchangeRate);


/* prog3-30.cpp is a driver program to test the library Exchange.
 *
 * Input:  US-to-Canadian exchange rate
 *         an amount in U.S. currency and
 *         an amount in Canadian currency
 * Output: equivalent amount in Canadian / U.S. currency
 *************************************************************/

#include <iostream.h>                    // cin, cout, >>, <<
#include "Exchange.h"
```

```cpp
int main()
{
   double exchRate,
          amountUS,
          amountCanadian;

   cout << "Please enter the US-to-Canadian exchange rate: ";
   cin >> exchRate;

   cout << "\nPlease enter an amount in US currency: $";
   cin >> amountUS;
   cout << "Equivalent amount in Canadian currency = $"
        << USToCanadian(amountUS, exchRate) << endl;

   cout << "\nPlease enter an amount in Canadian currency: $";
   cin >> amountUS;
   cout << "Equivalent amount in US currency = $"
        << CanadianToUS(amountUS, exchRate) << endl;

   return 0;
}
```

31.
```cpp
/* Geometry.h provides an interface for a library of geometric functions.
 ***********************************************************************/

double CircleCircumference(double radius);

double CircleArea(double radius);

double RectanglePerimeter(double height, double width);

double SquareArea(double side);

double TrianglePerimeter(double side1, double side2, double side3);

double TriangleArea(double side1, double side2, double side3);


/* Geometry.cpp provides the function implementations for Geometry,
 * a library of geometry functions.
 ***********************************************************************/

#include "Geometry.h"

//----------------------------------------------

double CircleCircumference(double radius)
{
   const double PI = 3.14159265358979323846;

   return 2.0 * PI * radius;
}
```

```
//----------------------------------------------

double CircleArea(double radius)
{
    const double PI = 3.14159265358979323846;

    return PI * radius * radius;
}

//----------------------------------------------

double RectanglePerimeter(double height, double width)
{
    return 2.0 * (height + width);
}

//----------------------------------------------

double SquareArea(double side)
{
    return side * side;
}

//----------------------------------------------

double TrianglePerimeter(double side1, double side2, double side3)
{
    return side1 + side2 + side3;
}

#include <math.h>           // sqrt

double TriangleArea(double side1, double side2, double side3)
{
    double s = (side1 + side2 + side3) / 2.0;

    return sqrt(s * (s - side1) * (s - side2) * (s - side3));
}


/* Geometry.doc provides the documentation for Exchange,
 * a library of monetary-conversion functions.
 ********************************************************************/

/* CircleCircumference returns the circumference of a circle of
 *given radius.
 *
 * Receive: radius, the radius of a circle
 * Return:  the circumference of the circle
 *********************************************************************/

double CircleCircumference(double radius);

/* CircleArea returns the area of a circle of given radius.
 *
 * Receive: radius, the radius of a circle
 * Return:  the area of the circle
 *********************************************************************/

double CircleArea(double radius);
```

```
/* RectanglePerimeter returns the perimeter of a rectangle of given height
 * and width.
 *
 * Receive: height, width, the dimensions of a rectangle
 * Return:  the perimeter of the rectangle
 ***************************************************************************/

double RectanglePerimeter(double height, double width);

/* SquareArea returns the area of a square with a given side length.
 *
 * Receive: side, the side of a square
 * Return:  the area of the square
 ***************************************************************************/

double SquareArea(double side);

/* TrianglePerimeter returns the perimeter of a triangle of given
 * side lengths.
 *
 * Receive: side1, side2, side3, the side lenghts of a triangle
 * Return:  the perimeter of the triangle
 ***************************************************************************/

double TrianglePerimeter(double side1, double side2, double side3);

/* TriangleArea returns the area of a triangle of given side lengths.
 *
 * Receive: side1, side2, side3, the side lenghts of a triangle
 * Return:  the area of the triangle
 ***************************************************************************/

double TriangleArea(double side1, double side2, double side3);


/* prog3-31.cpp is a driver program to test the Geometry library.
 *
 * Input:  radius of a circle
 *         sides of a rectangle
 *         side of a square
 *         sides of a triangle
 * Output: circumference and area of circle
 *         perimeter of the rectangle
 *         area of the square
 *         perimeter and area of the triangle
 ***********************************************************************/

#include <iostream.h>                    // cin, cout, >>, <<
#include "Geometry.h"

int main()
{
   double radius;

   cout << "Please enter the radius of a circle: ";
   cin >> radius;

   cout << "Circumference of circle is " << CircleCircumference(radius) << endl;

   cout << "Area of circle is " << CircleArea(radius) << endl;

   double side1, side2;
```

```
        cout << "Please enter the length and width of a rectangle: ";
        cin >> side1 >> side2;

        cout << "Perimeter of rectangle is "
             << RectanglePerimeter(side1, side2) << endl;

        cout << "Please enter the side of a square: ";
        cin >> side1;
        cout << "Area of circie is " << SquareArea(side1) << endl;

        double side3;

        cout << "Please enter the 3 sides of a triangle: ";
        cin >> side1 >> side2 >> side3;

        cout << "Perimeter of triangle is "
             << TrianglePerimeter(side1, side2, side3) << endl;

        cout << "Area of triangle is "
             << TriangleArea(side1, side2, side3) << endl;

        return 0;
}


/* prog3-32.cpp is a program that uses the library Geometry to
 * compute the perimeter and area of various figures.
 *
 * Input:   code for a geometric figure
 *          radius of a circle, sides of a rectangle
 *          side of a square, sides of a triangle
 * Output: circumference and area of circle
 *          perimeter of the rectangle
 *          area of the square
 *          perimeter and area of the triangle
 ***************************************************************/

#include <iostream.h>                   // cin, cout, >>, <<
#include "Geometry.h"

int main()
{
    char code;
    for (;;)
    {
        cout << "Enter C (circle), R (rectangle), T(triangle), Q(quit): ";
        cin >> code;
        if (code == 'Q') break;

        switch(code)
        {
            case 'C' :
                        double radius;
                        cout << "Enter radius of circle: ";
                        cin >> radius;
                        cout << "Circumference of circle is "
                             << CircleCircumference(radius) << endl;
                        cout << "Area of circle is "
                             << CircleArea(radius) << endl;
                        break;
```

```
        case 'R' :
                double length, width;
                cout << "Enter length and width of rectangle: ";
                cin >> length>> width;
                cout << "Perimeter of rectangle is "
                      << RectanglePerimeter(length, width) << endl;
                cout << "Area of rectangle is " << length * width << endl;
                break;

        case 'T' :
                double side1, side2, side3;
                cout << "Enter the 3 sides of triangle: ";
                cin >> side1 >> side2 >> side3;

                cout << "Perimeter of triangle is "
                      << TrianglePerimeter(side1, side2, side3) << endl;
                cout << "Area of triangle is "
                      << TriangleArea(side1, side2, side3) << endl;
    }
  }
  return 0;
}
```

33.

```
/* Time.h provides an interface for a library of geometric functions.
 ************************************************************************/

long int SecondsToMinutes(long int seconds);

long int MinutesToHours(long int minutes);

double HoursToDays(long int hours);

double SecondsToDays(long int seconds);


/* Time.cpp provides the function implementations for Time,
 * a library of time-conversion functions.
 ************************************************************************/

//---------------------------------------------

long int SecondsToMinutes(long int seconds)
{
    return seconds / 60;
}

//---------------------------------------------

long int MinutesToHours(long int minutes)
{
    return minutes / 60;
}

//---------------------------------------------

double HoursToDays(long int hours)
{
    return hours / 24.0;
}
```

```
    //---------------------------------------------

    double SecondsToDays(long int seconds)
    {
        return HoursToDays( MinutesToHours( SecondsToMinutes(seconds) ) );
    }


    /* Time.doc provides the documentation for Time,
     * a library of time-conversion functions.
     ***************************************************************************/

    /* SecondsToMinutes converts Seconds to Minutes.
     *
     *    Receive: seconds
     *    Return:  minutes
     ***********************************************/

    long int SecondsToMinutes(long int seconds);


    /* MinutesToHours converts Minutes to Hours.
     *
     * Receive: minutes
     * Return:  hours
     ***********************************************/

    long int MinutesToHours(long int minutes);


    /* HoursToDays converts Hours to Days.
     *
     * Receive: hours
     * Return:  days
     ***********************************************/

    double HoursToDays(long int hours);


    /* SecondsToDays converts Seconds to Days.
     *
     * Receive: seconds
     * Return:  days
     ***********************************************/

    double SecondsToDays(long int seconds);


    /* prog3-33.cpp is a driver program to test the library Time.
     *
     * Input:  initial population, time elapsed, and grown rate
     * Output: current population
     **********************************************************/

    #include <iostream.h>                // cin, cout, >>, <<
    #include "Time.h"

    int main()
    {
        long int seconds, minutes, hours;
        double days;
```

```
    cout << "Please enter number of seconds: ";
    cin >> seconds;

    minutes = SecondsToMinutes(seconds);
    hours = MinutesToHours(minutes);
    days = HoursToDays(hours);
    cout << "In minutes this is " << minutes << endl
         << "which in hours is  " << hours << endl
         << "which in days is   " << days << endl;

    cout << "\nComputing days directly from seconds using SecondsToDays() gives "
         << SecondsToDays(seconds) << " days" << endl;

    return 0;
}
```

34.

```
/* Sphere.h provides an interface for a library of functions for spheres.
 ************************************************************************/

const double PI = 3.14159265358979323846;

double SphereSurfaceArea(double radius);

double SphereVolume(double radius);


/* Sphere.cpp provides the function implementations for Sphere,
 * a library of formulas for spheres.
 ************************************************************************/

#include "Sphere.h"

//---------------------------------------------

double SphereSurfaceArea(double radius)
{
    return 4.0 * PI * radius * radius;
}

double SphereVolume(double radius)
{
    return 4.0 * PI * radius * radius * radius / 3.0;
}


/* Sphere.doc provides the documentation for Sphere,
 * a library of functions for spheres.
 ************************************************************************/

/* SphereSurfaceArea returns the surface area of a sphere with
 * a given redius.
 *
 * Receive: radius, the radius of a sphere
 * Return:  the surface area of the sphere
 ************************************************************************/

double SphereSurfaceArea(double radius);
```

```
/* SphereVolume returns the volume of a sphere with a given redius.
 *
 * Receive: radius, the radius of a sphere
 * Return:  the volume of the sphere
 ****************************************************************************/

double SphereVolume(double radius);

/* prog3-34.cpp is a driver program to test the Sphere library.
 *
 * Input:  radius of a sphere
 * Output: surface area and volume of the sphere
 ***********************************************************/

#include <iostream.h>              // cin, cout, >>, <<
#include "Sphere.h"

int main()
{
   double radius;

   cout << "Please enter the radius of a sphere: ";
   cin >> radius;

   cout << "Surface area of sphere is " << SphereSurfaceArea(radius) << endl;

   cout << "Volume of sphere is " << SphereVolume(radius) << endl;

   return 0;
}
```

35. This is much the same as Problem 34. Copy the definition of PI from #34 and the prototypes of the following functions into Cylinder.h, prototypes with specifications into Cylinder.doc, and the following function definitions into Cylinder.cpp.

```
//---------------------------------------------------------------------

double CylinderSurfaceArea(double Radius, double Height)
{
   return 2.0 * PI * radius * (radius + height);
}

//---------------------------------------------------------------------

double CylinderLateralSurfaceArea(double radius, double height)
{
   return 2.0 * PI * radius * height;
}

//---------------------------------------------------------------------

double CylinderVolume(double radius, double height)
{
   return PI * radius * radius * height;
}
```

36. Decide which conversions you will support, write the functions, put the function prototypes in Measure.h, prototypes with specifications in Measure.doc, function definitions into Measure.cpp.

Chapter 4: Class Types and Expressions

Exercises 4.3

```
1.  i1 = 1        r1 = 4.0
    i2 = 2        r2 = 5.5
    i3 = 3        r3 = 6.6

2.  i1 = 1        r1 = 4.0
    i2 = 2        r2 = 5.0
    i3 = 3        r3 = 6.0

3.  i1 = 1        r1 = 2.2
    i2 = 3        r2 = 4.4
    i3 = 5        r3 = 6.6
```

4. Error - attempting to assign a double value (2.2) to an integer variable (i2).

```
5.  i1 = 1        r1 = .2       c1 = '2'
    i2 = 3        r2 = .4       c2 = '4'
    i3 = 5        r3 = .6       c3 = '6'

6.  i1 = 1        r1 = 2.2      c1 = ' '
    i2 = 3        r2 = 4.4      c2 = ' '
    i3= 5         r3 = 6.6      c3 = ' '

7.  i1= 1         c1 = 'A'
    i2 = 2        c2 = 'B'
    i3 = 3        c3 = 'C'

8.  i1 = 12
    i2 = 345
    i3 = 678

9.  i1 = 12
    i2 = 345
    i3 = 678

10. i1 = 10
    i2 = 229
    i3 = 55      (Input stops at the character 8 since it's not a legal octal digit, so only 67 is read.)

11. i1 = 18
    i2 = 58
    i3 = 188

12. 436437438

13. 436 437438

14. 121314

15. 141516

16. 014015016
```

17.   cde

18.   0xc0xd0xe

19.   -567.392
      0.00040
    0.0004

20.   -5.7e+02
    4.0e-04
    Tolerance:4.000e-04

21.   New balance =2559.50   c   8.02

22. i =   15j =8.00000000
             15   8

For Exercises 23-26, many different answers are possible. Also, answers may vary, depending on your compiler.

23. **Two possible answers:**
```
cout << setw(8) << setprecision(4) << r1
     << "     " << ch
     << setw(5) << n1 << '\n'
     << n2 << "PDQ"
     << setprecision(5) << r2;

cout << left
     << setw(10) << r1 << ch
     << right
     << setw(4) << n1 << "  " << '\n'
     << n2 << "PDQ" << r2;
```

24. **Two possible answers:**
```
cout << setw(8) << setprecision(3) << r1
     << setw(11) << setprecision(4) << r2
     << "***" << n1 << ' ' << ch << '\n'
     << setw(9) << setprecision(2) << r1
     << setw(4) << n1 << n2;

cout << left << setprecision(5) << setw(10) << r1
     << setfill('*') << setprecision(2) << setw(10) << r2
     << setfill(' ') << setw(4) << n1
     << setw(3) << ch << '\n'
     << setprecision(4) << setw(7) << r1
     << n1 << setw(18) << n2;
```

25.
```
cout << "Roots are " << setw(7) << setprecision(3) << r1
     << " and " << setw(8) << setprecision(5) << r2;
```

26.
```
cout << "Approximate angles: "
     << fixed << showpoint <<
     << setw(5) << setprecision(1) << r1 << " and" << r1
     << "Magnitudes are" << setw(7) << n1 << " and"
     << setw(6) << -n2;
```

Exercises 4.4

1. `','`
2. 5
3. 0
4. true
5. `rowboat.`
6. `float a boat.`
7. Error — Can't extract a substring from an empty string
8. `ow,`
9. 1
10. 6
11. NPOS
12. 11
13. 11
14. 1
15. 1
16. 6
17. 0
18. 2
19. NPOS
20. 20
21. 22
22. Error — i = 22, so substring reference in output statement is not valid.
23. `go float.`
24. `Borrow your boat?`
25. `mow, mow, mow your goat`
26. Error in text: There should be a second statement in the loop that reads:

    ```
            if (i == NPOS) break;
    ```

    Then the output produced is: `rxxw, rxxw, rxxw yxxxxr bxxxxt`

    Without this statement, a run-time error occurs.

27. ```
    int pos = last_first.find(",", 0);
        first_last = last_first.substr(pos + 2, last_first.length() - pos - 2);
        first_last += " " + last_first.substr(0, pos);
    ```

28.
```
/* MonthName converts the number of a month to a string
 * of the corresponding month.
 *
 * Receive: int monthNumber
 * Return:  string (name of month)
 *************************************************/

string MonthName(int monthNumber)
{
    switch(monthNumber)
    {
        case(1): return "January";
        case(2): return "February";
        case(3): return "March";
        case(4): return "April";
        case(5): return "May";
        case(6): return "June";
```
```

```
        case(7): return "July";
        case(8): return "August";
        case(9): return "September";
        case(10): return "October";
        case(11): return "November";
        case(12): return "December";
        default : cout << "\nMonth:  illegal month number: "
                       << monthNumber<< endl;
                  return "";
    }
}
```

29.

```
/* MonthNumber converts the name of a month to its
 * corresponding number.
 *
 * Receive: string monthName
 * Return:  int (number of month)
 *************************************************/

int MonthNumber(string monthName)
{
    for(int i = 0; i < monthName.length(); i++)
        if(isupper(monthName[i]))
            monthName[i] = tolower(monthName[i]);

    if(monthName == "january")
        return 1;
    if(monthName == "february")
        return 2;
    if(monthName == "march")
        return 3;
    if(monthName == "april")
        return 4;
    if(monthName == "may")
        return 5;
    if(monthName == "june")
        return 6;
    if(monthName == "july")
        return 7;
    if(monthName == "august")
        return 8;
    if(monthName == "september")
        return 9;
    if(monthName == "october")
        return 10;
    if(monthName == "november")
        return 11;
    if(monthName == "december")
        return 12;
    cout << "\nMonthNumber:  illegal month name: " << monthName << endl;
    return 0;
}
```

30.

```
#include <ctype.h>     // islower(), toupper(), isupper(), tolower()

/* LowerToUpper turns a string into all uppercase.
 *
 * Receive: string lower
 * Return:  string lower (in uppercase)
 ****************************************************/

string LowerToUpper(string lower)
{
   for(int i = 0; i < lower.length(); i++)
      if(islower(lower[i]))
         lower[i] = toupper(lower[i]);

   return lower;
}

/* UpperToLower turns a string into all lowercase.
 *
 * Receive: string upper
 * Return:  string upper (in lowercase)
 ****************************************************/

string UpperToLower(string upper)
{
   for(int i = 0; i < upper.length(); i++)
      if(isupper(upper[i]))
         upper[i] = tolower(upper[i]);

   return upper;
}
```

31.

```
/* ReplaceAll replaces all occurrences of one string in another.
 *
 * Receive: strings str, substring, newSubstring
 * Return:  string str with all occurrences of substring
 *          replaced by newSubstring
 ***********************************************************/

string ReplaceAll(string str, string substring, string newSubstring )
{
   int pos = -1;
   for(;;)
   {
      pos = str.find(substring, pos + 1);
      if (pos == NPOS) return str;
      str.replace(pos, substring.length(),  newSubstring);
   }
}
```

32.
```
/* NameChange takes a full name (First Middle Last) and converts
 * it into another form ("Last, F. M.").
 *
 * Receive: strings firstName, middleName, lastName
 * Return:  the changed form string
 ****************************************************************/

string NameChange(string firstName, string middleName, string lastName)
{
    return lastName + ", " + firstName) + " " + middleName.substr(0,1) + ".";
}
```

33.
```
/* NameChange takes a full name(First Middle Last) and
 * converts it into another form ("Last, F. M.").
 *
 * Receive: string name
 * Return:  the changed form string
 ****************************************************************/
#include <ctype.h>

string NameChange(string name)
{
    unsigned endFirst,
             startMiddle,
             startLast;
    endFirst = name.find(" ", 0);
    startMiddle = endFirst + 1;
    while (isspace(name[startMiddle]))
        startMiddle++;

    startLast = name.find(" ", startMiddle);
    while (isspace(name[startLast ]))
        startLast++;

    return name.substr(startLast, name.length()-1) + ", " +
           name.substr(0, endFirst + 1) + name.substr(0,1) + ".";
}
```

34.
```
/* IsPalindrome returns true if the String is a palindrome;
 * that is, if it does not change when the order of the
 * characters in the string is reversed.
 *
 * Receive:  str, the string
 * Return:   true if str is a palindrome, false if not
 ****************************************************************/

bool IsPalindrome(string & str)
{
    int strLength = str.length(),
        limit = strLength / 2;

    for (int i = 0; i < limit ; i++)
        if (str[i] != str[strLength-i-1])
            return false;

    return true;
}
```

Programming Problems
Section 4.4

1-6. These are all similar to the example in Figure 4.1 of the text. Lyrics — at least approximations to them — are given here and programs for Problems 1 and 2.

1. Happy Birthday to you!
    Happy Birthday to you!
    Happy Birthday dear (name of person)!
    Happy Birthday to you!

```
/* prog4-1.cpp displays the lyrics for "Happy Birthday to You".
 *
 * Input:  person's name
 * Output: lyrics for the "Happy Birthday to You"
 ************************************************************/

#include <iostream.h>              // cin, cout, >>, <<
#include <string>                  // string

void PrintSong(string name);

int main()
{
   string person;
   cout << "Enter name of birthday person: ";
   getline(cin, person);

   PrintSong(person);

   return 0;
}

/* PrintSong() prints "Happy Birthday to You".
 *
 * Receive: name, a string.
 * Output:  the song with name inserted appropriately.
 ********************************************************/

void PrintSong(string name)
{
   cout << "Happy Birthday to you!\n"
        << "Happy Birthday to you!\n"
        << "Happy Birthday dear " << name << "!\n"
        << "Happy Birthday to you!\n";
}
```

2. Old Macdonald had a farm, E-I-E-I-O
    And on his farm he had a(n) (animal), E-I-E-I-O
    With a(n) (sound)-(sound) here and a(n) (sound)-(sound) there
    Here a(n) (sound) there a(n) (sound)
    Everywhere a(n) (sound)-(sound)
    Old Macdonald had a farm, E-I-E-I-O

```
/* prog4-2.cpp displays the lyrics for "Old MacDonald had a Farm".
 * using a function PrintVerse().
 *
 * Input:  none
 * Output: lyrics for the "Old MacDonald had a Farm"
 **********************************************************************/

#include <iostream.h>              // cin, cout, >>, <<
#include <string>                  // string

void PrintVerse(string animal, string sound);

int main()
{
    PrintVerse("cow", "moo");
    PrintVerse("pig", "oink");
    PrintVerse("dog", "woof");
    // etc.. . .

    return 0;
}

/* PrintVerse() prints one verse of "Old MacDonald had a Farm".
 *
 * Receive: strings animal and sound.
 * Output:  a verse with animal and soundinserted appropriately.
 **********************************************************************/

void PrintVerse(string animal, string sound)
{
    string a_an_1
           = (animal.find_first_of("aeiouAEIOU", 0) == 0 ? "an " : "a "),
           a_an_2
           = (sound.find_first_of("aeiouAEIOU", 0) == 0 ? "an " : "a ");

    cout << "\nOld MacDonald had a farm, E-I-E-I-O"
         << "\nAnd on this farm he had "
         << a_an_1 << animal << ", E-I-E-I-O"
         << "\nWith "<< a_an_2 << sound << '-' << sound << " here and "
         << a_an_2 << sound << '-' << sound << " there"
         << "\nHere " << a_an_2 << sound
         << " there " << a_an_2 << sound
         << "\nEverywhere " << a_an_2 << sound << '-' << sound
         << "\nOld MacDonald had a farm, E-I-E-I-O\n";
}
```

3.   This old man, he played one, he played knick-knack on my thumb
     With a knick-knack patty whack, give the dog a bone
     This old man came rolling home

     This old man, he played two, he played knick-knack on my shoe
     With a knick-knack patty whack, give the dog a bone
     This old man came rolling home

     ...three...on my knee...,   ...four...on my door...,   ...five...on my hive...

     ...six...on my sticks...,   ...seven...up to heaven...,   ...eight...on my gate...

     ...nine...all the time...,   ...ten...once again...

4. She'll be comin' round the mountain when she comes (toot toot)
    She'll be comin' round the mountain when she comes (toot toot)
    She'll be comin' round the mountain, she'll be comin' round the mountain
    She'll be comin' round the mountain when she comes (toot toot)

    She'll be drivin six white horses when she comes (whoa back!)...

    We'll all go out to meet her when she comes (Hi Babe!)...

    We'll all have chicken and dumplings when she comes (Yum Yum!)...

    We'll have to sleep at grandma's when she comes (scratch scratch!)...

    The dogs'll start to holler when she comes (woof woof!)...

5. Oh, when the Saints go marching in
    Oh, when the Saints go marching in
    Lord, I want to be in that number
    When the Saints go marching in.

    ... when the sun refuses to shine, ...

    ... when the dead, in Christ shall rise ...

6. You put your right foot in
    You put your right foot out
    You put your right foot in and you shake it all about
    You do the Hokey Pokey and you turn yourself around
    That's what it's all about

    ... left foot ...   ... right hand ...   ... left hand ...   ... right shoulder ...

    ... left shoulder ...   ... head ...   ... rear end ...   ... elbows ...

    ... knees ...   ... nose ...   ... thumb ...   ... whole self ...

7.

```
/* prog4-7.cpp is a driver program to test the function
 * MonthName() from Exercise 28.
 *
 * Input:  a nonnegative integer (number of a month)
 * Output: Name of month (or error message)
 ********************************************************/

#include <iostream.h>                // cin, cout, >>, <<
#include <string>                    // string

string MonthName(int monthNumber);

int main()
{
    int n;

    cout << "Enter a number from 1 throough 12: ";
    cin >> n;

    cout << "Month name is " << MonthName(n) << endl;

    return 0;
}
```

```
/* Insert definition of function MonthName()
   from Exercise 28 here. */
```

8.
```
/* prog4-8.cpp is a driver program to test the function
 * MonthNumber() from Exercise 29.
 *
 * Input:  a string (name of a month)
 * Output: number of month (or error message)
 ************************************************************/

#include <iostream.h>              // cin, cout, >>, <<
#include <string>                  // string

int MonthNumber(string monthName);

int main()
{
   string name;

   cout << "Enter the name of a month: ";
   cin >> name;

   cout << "Month number is " << MonthNumber(name) << endl;

   return 0;
}


/* Insert definition of function MonthNumber()
   from Exercise 29 here. */
```

9.
```
/* prog4-9.cpp is a driver program to test the functions
 * LowerToUpper() and UpperToLower from Exercise 30.
 *
 * Input:  a string
 * Output: the string in all upper case, then in all lower case
 ************************************************************/

#include <iostream.h>              // cin, cout, >>, <<
#include <string>                  // string

string LowerToUpper(string lower);
string UpperToLower(string lower);

int main()
{
   string str;

   cout << "Enter a string: ";
   getline(cin, str);

   cout << LowerToUpper(str) << endl;
   cout << UpperToLower(str) << endl;

   return 0;
}
```

```
/* Insert definition of functions LowerToUpper() and
   UpperToLower from Exercise 30 here. */
```

10.

```
/* prog4-10.cpp is a driver program to test the function
 * ReplaceAll() from Exercise 31.
 *
 * Input:  strings str1, str2, str3
 * Output: str1 with all occurrences of str2 replaced by str3
 ****************************************************************/

#include <iostream.h>              // cin, cout, >>, <<
#include <string>                  // string

string ReplaceAll(string str, string substring, string newSubstring);

int main()
{
    string str1, str2, str3;

    cout << "This program replaces all occurrences of str2 in str1 by str3.\n";
    cout << "Enter str1: ";
    getline(cin, str1);
    cout << "Enter str2: ";
    getline(cin, str2);
    cout << "Enter str3: ";
    getline(cin, str3);

    cout << "New string is :\n" << ReplaceAll(str1, str2,str3) << endl;

    return 0;
}

/* Insert definition of function ReplaceAll()
   from Exercise 31 here. */
```

11.

```
/* prog4-11.cpp is a driver program to test the function
 * NameChange() from Exercise 32.
 *
 * Input:  strings first, middle, last
 * Output: name in the form, last, first m.
 ****************************************************************/

#include <iostream.h>              // cin, cout, >>, <<
#include <string>                  // string

string NameChange(string firstName, string middleName, string lastName);

int main()
{
    string first, middle, last;

    cout << "Enter first, middle, and last names (no spaces in names): ";
    cin >> first >> middle >> last;
    cout << "Changed string is :\n" << NameChange(first, middle, last) << endl;

    return 0;
}
```

```
/* Insert definition of function NameChange()
   from Exercise 32 here. */
```

12.
```
/* prog4-12.cpp is a driver program to test the function
 * NameChange() from Exercise 33.
 *
 * Input:  string name
 * Output: name in the form, last, first m.
 *************************************************************/

#include <iostream.h>              // cin, cout, >>, <<
#include <string>                  // string

string NameChange(string name);

int main()
{
   string name;

   cout << "Enter a name (no spaces in first, middle, or last): ";
   getline(cin, name);
   cout << "Changed string is:\n" << NameChange(name) << endl;

   return 0;
}

/* Insert definition of function NameChange()
   from Exercise 33 here. */
```

13.
```
/* prog4-13.cpp is a driver program to test the function
 * IsAPalindrome() from Exercise 34.
 *
 * Input:  a string str
 * Output: true (1) if str is a palindrome, false (0) otherwise
 *************************************************************/

#include <iostream.h>              // cin, cout, >>, <<
#include <string>                  // string

bool IsPalindrome(string & str);

int main()
{
   string str;

   cout << "Enter a string: ";
   getline(cin, str);

   cout << "This " << (IsPalindrome(str) ? "is " : "is not ")
        << "a palindrome\n";

   return 0;
}

/* Insert definition of function IsPalindrome()
   from Exercise 34 here. */
```

14.

```
/* prog4-14 is a driver program to test the function StringCount().
 *
 * Input:  a string searchStringand several lines of text
 * Output: a count of the number of occurrences of searchString
 *         in the text
 *************************************************************************/

#include <iostream.h>          // cin, cout, <<, >>
#include <string>              // string

int StringCount(string str);

int main()
{
   cout << "This program searches text for a given string.\n"
           "Enter the string being sought: ";
   string searchString;
   getline(cin, searchString);

   cout << "\n*** " << StringCount(searchString)
        << " occurrences of "  << searchString << " were found\n";

   return 0;
}

/* StringCount() counts occurrences of a string in several lines
 * of text.
 *
 * Receive:  str, the string
 * Input:    several lines of text
 * Return:   # of occurrences of str in the text
 *************************************************************************/

int StringCount(string str)
{
   int count = 0;
   string lineOfText;

   cout << "Enter lines of text (^D to stop)\n";
   for (;;)
   {
      getline(cin, lineOfText);
      if (cin.eof()) break;
      int position = -1;
      for (;;)
      {
         position = lineOfText.find(str, position + 1);
         if (position == NPOS) break;
         count ++;
      }
   }

   return count;
}
```

15.

```
/* prog4-15 is a driver program to test the function StringCount().
 *
 * Input:  a string searchStringand several lines of text
 * Output: a count of the number of occurrences of searchString
 *         in the text
 ********************************************************************/

#include <iostream.h>              // cin, cout, <<, >>
#include <iomanip.h>               // setw()
#include <string>                  // string

void FindString(string str);

int main()
{
    cout << "This program searches text for a given string.\n"
            "Enter the string being sought: ";
    string searchString;
    getline(cin, searchString);
    FindString(searchString);

    return 0;
}

/* FindString() finds occurrences of a string in several lines
 * of text and places asterisks under all of them.
 *
 * Receive: str, the string
 * Input:   several lines of text
 * Output:  *'s under all occurrences of str in the text
 ****************************************************************/

void FindString(string str)
{
    string lineOfText;
    int strLength = str.length();

    cout << "Enter lines of text (^D to stop)\n";
    for (;;)
    {
        getline(cin, lineOfText);
        if (cin.eof()) break;
        int oldPosition = -1,
            newPosition;
        for (;;)
        {
            newPosition = lineOfText.find(str, oldPosition + 1);
            if (newPosition == NPOS) break;

            int offset = (oldPosition == -1 ? 1 : strLength);
            for (int i = 1; i <= newPosition - oldPosition - offset; i++)
              cout << " ";
            for (int i = 1; i <= strLength;i++)
                cout << '*';

            oldPosition = newPosition;
        }
        if (oldPosition != -1)
            cout << endl;
    }
}
```

16. This program is very straightforward and is much like Problems 1-6. Simply read in the necessary strings (like
title, firstName, middleName, etc.) and then output the contest letter to the screen, substituting the strings
you input for the underlined locations.

17.

```
/* prog4-17.cpp converts units in cooking.
 *
 * Input:  amount, units, and desired units
 * Output: the conversion
 **********************************************/

#include <iostream.h>            // cin, cout, <<, >>
#include <string>                // string

double CookingConversion(string Units, string NewUnits);

int main()
{
    double amount;
    string units,
           newUnits;

    cout << "\nPlease enter the amount: ";
    cin >> amount;

    cout << "Please enter the units: ";
    cin >> units;

    cout << "Please enter the new units desired: ";
    cin >> newUnits;

    double factor = CookingConversion(units, newUnits);

    if (factor == 0.0)
       cout << "\nOne or both of the units unrecognized."
               "\nMust be TEASPOONS, TABLESPOONS, CUPS, PINTS, QUARTS.\n";
    else
       cout << "\nThere are " << factor * amount << ' '
            << newUnits << " in " << amount << ' ' << units << ".\n";

    return 0;
}

/* CookingConversion converts among teaspoons, tablespoons, cups, pints,
 * and quarts.
 *
 * Receive:  units, the type of units given
 *           newUnits, the type of units desired
 * Return:   the number of 1 'newUnits' in 1 'unit'
 ********************************************************************/

double CookingConversion(string units, string newUnits)
{
    const char TEASPOONS[] = "TEASPOONS",
               TABLESPOONS[] = "TABLESPOONS",
               CUPS[] = "CUPS",
               PINTS[] = "PINTS",
               QUARTS[] = "QUARTS";
```

```
if (units == TEASPOONS)
{
   if (newUnits == TEASPOONS)
      return 1.0;
   if (newUnits == TABLESPOONS)
      return 1.0 / 3.0;
   if (newUnits == CUPS)
      return 1.0 / 3.0 / 16.0;
   if (newUnits == PINTS)
      return 1.0 / 3.0 / 16.0 / 2.0;
   if (newUnits == QUARTS)
      return 1.0 / 3.0 / 16.0 / 2.0 / 2.0;
   //else
      return 0.0;
}
if (units == TABLESPOONS)
{
   if (newUnits == TEASPOONS)
      return 3.0;
   if (newUnits == TABLESPOONS)
      return 1.0;
   if (newUnits == CUPS)
      return 1.0 / 16.0;
   if (newUnits == PINTS)
      return 1.0 / 16.0 / 2.0;
   if (newUnits == QUARTS)
      return 1.0 / 16.0 / 2.0 / 2.0;
   //else
      return 0.0;
}
if (units == CUPS)
{
   if (newUnits == TEASPOONS)
      return 16.0 * 3.0;
   if (newUnits == TABLESPOONS)
      return 16.0;
   if (newUnits == CUPS)
      return 1.0;
   if (newUnits == PINTS)
      return 1.0 / 2.0;
   if (newUnits == QUARTS)
      return 1.0 / 2.0 / 2.0;
   //else
      return 0.0;
}
if (units == PINTS)
{
   if (newUnits == TEASPOONS)
      return 2.0 * 16.0 * 3.0;
   if (newUnits == TABLESPOONS)
      return 2.0 * 16.0;
   if (newUnits == CUPS)
      return 2.0;
   if (newUnits == PINTS)
      return 1.0;
   if (newUnits == QUARTS)
      return 1.0 / 2.0;
   //else
      return 0.0;
}
```

```
    if (units == QUARTS)
    {
        if (newUnits == TEASPOONS)
            return 2.0 * 2.0 * 16.0 * 3.0;
        if (newUnits == TABLESPOONS)
            return 2.0 * 2.0 * 16.0;
        if (newUnits == CUPS)
            return 2.0 * 2.0;
        if (newUnits == PINTS)
            return 2.0;
        if (newUnits == QUARTS)
            return 1.0;
        //else
            return 0.0;
    }
    return 0.0;
}
```

18.
```
/* prog4-18.cpp tests AreAnagrams().
 *
 * Input:  two strings
 * Output: whether or not they are anagrams
 **********************************************/

#include <iostream.h>                  // cin, cout, <<, >>
#include <string>                      // string

bool AreAnagrams(string Str1, string str2);

int main()
{
    string string1, string2;

    cout << "\nPlease enter two words: ";
    cin >> string1 >> string2;

    cout << "\nThese strings are ";
    if (!AreAnagrams(string1, string2))
        cout << "not ";
    cout << "anagrams.\n";

    return 0;
}

/* AreAnagrams returns true if the two strings are anagrams;
 * that is, if one string is a permutation of the characters
 * of the other string.
 *
 * Receive:  str1, str2, two strings
 * Return:   true if str1 and Str2 are anagrams, false if not
 ***************************************************************/

bool AreAnagrams(string str1, string str2)
{
    string temp = str2;
    int pos;
```

```
    for (int i = 0; i < str1.length(); i++)
    {
        pos = temp.find(str1.substr(i,1));

        if (pos == NPOS)
            return false;

        temp.remove(pos, 1);
    }

    return true;
}
```

19.

```
/* prog4-19.cpp plays the game of Hangman.
 *
 * Input:  individual guesses
 * Output: success or failure
 **********************************************/

#include <iostream.h>              // cin, cout, <<, >>
#include <string>                  // string
#include <ctype.h>                 // isalpha()

void PlayHangman(string word);
void ConvertToLower(string & word);

int main()
{
    string word;                   // word to be guessed

    for (;;)
    {
        cout << "\nEnter word to guess (*** to stop): ";
        cin >> word;
        if (word == "***") break;

        PlayHangman(word);         // play the game
    }

    return 0;
}


/* PlayHangman plays one game of Hangman with a given word.
 *
 * Receive:  the word with which to play
 ****************************************************************/

void PlayHangman(string word)
{
    const int BODY_PARTS = 8;              // number of wrong guesses allowed

    string guessWord = word,               // has '_' on letters not found
           checkWord = word;               // has '_' on letters found

    ConvertToLower(checkWord);
```

```
for (int i = 0; i < checkWord.length(); i++)
    if (isalpha(guessWord[i]))
        guessWord[i] = '_';

int partsLeft = BODY_PARTS,        // number of guesses left
    pos;                           // used in string searches
string guess;                      // current character guess

for (;;)
{
    cout << "\nThe word: " << guessWord << endl;

    cout << "\nPlease enter a character: ";
    cin >> guess;

    ConvertToLower(guess);

    pos = checkWord.find(guess, 0);
    if (pos != NPOS)
    {
        for(;;)
        {
            cout << "\nGood choice!\n";
            guessWord[pos] = word[pos];
            checkWord[pos] = '_';
            pos = checkWord.find(guess, 0);
            if (pos == NPOS) break;
        }
        if (guessWord.find("_", 0) == NPOS)
        {
            cout << "\nYou win!  The word you completed is: "
                << word << endl;
            break;
        }
    }

    else
    {
        partsLeft--;

        if (partsLeft == 0)
        {
            cout << "\nSorry -- you lose!\n"
                    "\nThe word was: " << word << endl;
            break;
        }
        else
        {
            cout << "\nBad choice -- you have "
                << partsLeft << " body parts left!\n";
        }
    }
}
}
```

```
/* ConvertToLower makes a string all lowercase.
 *
 * Receive:  str, a string
 * Return:   str, the string with no uppercase letters
 ***********************************************************/

void ConvertToLower(string & str)
{
   for (int i = 0; i < str.length(); i++)
      if (isupper(str[i]))
         str[i] = tolower(str[i]);
}
```

20.

```
/* prog4-20.cpp uses Rev. Zeller's method to find the day of the week
 * on which a given date fell or will fall.
 *
 * Input:   Values for Month, Day, and Year; Response
 * Output:  Day on which date fell or will fall
 *****************************************************************************/

#include <iostream.h>              // cin, cout, <<, >>
#include <string>                  // string

string DayOfTheWeek(string month, int day, int year);

int main()
{
   string month;                   // month,
   int day, year;                  //    day,&  year to be processed

   for (;;)
   {
      cout << "\nEnter month, day, and year (STOP 0 0 to stop): ";
      cin >> month >> day >> year;
      if (month == "STOP") break;

      cout << "That date fell or will fall on "
           << DayOfTheWeek(month, day, year) << endl;
   }
   return 0;
}

/* DayOfTheWeek uses Rev. Zeller's formula to find the day of
 * the week on which a given date falls.
 *
 * Receive:  month name, day, and year
 * Return :  day of the week
 *
 ***********************************************************/

string DayOfTheWeek(string month, int day, int year)
{
   int a, b, c, d, w, x, y, z, r;
   // variables in Zeller's formulas a = month (March = 1, April = 2,
   // ..., February = 12), b = day, c = year of century, d = year

   if (month == "March") a = 1;
   else if (month == "April") a = 2;
   else if (month == "May") a = 3;
   else if (month == "June") a = 4;
```

```
      else if (month == "July") a = 5;
      else if (month == "August") a = 6;
      else if (month == "September") a = 7;
      else if (month == "October") a = 8;
      else if (month == "November") a = 9;
      else if (month == "December") a = 10;
      else if (month == "January") a = 11;
      else if (month == "February") a = 12;
      else
      {
         cerr << "Illegal month name -- " << month << endl;
         return "****";
      }
      if (a >= 11) year--;
      b = day;
      c = year %   100;
      d = year / 100;
      w = (13*a - 1) / 5;
      x = c / 4;
      y = d / 4;
      z = w + x + y + b + c - 2*d;
      r = z % 7;

      switch (r)
      {
         case 0 : return "Sunday";
         case 1 : return "Monday";
         case 2 : return "Tuesday";
         case 3 : return "Wednesday";
         case 4 : return "Thursday";
         case 5 : return "Friday";
         case 6 : return "Saturday";
      }
}



21.
/* prog4-21.cpp simulates playing the coin tossing game discussed in
 * the text and prints the average payoff for the games.
 *
 * Input:  the number of times to play
 * Output: the simulation and average payoff
 ***********************************************************************/

#include <iostream.h>              // cin, cout, <<, >>
#include <iomanip.h>               // setiosflags(), setprecision()
#include "RandomInt.h"

int main()
{
   const int HEADS = 0,
             TAILS = 1;
   int times;

   cout << "\nHow many times would you like to play? ";
   cin >> times;

   RandomInt coin (HEADS, TAILS);
   long int payoff,
            totalPayoff = 0;
   int totalTails;
```

```
        for (int i = 0; i < times; i++)
        {
            payoff = 2;
            totalTails = 0;

            cout << "\nTossing... ";

            coin.Generate();

            for (;;)
            {
                if ((coin == HEADS) break;

                cout << "Tails, ";
                payoff *= 2;
                totalTails++;
                coin.Generate();
            }

            cout << "Heads.  Payoff: $" << payoff;

            totalPayoff += payoff;
        }

        cout << "\n\nTotal payoff: $" << totalPayoff
             << setiosflags(ios::showpoint | ios::fixed)
             << setprecision(2)
             << "\nAverage payoff: $"
             << double(totalPayoff) / double(times) << '\n';

        return 0;
}


22.
/* prog4-22.cpp simulates the gambling game described in the text and
 * displays his average winnings.
 *
 * Input:  number of times to play
 * Output: simulation and average winnings
 *******************************************************************/

#include <iostream.h>            // cin, cout, <<, >>
#include <iomanip.h>             // setiosflags(), setprecision()
#include "RandomInt.h"

int main()
{
    int times;

    cout << "\nHow many times would you like to play? ";
    cin >> times;

    RandomInt die1 (1, 12),
              die2 (1, 12),
              card (1, 13);

    long int payoff,
             totalPayoff = 0;
```

```
    for (int i = 0; i < times; i++)
    {
        payoff = 0;

        cout << "\nRolling... ";

        die1.Generate();
        die2.Generate();

        cout << die1 << ' ' << die2;

        if ( (die1 + die2) % 2 == 0)
        {
            cout << " Drawing... ";
            card.Generate();
            cout << card;
            if ( (card == 1) || (card == 3) || (card == 5) ||
                 (card == 7) || (card == 9) )
                payoff = int(card);
        }

        if (payoff == 0)
            cout << " ...lost.";
        else
            cout << " ...won $" << payoff << '!';

        totalPayoff += payoff;
    }

    double averageWinnings = ( double(totalPayoff) - double(times) * 5.0 ) /
                             double(times);

    cout << setiosflags(ios::showpoint | ios::fixed) << setprecision(2);

    if (averageWinnings > 0)
        cout << "\n\nAverage winnings: $" << averageWinnings << '\n';
    else
        cout << "\n\nAverage losses: $" << -averageWinnings << '\n';

    return 0;
}
```

23.

```
/* prog4-23 simulates a number of times at bat and calculates the
 * batting average of the simulated times at bat.
 *
 * Input:  the number of times at bat
 * Output: the batting average
 **********************************************************************/

#include <iostream.h>              // cin, cout, <<, >>
#include <iomanip.h>               // setiosflags(), setprecision()
#include "RandomInt.h"

int main()
{
    int times;

    cout << "\nHow many times at bat? ";
    cin >> times;

    RandomInt atBat (1, 1000);
```

```
    int outs = 0,
        walks = 0,
        singles = 0,
        doubles = 0,
        triples = 0,
        homeRuns = 0;

    for (int i = 0; i < times; i++)
    {
        atBat.Generate();

        if (atBat <= 634)
            outs++;
        else if (atBat <= 737)
            walks++;
        else if (atBat <= 927)
            singles++;
        else if (atBat <= 976)
            doubles++;
        else if (atBat <= 987)
            triples++;
        else
            homeRuns++;
    }

    cout << "\nStats for Johann after " << times << " at bats: "
         << "\n\tOuts: " << outs
         << "\n\tWalks: " << walks
         << "\n\tSingles: " << singles
         << "\n\tDoubles: " << doubles
         << "\n\tTriples: " << triples
         << "\n\tHome Runs: " << homeRuns;

    int  hits = singles + doubles + triples + homeRuns;
    double average = double(hits) / double(times - walks);

    cout << setiosflags(ios::showpoint | ios::fixed) << setprecision(3)
         << "\n\nBatting average: " << average << '\n';

    return 0;
}
```

24.

```
/* prog4-24.cpp simulates the "drunkard's walk problem," displaying the
 * percentage of time the person ends up at home and the average number
 * of blocks walked on each trip.
 *
 * Output:  the information
 ********************************************************************/

#include <iostream.h>                // cin, cout, <<, >>
#include "RandomInt.h"

int main()
{
    const int TIMES = 500;

    RandomInt walk (1,3);

    int location;
```

```
     long int totalHome,
             totalBlocks;

     for (int start = 2; start <= 7; start++)
     {
        totalHome = totalBlocks = 0;

        for (int trip = 1; trip <= TIMES; trip++)
        {
           location = start;

           for (;;)
           {
              walk.Generate();
              totalBlocks++;

              if (int(walk) == 1)
                 ;ocation++;
              else
                 location--;

              if (location == 1 || location == 8) break;
           }

           if (location == 8)
              totalHome++;
        }

        double averageBlocks = double(totalBlocks) / double(TIMES),
               percentHome = double(totalHome) * 100.0 / double(TIMES);

        cout << "From block " << start
             << ", he averaged " << averageBlocks
             << " blocks, reaching home " << percentHome
             << "% of the time.\n";
     }

     return 0;
}
```

25.

```
/* prog4-25.cpp simulates particles entering the shield described in the
 * text and determines what percentage of them reaches the outside.
 *
 * Input:  the number of particles
 * Output: the percentage of particles reaching the outside
 *********************************************************************/

#include <iostream.h>            // cin, cout, <<, >>
#include "RandomInt.h"

int main()
{
   const int COLLISION_LIMIT = 10,
             THICKNESS = 5;

   int particles;

   cout << "\nPlease enter the number of particles: ";
   cin >> particles;

   RandomInt direction (1,4);
```

```
   int distance,
       collisions,
       oldDirection,
       outsiders = 0;

   for (int i = 1; i <= particles; i++)
   {
      distance = 1;
      collisions = 0;
      oldDirection = 1;

      for (;;)
      {
         direction.Generate();

         if (int(direction) != oldDirection)
            collisions++;

         if (int(direction) == 1)
            distance++;
         else if (int(direction) == 2)
            distance--;

         oldDirection = int(Direction);
         if (collisions > COLLISION_LIMIT ||
             distance <= 0 || distance >= THICKNESS) break;
      }

      if (distance == THICKNESS)
         outsiders++;
   }

   double percentOutside = double(outsiders) * 100.0 / double(particles);

   cout << endl << percentOutside << "% of the particles escaped!\n";

   return 0;
}
```

26.

```
/* prog 4-26.cpp approximates pi using the dart-throwing method.
 *
 * Input:  the number of darts to throw
 * Output: the approximation to pi
 ********************************************************************/

#include <iostream.h>              // cin, cout, <<, >>
#include "RandomInt.h"

int main()
{
   int darts;

   cout << "\nPlease enter the number of darts: ";
   cin >> darts;

   int dartsInCircle = 0;

   RandomInt X(0,9999),
             Y (0,9999);
```

```
double realX,
       realY;

for (int i = 1; i <= darts; i++)
{
   X.Generate();
   Y.Generate();

   realX = double(int(X)) / 10000.0;    // simulate random real numbers
   realY = double(int(Y)) / 10000.0;    //   by dividing integers by 10000

   if (realX * realX + realY * realY <= 1)
      dartsInCircle++;
}

cout << "\nApproximation to pi: "
     << 4.0 * double(dartsInCircle) / double(darts) << endl;

return 0;
}
```

27. The experiment can be simulated by assuming two parallel lines, both vertical, say x = 0 and
    x = 2. Then generate a random real number C between 0 and 2, representing the center of the dropped needle, and
    another random number Theta between 0 and $\pi/2$, representing the angle the needle makes with the positive x
    axis:

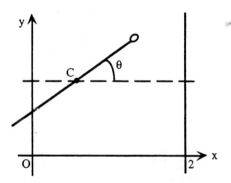

    The left and right endpoints of the needle can then be calculated by:

```
horizontal = cos(theta)
left = c - horizontal
right = c + horizontal
```

    if left ≤ 0 or right ≥ 2, the needle has crossed one of the lines.

```
/* prog 4-27.cpp solves the Buffon Needle problem.
 *
 * Input:  the number of times to drop the needle
 * Output: probability p of crossing a line and 2/p (approx. to pi)
 ************************************************************************/

#include <iostream.h>              // cin, cout, <<, >>
#include "RandomInt.h"
```

```
int main()
{
   double HALF_PI = 1.5705796327;
   int numDrops;

   cout << "\nPlease enter the number of times to drop needle: ";
   cin >> numDrops;

   double c,            // location of needle's center (between x = 0 and x = 2)
        theta,          // angle from x axis to needle (0 <= theta <= pi/2)
        horizontal,     // horizontal distnace from needle's center to its end(s)
        left, right;    // locations of needle's left, right end

   int crossings = 0;// # of times needle crosses x = 0 or x = 2

   // Begin the simulation

   RandomInt a(0,9999),
             b (0,9999);
   for(int i = 1; i <= numDrops; i++)
   {
      a.Generate();
      b.Generate();
                                         // simulate random real numbers
      c = 2.0 * double(int(a)) / 10000.0; // by dividing integers by 10000
      theta = HALF_PI * double(int(b)) / 10000.0;
      horizontal = cos(theta);
      left = c - horizontal;
      right = c + horizontal;
      if (left <= 0.0 || right >= 2.0)
         crossings++;
   }

   double probability = double(crossings) / double(numDrops);
   cout << "Calculated probability of needle crossing line is "
        << probability
        << "\nPi approx. equal to 2/probability = " << 2.0 / probability
        << endl;
}
```

28.

```
/* prog 4-28.cpp uses a function NormalRandom() to generate normally
 * distributed random numbers representing tensile strengths of metal
 * components and determine how many must be rejected
 *
 * Input:  mean and std. deviation of normal distribution, lower
 *         limit on tensile strengt
 * Output: number of components tested and number to be rejected
 ***********************************************************************/

#include <iostream.h>        // cin, cout, <<, >>
#include "RandomInt.h"

double NormalRandom (RandomInt & x, double mu, double sigma);
```

```
int main()
{
   double mean,            // mean and
          stdDeviation,    // standard deviation of normal distribution
          lowerLimit;      // lower limit on tensile strength (reject if below)
   int numComponents;      // number of components tested

   cout << "Enter mean, standard deviation and the lowest acceptable "
           "\nvalue for tensile strength: ";
   cin >> mean >> stdDeviation >> lowerLimit;
   cout << "Enter number of components to simulate: ";
   cin >> numComponents;

   // Carry out the simulation
   int numRejected = 0;    // number of rejected components
   double tensileStrength;
   RandomInt x(0,9999);
   for(int i = 1; i <= numComponents; i++)
   {
     tensileStrength = NormalRandom(x, mean, stdDeviation);
     if (tensileStrength < lowerLimit)
        numRejected++;
   }

   cout << "Out of " << numComponents << " components, "
        << numRejected << " were rejected.\n";
}

/* NormalRandom generates normally distributed random numbers.
 *
 * Receive:   mean (mu) and standard deviation (sigman) of a normal
 *            distribution; random integer x
 * Pass back: last random int x generated (used in next call)
 * Return:    a normally-distributed random number
 ********************************************************************/

double NormalRandom (RandomInt & x, double mu, double sigma)
{
   double sum = 0;
   for (int i = 1; i <= 12; i++)
   {
      x.Generate();
      sum += double(x)/10000.0;
   }

   return mu + sigma * (sum - 6.0);
}
```

Chapter 5: Selective Execution

Exercises 5.2

1. second
    third

2.  ```
    if ((honors) && (awards))
        goodStudent = true;
    else
        goodStudent = false;
    ```

3. goodStudent = honors && awards;

4.
```
/* OKToSpray determines if weather conditions will allow pesticide
 * spraying.
 *
 * Receive: temperature, a double
 *          relativeHumidity, a double
 *          windSpeed, a double
 * Return:  true if temperature >= 70 degrees F and
 *                  relativeHumidity is between 15% and 25% and
 *                  windSpeed <= 10 mph
 *          false otherwise
 ********************************************************************/

bool OkToSpray(double temperature, double relativeHumidity,
               double windSpeed)
{
    return (temperature >= 70.0) &&
           (15 <= relativeHumidity) && (relativeHumidity <= 35) &&
           (windSpeed <= 10);
}
```

5.
```
/* CreditApproved determines if a loan should be approved.
 *
 * Receive: income, a double
 *          assets, a double
 *          liabilities, a double
 * Return:  true if income >= $25,000 or assets >= $100,000
 *                  and
 *                  liabilities < $50,000
 *          false otherwise
 ********************************************************************/

bool CreditApproved(double income, double assets, double liabilities)
{
    return ( (income >= 70.0) || (assets >= 100000) )
           && (liabilities < 50000);
}
```
```

6.

```
/* IsLeapYear determines if a year is a leap year.
 *
 * Receive: year, an int
 * Return:  true if year is a leap year, false otherwise
 ************************************************************/

bool IsLeapYear(int year)
{
   return (year % 4 == 0) &&
          (!(year % 100 == 0) || (year % 400 == 0));
}
```

7.

```
/* DaysInMonth determines the number of days in a month.
 *
 * Receive: ints month and year
 * Return:  number of days in month of specified year
 ************************************************************/

int DaysInMonth(int month, int year)
{
   if (month == 2)
      if (IsLeapYear(year))
         return 29;
      else
         return 28;
   else if ( (month == 4) || (month == 6) ||
             (month == 9) || (month == 11) )
      return 30;
   else
      return 31;
}
```

8.

```
/* DaysInMonth determines the number of days in a month.
 *
 * Receive: month, a string
 *          year, an int
 * Return:  number of days in month of specified year
 ************************************************************/

#include <ctype.h>

int DaysInMonth(string month, int year)
{
   for (int i = 0; i < month.size(); i++)
      if (islower(month[i]))
         month[i] = toupper(month[i]);

   if (month == "FEBRUARY")
      if (IsLeapYear(year))
         return 29;
      else
         return 28;
   else if ( (month == "APRIL") || (month == "JUNE") ||
             (month == "SEPTEMBER") || (month == "NOVEMBER") )
      return 30;
   else
      return 31;
}
```

Exercises 5.4

1.
```
switch (transCode)
{
    case 'D':
                balance += amount;
                break;
    case 'W':
                balance -= amount;
                break;
    case 'P':
                cout << "Current balance: " << balance;
                break;
    default:
                cerr << "*** Invalid transaction code: " << transCode << endl;
}
```

2.
```
switch (operatorSymbol)    // NOTE:  operator  is a keyword
{
    case '+':
                cout << a + b;
                break;
    case '-':
                cout << a - b;
                break;
    case '*':
                cout << a * b;
                break;
    case '/':
                cout << a / b;
                break;
    default:
                cerr << "*** Invalid operator: " << operatorSymbol << endl;
}
```

3.
```
/* CallLetters finds the call letters for a TV channel.
 *
 * Receive: channel, an int
 * Return:  a string containing call letters for channel
 ******************************************************/

string CallLetters(int channel)
{
    switch (channel)
    {
        case 2:   return "WCBS";
        case 4:   return "WNBC";
        case 5:   return "WNEW";
        case 7:   return "WABC";
        case 9:   return "WOR";
        case 11:  return "WPIX";
        case 13:  return "WNET";
        default:  cerr << channel << " not available";
                  return "";
    }
}
```

4.
```
/* ShippingCost finds shipping cost for a given distance.
 *
 * Receive: distance, an int
 * Return:  cost to ship an item that distance
 ********************************************************/

double ShippingCost (int distance)
{
    switch (distance / 100)
    {
        case 0:            return 5.00;
        case 1: case 2:    return 8.00;
        case 3: case 4:
        case 5:            return 10.00;
        case 6: case 7:
        case 8: case 9:    return 12.00;
        default:           cerr << "*** Invalid Distance: " << distance;
                           return 0.0;
    }
}
```

5.
```
/* MonthName finds the name of a month.
 *
 * Receive: month, an int
 * Return:  a string containing name of month
 ***********************************************/

string MonthName(int month)
{
    switch (month)
    {
        case 1:    return "January";
        case 2:    return "February";
        case 3:    return "March";
        case 4:    return "April";
        case 5:    return "May";
        case 6:    return "June";
        case 7:    return "July";
        case 8:    return "August";
        case 9:    return "September";
        case 10:   return "October";
        case 11:   return "November";
        case 12:   return "December";
        default:   cerr << "*** Invalid Month: " << month;
                   return "";
    }
}
```

6.
```
/* DaysInMonth determines the number of days in a month.
 *
 * Receive: ints month and year
 * Return:  number of days in month of specified year
 ***********************************************************/

int DaysInMonth(int month, int year)
{
   switch (month)
   {
      case 2:            if (IsLeapYear(year))
                            return 29;
                         else
                            return 28;
      case 1: case 3:
      case 5: case 7:
      case 8: case 10:
      case 12:           return 31;

      case 4: case 6:
      case 9: case 11:   return 30;

      default:           cerr << "*** Invalid Month: " << month;
                         return 0;
   }
}
```

Exercises 5.5

1. This function returns the absolute value of its argument.

2. If the argument is an upper-case letter, the function returns its lowercase equivalent (see the ASCII table in Appendix A); otherwise, it simply returns the argument unchanged.

3. ```
   month < 10 ? '0' : ""
   day < 10 ? '0' : ""
   year % 100 < 10 ? '0' : ""
   ```

4. ```
   (number < 10) ? "00" : ( (number < 100) ? '0' : "" )
   ```

5. ```
   int SmallerOf(int x, int y)
   {
      return (x < y) ? x : y;
   }
   ```

6. (a) ```
       int LargestOf(int x, int y, int z)
       {
          return (x > y) ?
              ((x > z) ? x : z) :
              ((y > z) ? y : z);
       }
       ```

   (b) ```
       int SmallestOf(int x, int y, int z)
       {
          return (x < y) ?
              ((x < z) ? x : z)
              ((y < z) ? y : z);
       }
       ```
       ```

```
7.  int Sum(int n)
    {
        return (n > 0) ? (n * (n + 1) / 2) : 0;
    }
```

Programming Problems

Section 5.2

1.
```
/* prog5-1.cpp is a driver program to test the function
 * OkToSpray() from Exercise 4.
 *
 * Input:  temp, relHumid, wind
 * Output: 1 (true) if it is OK to spray, 0 (false) if not
 ****************************************************************/

#include <iostream.h>                    // cin, cout, >>, <<

bool OToSpray(double temperature, double  relativeHumidity,
              double  windSpeed);

int main()
{
    double tempF,
           relHumid,
           wind;

    cout << "Please enter the temperature (degrees Fahrenheit): ";
    cin >> tempF;

    cout << "Please enter the relative humidity (percent): ";
    cin >> relHumid;

    cout << "Please enter the wind speed (miles per hour): ";
    cin >> wind;

    cout << "OK to spray? " << OkToSpray(tempF, relHumid, wind)<< endl;

    return 0;
}

/* Insert definition of OkToSpray() from Exercise 4 here */
```

2.
```
/* prog5-2.cpp is a driver program to test the function
 * CreditApproved() from Exercise 5.
 *
 * Input:  income, assets, liabilities
 * Output: 1 (true) if it is credit is approved, 0 (false) if not
 ****************************************************************/

#include <iostream.h>                    // cin, cout, >>, <<

bool CreditApproved(double income, double assets, double liabilities);
```

```
int main()
{
    double income,
           assets,
           liabilities;

    cout << "Please enter the applicant's income: ";
    cin >> income;

    cout << "Please enter the value of his or her assets: ";
    cin >> assets;

    cout << "Please enter his or her total liabilities: ";
    cin >> liabilities;

    cout << "Credit approved? "
         << CreditApproved(income, assets, liabilities )<< endl;

    return 0;
}

/* Insert definition of CreditApproved() from Exercise 5 here */
```

3.
```
/* prog5-3.cpp is a driver program to test the function
 * IsLeapYear() from Exercise 6.
 *
 * Input:  year
 * Output: 1 (true) if year is a leap year is approved, 0 (false) if not
 **********************************************************************/

#include <iostream.h>              // cin, cout, >>, <<

bool IsLeapYear(int year);

int main()
{
    int year;

    cout << "Please enter enter a year: ";
    cin >> year;

    cout << "Leap year? " << IsLeapYear(year)<< endl;

    return 0;
}

/* Insert definition of IsLeapYear() from Exercise 6 here */
```

4.
```
/* prog5-4.cpp is a driver program to test the function
 * DaysInMonth() from Exercise 7.
 *
 * Input:  month and year
 * Output: number of days in the specified month
 *******************************************************************/

#include <iostream.h>              // cin, cout, >>, <<
#include <string>                  // string
```

```
int DaysInMonth(int month, int year);

int main()
{
   int month,
       year;

   cout << "Please enter enter a month and a year: ";
   cin >> month >> year;

   cout << "Month " << month << " of " << year << " had "
        << DaysInMonth(month, year) << " days\n";

   return 0;
}

/* Insert definition of IsLeapYear() from Exercise 6 here */

/* Insert definitions of DaysInMonth() from Exercise 7 here */
```

5.
```
/* prog5-5.cpp is a driver program to test the function
 * DaysInMonth() from Exercise 8.
 *
 * Input:   month and year
 * Output: number of days in the specified month
 ******************************************************************/

#include <iostream.h>                // cin, cout, >>, <<

int DaysInMonth(string month, int year);

int main()
{
   string month;
   int year;

   cout << "Please enter enter the name of a month and a year: ";
   cin >> month >> year;

   cout << month << " of " << year << " had "
        << DaysInMonth(month, year) << " days\n";

   return 0;
}

/* Insert definition of IsLeapYear() from Exercise 6 here */

/* Insert definitions of DaysInMonth() from Exercise 8 here */
```

6.
```
/* prog5-6.cpp reads the previous and current gas meter readings and
 * displays the charges for usage.
 *
 * Input:   previous and current meter readings
 * Output: gas charge
 ******************************************************************/

#include <iostream.h>                // cin, cout, >>, <<
```

```
#include <iomanip.h>                    // setiosflags(), setprecision()

double GasCharge(int cubicMeters);

int main()
{
    int previous,
        current;

    cout << "Please enter previous meter reading: ";
    cin >> previous;

    cout << "Please enter current meter reading: ";
    cin >> current;

    int actual = (previous < current) ?
                 (current - previous) :
                 (current + 10000 - previous);

    double price = GasCharge(actual);

    cout << setiosflags(ios::showpoint | ios::fixed)
         << setprecision(2)
         << "\nCharge for gas usage: $" << price << endl;

    return 0;
}

/* GasCharge computes the charges for a given amount of gas usage
 *    (based on the table in the text).
 *
 * Receive:  cubicMeters, the cubic meters of gas used
 * Return:    the charge in dollars
 ******************************************************************/

double GasCharge(int cubicMeters)
{
    double charge = 5.00;
    if (cubicMeters <= 70)
       return charge;
    else
       charge += 0.05 * (cubicMeters - 70);

    if (cubicMeters <= 170)
       return charge;
    else
       charge += 0.025 * (cubicMeters - 170);

    if (cubicMeters <= 400)
       return charge;
    else
       return charge + 0.015 * (cubicMeters - 400);
}
```

7.   For this problem, the warnings given in Chapters 2 and 5 about comparing real numbers with == and ! = is appropriate. See Potential problem #2 at the end of Chapter 5 in this connection. For lines $Ax + By + Cz = 0$ and $Dx + Ey + Fz = 0$, it is easy to verify that the lines are parallel if and only if $A*E - B*F$ is 0 and they are perpendicular if and only if $A*D + B*E$ is 0. The following program uses these criteria, but because of roundoff error, it checks if these differences are small in absolute value.

```
/* prog5-7.cpp reads coefficients of two linear equations and
 * and determines if the lines are parallel or intersect, and if
 * they intersect, whether they are perpendicular.
 *
 * Input:  coefficients A, B, C, D, E, F of linear equations
 * Output: message indicating the lines' relationship to each other
 ****************************************************************/

#include <iostream.h>              // cin, cout, >>, <<

bool Parallel(double A, double B, double C,
              double D, double E, double F);

bool Perpendicular(double A, double B, double C,
                   double D, double E, double F);

int main()
{
   double A, B, C, D, E, F;

   cout << "Please enter coefficients A, B, C for first line:  ";
   cin >> A >> B >> C;

   cout << "Please enter coefficients D, E, F for first line: ";
   cin >> D >> E >> F;

   cout << "\n Lines ";
   if (Parallel(A, B, C, D, E, F))
      cout << "are parallel (or nearly so)\n";
   else
   {
      cout << "intersect";
      if (Perpendicular(A, B, C, D, E, F))
         cout << " and are perpendicular (or nearly so)\n";
      else
         cout << " but are not perpendicular\n";
   }
}


#include <math.h>  // abs -- fabs in older non-ANSI-standard versions

/* Parallel checks if two lines are parallel
 *
 * Receive:  doubles A, B, C, D, E, F
 * Return:   true if lines are (nearly) parallel, false otherwise
 ****************************************************************/

bool Parallel(double A, double B, double C,
              double D, double E, double F)

{
   const double EPSILON = 1E-7;    // roundoff error allowance

   return abs(A*E - B*D) < EPSILON;
}
```

```
/* Perpendicular checks if two lines are perpendicular
 *
 * Receive:  doubles A, B, C, D, E, F
 * Return:   true if lines are (nearly) perpendicular, false otherwise
 *****************************************************************/

bool Perpendicular(double A, double B, double C,
                   double D, double E, double F)
{
   const double EPSILON = 1E-7;    // roundoff error allowance

   return abs(A*D + B*E) < EPSILON;
}
```

8.   This program also requires that roundoff error be taken into acount. One way to check for collinearity of three points is to calculate the slopes of lines determined by two pairs of the points and see if they are equal. Function Collinear() first checks if the points lie on a vertical line; if no two do, then it checks slopes.

```
/* prog5-8.cpp determines whether three points are collinear.
 *
 * Input:  coordinates x1, y1,  x2, y2.  x3, y3 of the points
 * Output: message indicating if the points are collinear
 *****************************************************************/

#include <iostream.h>            // cin, cout, >>, <<

bool Collinear(double x1, double y1, double x2, double y2,
               double x3, double y3);

int main()
{
   double x1, y1, x2, y2, x3, y3;

   cout << "Please enter coordinates of three points: ";
   cin >> x1 >> y1 >> x2 >> y2 >> x3 >> y3;

   cout << "\nPoints are ";
   if (Collinear(x1, y1, x2, y2, x3, y3))
      cout << "collinear (or nearly so)\n";
   else
      cout << "not collinear\n";
   }
}


#include <math.h>  // abs -- fabs in older non-ANSI-standard versions

/* Collinear checks if three points are collinear.
 *
 * Receive:  doubles x1, y1, x2, y2, x3, y3  (coordinates of points)
 * Return:   True if points are (nearly) collinear, false otherwise
 *****************************************************************/

bool Collinear(double x1, double y1, double x2, double y2,
               double x3, double y3)
```

```
{
   const double EPSILON = 1E-7;    // roundoff error allowance

   if (x1 == x2)
      return (x1 == x3);
   else
      if (x1 == x3)        // and x1 != x2
         return true;
      else
      {
         double slope1 = (y2 - y1) / (x2 - x1),
                slope2 = (y3 - y1) / (x3 - x1);
         return abs(slope1 - slope2) < EPSILON;
      }
}
```

9.
```
/* prog5-9.cpp is a driver program to test the function
 * CallLetters() from Exercise 3.
 *
 * Input:  a TV channel number
 * Output: call letters of that channel or message that there is none
 *********************************************************************/

#include <iostream.h>              // cin, cout, >>, <<
#include <string>                  // string

string CallLetters(int channel);

int main()
{
   int TVChannel;

   cout << "Please enter a TV channel number: ";
   cin >> TVChannel;

   cout << "Call letters for " << TVChannel <<
           " are " << CallLetters(TVChannel) << endl;

   return 0;
}

/* Insert definition of CallLetters() from Exercise 3 here */
```

10.
```
/* prog5-10.cpp is a driver program to test the function
 * ShippingCost() from Exercise 4.
 *
 * Input:  a distance
 * Output: cost to ship that distance
 *********************************************************/

#include <iostream.h>              // cin, cout, >>, <<
#include <iomanip.h>               // setiosflags(), setprecision()

double ShippingCost (int distance);
```

```
int main()
{
   int distanceToShip;

   cout << "Please enter distance to ship: ";
   cin >> distanceToShip;

   cout << setiosflags(ios::showpoint | ios::fixed)
        << setprecision(2)
        << "Cost to ship: $" << ShippingCost (distanceToShip) << endl;

   return 0;
}

/* Insert definition of ShippingCost() from Exercise 4 here */
```

11.
```
/* prog5-11.cpp is a driver program to test the function
 * MonthName() from Exercise 5.
 *
 * Input:  a month number
 * Output: the name of that month or an error message
 *************************************************************/

#include <iostream.h>              // cin, cout, >>, <<
#include <string>                  // string

string MonthName(int month);

int main()
{
   int month;

   cout << "Please enter the number of a month: ";
   cin >> month;
   cout << MonthName(month) << endl;

   return 0;
}

/* Insert definition of MonthName() from Exercise 5 here */
```

12.
```
/* prog5-12.cpp is a driver program to test the function
 * DaysInMonth() from Exercise 6.
 *
 * Input:  a month number and a year
 * Output: number of days in that month
 *************************************************************/

#include <iostream.h>              // cin, cout, >>, <<

int DaysInMonth(int month, int year);

int main()
{
   int month,
       year;
```

```
   cout << "Please enter the number of a month and a year: ";
   cin >> month >> year;
   cout << "That month had " << DaysInMonth(month, year) << " days\n";

   return 0;
}

/* Insert definition of IsLeapYear() from Exercise 6 of Section 5.2 here */

/* Insert definition of DaysInMonth() from Exercise 6 here */
```

13..

```
/* prog5-13.cpp finds the nearest cross street to an avenue address
 * in midtown Manhattan..
 *
 * Input:  address and avenue number
 * Output: name of nearest cross street
 ******************************************************************/

#include <iostream.h>                    // cin, cout, >>, <<

int NearestCrossStreet(int address, int avenue);


int main()
{
   int address, avenue;

   cout << "Please enter an address and an avenue: ";
   cin >> address >> avenue;
   cout << "Nearest cross street is: " <<
           NearestCrossStreet(address, avenue) << endl;

   return 0;
}

/* NearestCrossStreet determines the number of the nearest cross street
 * for a given address and avenue number according to the algorithm
 * given in the text.
 *
 * Receive:  address, the address number
 *           avenue, the avenue number
 * Return:   the nearest cross street number
 ******************************************************************/

int NearestCrossStreet(int address, int avenue)
{
   int street = address / 20;           // cancel last digit and
                                        //   divide by 2
   switch (avenue)
   {
      case 1:
      case 2:
              street += 3;
              break;
      case 3:
      case 8:
              street += 10;
              break;
```

```
        case 4:
                street += 8;
                break;
        case 5:
                if (address <= 200)
                    street += 13;
                else
                    street += 16;
                break;
        case 6:
                street -= 12;
                break;
        case 7:
                street += 12;
                break;
        case 10:
                street += 14;
                break;
        default:
                cerr << "*** Invalid Avenue" << avenue << '\n';
    }

    return street;
}
```

14.
```
/* prog5-14.cpp reads the number of units bought and the unit price
 * and then calculates and prints the total full cost, the total
 * amount of the discount, and the total discounted cost.
 *
 * Input:  units and unitPrice
 * Output: fullCost, discount, and discountedCost
 *****************************************************************/

#include <iostream.h>              // cin, cout, >>, <<
#include <iomanip.h>               // setiosflags(), setprecision()

double PercentDiscount(long units, double unitPrice);

int main()
{
    long int units;
    double unitPrice;

    cout << "Enter the number of units bought and the unit price: ";
    cin >> units >> unitPrice;

    double fullCost = units * unitPrice,
           percent = PercentDiscount(units, unitPrice),
           discount = (percent / 100.0) * fullCost,
           discountedCost = fullCost - discount;

    cout << setiosflags(ios::showpoint | ios::fixed)
         << setprecision(2)
         << "\nTotal full cost: $" << fullCost
         << "\nTotal amount of discount: $" << discount
         << "\nTotal discounted cost: $" << discountedCost << '\n';

    return 0;
}
```

```
/* PercentDiscount calculates the percentage discount for a specified
 * number of units and unit price based on the table in the text.
 *
 * Receive:  units, the number of units bought
 *           unitPrice, the unit price in dollars
 * Return:   the percent discount
 *********************************************************************/

double PercentDiscount(long units, double unitPrice)
{
    switch (units / 10)
    {
        case 0:                                 // 1-9
                if (unitPrice <= 10.00)
                    return 0;
                else if (unitPrice <= 100.00)
                    return 2;
                else
                    return 5;
        case 1:                                 // 10-19
                if (unitPrice <= 10.00)
                    return 5;
                else if (unitPrice <= 100.00)
                    return 7;
                else
                    return 9;
        case 2:                                 // 20-29
        case 3:                                 // 30-39
        case 4:                                 // 40-49
                if (unitPrice <= 10.00)
                    return 9;
                else if (unitPrice <= 100.00)
                    return 15;
                else
                    return 21;
        case 5:                                 // 50-59
        case 6:                                 // 60-69
        case 7:                                 // 70-79
        case 8:                                 // 80-89
        case 9:                                 // 90-99
                if (unitPrice <= 10.00)
                    return 14;
                else if (unitPrice <= 100.00)
                    return 23;
                else
                    return 32;
        default:                                // 100+
                if (unitPrice <= 10.00)
                    return 21;
                else if (unitPrice <= 100.00)
                    return 32;
                else
                    return 43;
    }
}
```

15.

```
/* prog5-15.cpp reads an estimated flight time and an actual flight
 * time and then prints whether the estimated time is too large,
 * acceptable, or too small.
 *
 * Input:  Estimated and actual flight times
 * Output: Acceptability of estimated flight time
 *****************************************************************/

#include <iostream.h>              // cin, cout, >>, <<

int CalcAcceptableError(int estimated);

int main()
{
   int estimated,
       actual;

   cout << "Enter estimated flight time in minutes: ";
   cin >> estimated;

   cout << "Please enter the actual flight time in minutes: ";
   cin >> actual;

   int actualError = actual - estimated,
       acceptableError = CalcAcceptableError(estimated);

   if (actualError > acceptableError)
      cout << "\nEstimated time too large (by "
           << actualError << " minutes).\n";
   else if (actualError < -acceptableError)
      cout << "\nEstimated time too small (by "
           << -actualError << " minutes).\n";
   else
      cout << "\nEstimated time acceptable.\n";
   return 0;
}

/* CalcAcceptableError determines the acceptable error for a given
 * estimated flight time, according to the table in the text.
 *
 * Receive:  Estimated, the estimated flight time
 * Return:   The acceptable error margin in minutes
 *****************************************************************/

int CalcAcceptableError(int estimated)
{
   switch (estimated / 30)
   {
      case 0:                       // 0-29
              return 1;
      case 1:                       // 30-59
              return 2;
      case 2:                       // 60-89
              return 3;
      case 3:                       // 90-119
              return 4;
      case 4:                       // 120-149
      case 5:                       // 150-179
              return 6;
```

```
      case 6:                             // 180-209
      case 7:                             // 210-239
              return 8;
      case 8:                             // 240-269
      case 9:                             // 270-299
      case 10:                            // 300-329
      case 11:                            // 330-359
              return 13;
      default:                            // 360+
              return 17;
   }
}
```

16 - 19 are all similar programs. Here is a solution for Problem 16.

16.

```
/* prog5-16.cpp is a driver program to test the function ConvertLength()
 *
 * Input:  a length and the unit of measurement used and a unit of
 *          measurement to which it is to be converted
 * Output: converted measurement
 ********************************************************************/

#include <iostream.h>                    // cin, cout, >>, <<

void ConvertLength(double length, char inUnits, char outUnits);

int main()
{
   double length;
   char inUnits, outUnits;

   cout << "This program will perform the following conversions:\n"
           "  I --> c  (inches to centimers)\n"
           "  F --> c  (feet to centimers)\n"
           "  F --> m  (feet to meters)\n"
           "  Y --> m  (yards to meters)\n"
           "  M --> k  (miles to kilometers)\n\n"
           " Enter length and letters for conversion desired: ";
   cin >> length >> inUnits >> outUnits;

   cout << length;
   switch (inUnits)
   {
      case 'I':
              cout << " inches ";
              break;
      case 'F':
              cout << " feet ";
              break;
      case 'Y':
              cout << " yards ";
              break;
      case 'M':
              cout << " miles ";
              break;
      default:
              cout << ' ' <<  inUnits << "-units cannot be converted.\n";
              return 1;
   }
```

```
    cout << "is equivalent to ";

    ConvertLength(length, inUnits, outUnits);

    return 0;
}

/* ConvertLength converts a length from inUnits to outUnits
 *
 * Receive:  length, inUnits, outUnits
 * Output:   length converted to outUnits
 ********************************************************************/

void ConvertLength(double length, char inUnits, char outUnits)
{
    switch (inUnits)
    {
        case 'I':
                if (outUnits == 'c')
                {
                    cout << 2.5004 * length << " centimeters\n";
                    return;
                }
                break;
        case 'F':
                if (outUnits == 'c')
                {
                    cout << 30.4801 * length << " centimeters\n";
                    return;
                }
                else if (outUnits == 'm')
                {
                    cout << 0.304801 * length << " meters\n";
                    return;
                }
                break;
        case 'Y':
                if (outUnits == 'm')
                {
                    cout << 0.914402 * length << " meters\n";
                    return;
                }
                break;
        case 'M':
                if (outUnits == 'k')
                {
                    cout << 1.60935 * length << " kilometers\n";
                    return;
                }
    }

    cout << "*** --  Cannot be converted to " << outUnits << "-units\n";
}


20. (a) (i)  sum1 = (a && !b) || (!a && b);
            carry1 = a && b;
        (ii) sum = (sum1 && !cIn) || (!sum1 && cIn);
            carry = carry1 || (sum1 && cIn);
```

(b)

```
/* prog5-20.cpp simulates a binary full-adder.
 *
 * Input:  a, b, and cIn
 * Output: sum and carry
 **************************************************/

#include <iostream.h>                // cin, cout, >>, <<

int main()
{
   bool a,
        b,
        cIn;

   cout << "Enter two binary inputs and the carry-in: ";
   cin >> a >> b >> cIn;

   bool sum1 = (a && !b) || (!a && b),
        carry1 = a && b,
        sum = (sum1 && !cIn) || (!sum1 && cIn),
        carry = carry1 || (sum1 && cIn);

   cout << "\nSum = " << sum
        << " - Carry = " << carry << endl;

   return 0;
}
```

21. (a) (i) `s1 = (a1 && !b1) || (!a1 && b1);`
            `xOut1 = a1 && b1;`
   (ii) `sum1 = (a2 && !b2) || (!a2 && b2);`
            `carry1 = a2 && b2;`
            `s2 = (sum1 && !cOut1) || (!sum1 && cOut1);`
            `cOut = carry1 || (sum1 && cOut1);`

(b)

```
/* prog5-21.cpp simulates a two-bit adder.
 *
 * Input:  a1, b1, a2, b2
 * Output: s1, s2, cOut
 **************************************************/

#include <iostream.h>                // cin, cout, >>, <<

int main()
{
   short int a, b;

   cout << "Enter two two-bit inputs: ";
   cin >> a >> b;

   bool a1 = a % 10,
        a2 = a / 10,
        b1 = b % 10,
        b2 = b / 10;
```

```
    bool s1 = (a1 && !b1) || (!a1 && b1),
         cOut1 = a1 && b1;

    bool sum1 = (a2 && !b2) || (!a2 && b2),
         carry1 = a2 && b2,
         s2 = (sum1 && !cOut1) || (!sum1 && cOut1),
         cOut = carry1 || (sum1 && cOut1);

    cout << "\nSum = " << cOut << s2 << s1 << '\n';

    return 0;
}
```

Chapter 6: Repetition

Exercises 6.4

1.
```
10 cubed = 1000
 9 cubed = 729
 8 cubed = 512
 7 cubed = 343
 6 cubed = 216
 5 cubed = 125
 4 cubed = 64
 3 cubed = 27
 2 cubed = 8
 1 cubed = 1
```

2.
```
10 squared = 1000
 8 squared = 512
 6 squared = 216
 4 squared = 64
 2 squared = 8
```

3.
```
1
1
2
2
3
3
1
4
4
2
5
5
3
1
```

4.
```
3
1
3
5
```

5.
```
313
312
311
323
322
333
212
211
222
111
```

6.
```
111

121
122

131
132
133


222

232
233


333
```

7.
```
519
426
333
240
15-3
```

8.
```
01010
1911
2812
3713
4614
5515
6416
```

9.
```
01010
1911
2812
3713
4614
5515
6416
7317
8218
9119
10020
11-121
```

10.
```
5123###
31###
1***
```

11.
```
base-2 log of 32 = 5
base-2 log of 16 = 4
base-2 log of 8 = 3
base-2 log of 4 = 2
base-2 log of 2 = 1
base-2 log of 1 = 0
```

12. Infinite loop — displays 0 ad infinitum.   On the first pass, i is 0, so j is 0, and the statement j *= 2;
    never changes the value of j so the condition j * j < 100 is always true.

    If the first statement is changed to: i = 1;
    then the output produced will be:

    ```
    2
    3
    5
    9
    4
    6
    10
    6
    9


    *****
    ```

13. ```
    01
    1-1
    23
    ```

14. `0002448612`

15.

While loop		Do-while loop		Forever loop	
number	product	number	product	number	product
0	1	0	1	0	1
1	1	1	1	1	1
2	2	2	2	2	2
3	6	3	6	3	6
4	24	4	24	4	24
				5	24

16.

While loop		Do-while loop		Forever loop	
number	product	number	product	number	product
0	1	0	1	0	1
1	1	1	1	1	1
2	2	2	2	2	2
				3	2

17.

While loop		Do-while loop		Forever loop	
number	product	number	product	number	product
0	1	0	1	0	1
		1	1	1	1
				2	2
				3	2

NOTE: Answers may vary for Exercises 18-22.

18. ```
    do
    {
        cout << x << endl;
        x -= 0.5;
    }
    while (x > 0);
    ```

19.
```
for (int i = 1; i <= 50 ; i++)
    cout << (2*i) * (2*i) << endl;
```

20.
```
for (double x = 1.0; x <= 5.0; x += 0.25)
    cout << sqrt(x) << endl;
```

21.
```
int fib1 = fib2 = 1;
cout << 1 << endl << 1 << endl;
for (;;)
{
    fib3 = fib1 + fib2;
    if (fib3 >= 500) break;
    cout << fib3 << endl;
    fib1 = fib2;
    fib2 = fib3;
}
```

22.
```
double x;
do
{
    cout << "Enter a real number: ";
    cin >> x;
    cerr << "*** Number must be positive ***\n\n";
}
while (x <= 0);
```

23.
```
/* Power returns the n-th power of x.
 *
 * Receive: x, a double, and n, an unsigned int
 * Return:  n-th power of x
 ****************************************************/

double Power(double x, unsigned n)
{
    double product = 1.0;
    for (int i = 0; i < n; i++)
        product *= x;
    return product;
}
```

24.
```
/* Power returns the n-th power of x.
 *
 * Receive: x, a double, and n, an int
 * Return:  n-th power of x
 ****************************************************/

#include <math.h>            // abs()   ( or fabs() )
double Power(double x, int n)
{
    double product = 1.0;
    for (int i = 0; i < abs(n); i++)
        product *= x;
    if (n >= 0)
        return product;
    else if (x != 0)
        return 1.0 / product;
    else
    {
        cerr << "0 to a negative power is undefined -- returning 0\n";
        return 0;
    }
}
```

25.
```
/* DivisorSum returns the sum of the proper divisors of an integer.
 *
 * Receive: n, an unsigned int
 * Return:  sum of proper divisors of n
 ********************************************************************/

unsigned DivisorSum (unsigned n)
{
   unsigned sum = 0;
   for (int i = 1; i <= n/2; i++)
      if (n % i == 0) sum += i;
   return sum;
}
```

26.
```
/* IsPrime checks if an integer n is prime.
 *
 * Receive: n, an unsigned int
 * Return:  true if n is a prime, false otherwise
 ***************************************************/

bool IsPrime(unsigned n)
{
   if (n < 2)
      return false;              // 0 & 1 aren't primes
   if (n == 2)
      return true;               // 2 is prime
   if (n % 2 == 0)
      return false;              // evens > 2 aren't prime

   for (int d = 3; d*d <= n; d++) // check if any odd integer in the range
      if (n % d == 0)            // 3 through square root of n divides n
         return false;           //  d divides n, so n not prime
   return true;                  // no such number divides n, so it's prime
}
```

27.
```
/* IntLog2 returns the integer base-2 logarithm of an integer.
 *
 * Receive: n, an unsigned int
 * Return:  integer base-2 logarithm of n
 ********************************************************************/

unsigned IntLog2(unsigned n)
{
   unsigned count = 0;
   while (n > 1)
   {
      count++;
      n /= 2;
   }
   return count;
}
```

Programming Problems

Sections 6.1-6.4

1.

```cpp
/* prog6-1.cpp is a driver program to test the function
 * Power() from Exercise 23.
 *
 * Input:  a double x and a nonnegative integer n
 * Output: the n-th power of x
 *********************************************************/

#include <iostream.h>                // cin, cout, >>, <<

double Power(double x, unsigned n);

int main()
{
   double x;
   int n;

   for (;;)
   {
      cout << "Program computes x to the n-th power.  Enter x and n (0 0 to stop): ";
      cin >> x >> n;
      if (x == 0 && n == 0) break;

      cout << x << " to the power " << n <<" is " << Power(x, n) << endl;
   }

   return 0;
}

/* Insert definition of the function Power()  from Exercise 23 here */
```

2.

```cpp
/* prog6-2.cpp is a driver program to test the function
 * Power() from Exercise 24.
 *
 * Input:  a double x and an integer n
 * Output: the n-th power of x
 *********************************************************/

#include <iostream.h>                // cin, cout, >>, <<

double Power(double x, int n);

int main()
{
   double x;
   int n;
```

```
    for (;;)
    {
        cout << "Program computes x to the n-th power.  Enter x and n (0 0 to stop): ";
        cin >> x >> n;
        if (x == 0 && n == 0) break;

        cout << x << " to the power " << n <<" is " << Power(x, n) << endl;
    }

    return 0;
}
/* Insert definition of the function Power()  from Exercise 24 here */
```

3.
```
/* prog6-3.cpp is a driver program to test the function
 * DivisorSum() from Exercise 25.
 *
 * Input:  a positive integer number
 * Output: the sum of the divisors of number
 ********************************************************/

#include <iostream.h>              // cin, cout, >>, <<

unsigned DivisorSum (unsigned n);

int main()
{
    int number;

    cout << "Enter a positive integer: ";
    cin >> number;

    cout << "Sum of its divisors is " << DivisorSum (number) << endl;

    return 0;
}

/* Insert definition of the function DivisorSum ()
   from Exercise 25 here */
```

4.
```
/* prog6-4.cpp is a driver program to test the function
 * IsPrime() from Exercise 26.
 *
 * Input:  a positive integer number
 * Output: indication of whether the number is a prime
 ********************************************************/

#include <iostream.h>              // cin, cout, >>, <<

bool IsPrime(unsigned n);
```

```
int main()
{
   int number;

   for (;;)
   {
      cout << "Enter a positive integer (0 to stop): ";
      cin >> number;
      if (number == 0) break;

      cout << "This number is";
      if (!IsPrime(number))
         cout << " not";
      cout << " prime\n";
   }

   return 0;
}

/* Insert definition of the function IsPrime()
   from Exercise 26 here */
```

5.
```
/* prog6-5.cpp is a driver program to test the function
 * IntLog2() from Exercise 27.
 *
 * Input:  a positive integer number
 * Output: the higest exponent e so that 2^e <= number
 *****************************************************/

#include <iostream.h>              // cin, cout, >>, <<

unsigned IntLog2(unsigned n);

int main()
{
   int number;

   cout << "Enter a positive integer: ";
   cin >> number;

   cout << "Integer base-two logarithm is " << IntLog2(number) << endl;

   return 0;
}

/* Insert definition of the function IntLog2()
   from Exercise 27 here */
```

6.
```
/* prog6-6.cpp prints a multiplication table.
 *
 * Output:  The multiplication table
 ***************************************************/

#include <iostream.h>                  // cin, cout, >>, <<
#include <iomanip.h>                   // setw()
```

```
int main()
{
  const int SIZE = 9;

    for (int column = 1; column <= SIZE; column++)
       cout << setw(3) << column;

    for (int row = 1; row <= SIZE; row++)
    {
       cout << '\n' << setw(3) << row;
       for (int column = 1; column <= row; column++)
          cout << setw(3) << (row * column);
    }

    cout << endl;
    return 0;
}
```

7.
```
/* prog6-7.cpp classifies n as being deficient, perfect, or abundant,
 * and finds the smallest odd abundant number.
 *
 * Output:  The answers
 *********************************************************************/

#include <iostream.h>                    // cin, cout, >>, <<

unsigned DivisorSum (unsigned n);
void PrintDescription(unsigned Number);

int main()
{
   unsigned number;

   for (number = 1; number <= 30; number++)
      PrintDescription(number);

   for (number = 490; number <= 500; number++)
      PrintDescription(number);

   for (number = 8120; number <= 8130; number++)
      PrintDescription(number);

   cout << "\nExtra: The smallest odd abundant number is: ";

   number = 1;
   for (;;)
   {
      if (DivisorSum(number) > number) break;
      number += 2;
   }

   cout << number << endl;

   return 0;
}
```

```
/* PrintDescription prints the description of the specified number --
 * deficient, abundant, or perfect.
 *
 * Receive: number
 * Return:  number and description
 ***********************************************************************/

void PrintDescription(unsigned number)
{
   cout << number << " is ";

   if (DivisorSum(number) < number)
      cout << "deficient.\n";
   else if (DivisorSum(number) > number)
      cout << "abundant.\n";
   else
      cout << "perfect!\n";
}



/* Insert definition of the function DivisorSum ()
   from Exercise 25 here */
```

8.
```
/* prog6-8.cpp prints, under appropriate headings, the amount spent on
 * advertising, the number of sales made, and the net profit.  It begins
 * with the company's current status and doubles the amount spent on
 * advertising until the net profit begins to decline.
 *
 * Output:  the information
 ***********************************************************************/

#include <iostream.h>                 // cin, cout, >>, <<
#include <iomanip.h>                  // setw(), setiosflags(), setprecison()

int main()
{
   const double PROFIT_PER_ITEM = 300.00,
                FIXED_COSTS = 1000.00;

   double currentSales = 200,
          currentAdCost = 2000.00,
          currentProfit = currentSales * PROFIT_PER_ITEM -
                          currentAdCost - FIXED_COSTS ,
      newSales,
      newProfit,
      newAdCost;

   cout << "\nAdvertising   Projected Sales   Net Profit"
           "\n===========   ===============   ==========\n";

   cout << setiosflags(ios::showpoint | ios::fixed)
        << setprecision(2);
```

```cpp
   for (;;)
   {
      cout << " $" << setw(8) << currentAdCost
           << "         $" << setw(7) << currentSales
           << "         $" << setw(9) << currentProfit << endl;

      newAdCost = 2.0 * currentAdCost;
      newSales = 1.2 * currentSales;
      newProfit = newSales * PROFIT_PER_ITEM -
                    newAdCost - FIXED_COSTS ;

      if (newProfit <= currentProfit) break;

      currentAdCost = newAdCost;
      currentSales = newSales;
      currentProfit = newProfit;
   }

   cout << " $" << setw(8) << newAdCost
        << "         $" << setw(7) << newSales
        << "         $" << setw(9) << newProfit << endl;

   return 0;
}
```

9.
```cpp
/* prog6-9.cpp uses the "divide-and-average" algorithm to approximate
 * square roots.
 *
 * Input:  a positive real number, an approximation of its square root,
 *         and the maximum allowable error
 * Output: the approximate square root of the real number
 ************************************************************************/

#include <iostream.h>              // cin, cout, >>, <<
#include <math.h>                  // fabs, sqrt()

int main()
{
   double  posReal,
           approx,
           epsilon;

   cout << "Enter a positive real number: ";
   cin >> posReal;

   cout << "Enter an approximation of its square root: ";
   cin >> approx;

   cout << "Enter the maximum allowable error: ";
   cin >> epsilon;

   if ( (posReal <= 0) || (approx <= 0) || (epsilon <= 0) )
   {
      cout << "\nAll numbers must be positive!\n";
      return 1;
   }

   double newApprox = (posReal / approx + approx) / 2.0;
```

```
   while (fabs(newApprox - approx) > epsilon)
   {
       cout << "\nApproximation: " << approx;

       approx = newApprox;
       newApprox = (posReal / approx + approx) / 2.0;
   }

   cout << "\n\nFinal approximation: " << approx;
   cout << "\n Actual square root: " << sqrt(posReal) << endl;

   return 0;
}
```

10.

```
/* prog6-10.cpp accepts a positive integer and gives its prime factorization.
 *
 * Input:  a positive integer
 * Output: its prime factorization
 ************************************************************************/

#include <iostream.h>              // cin, cout, >>, <<

int main()
{
   unsigned number,               // the number to be factored
            divisor = 2;          // the current divisor
   bool isPrime = true;           // true if the number is prime

   cout << "Enter the number to be factored: ";
   cin >> number;

   if (number < 2)
   {
       cout << "\nNumber must be 2 or more!\n";
       return 1;
   }

   cout << "\nFactorization:\n";

   while (divisor <= number)
   {
       while (number % divisor == 0)
       {
          cout << divisor;
          if (number != divisor)
          {
              cout << " * ";
              isPrime = false;
          }
          number /= divisor;
       }
       divisor++;
   }

   if (isPrime)
       cout << " is prime!";

   cout << endl;

   return 0;
}
```

Sections 6.5 & 6.6

11.

```
/* prog6-11.cpp reads a list of numbers, counts them, finds the
 * smallest and largest numbers in the list and their positions
 * in the list
 *
 * Input:  a list of numbers
 * Output: count, smallest and largest numbers, their positions
 ************************************************************************/

#include <iostream.h>          // cin, cout, >>, <<

int main()
{
   const int SENTINEL = -1;     // the end of data indicator

   int value,                   // the current value being processed
       minValue, minPos,        // smallest value read so far & its position
       maxValue, maxPos,        // largest value read so far & its position
       count = 0;               // ocunt of values;

   cout << "Enter nonegative integers ("
        << SENTINEL << " to stop).\n";

   cout << "First number: ";
   cin >> value;

   if (value == SENTINEL)
   {
      cout << "\nNo numbers entered!\n";
      return 1;
   }

   minValue = maxValue = value;
   minPos = maxPos = count = 1;

   for (;;)
   {
      cout << "Next number:  ";
      cin >> value;

      if (value == SENTINEL) break;

      count ++;
      if (value < minValue)
      {
         minValue = value;
         minPos = count;
      }
      else if (value > maxValue)
      {
         maxValue = value;
         maxPos = count;
      }
   }
```

```
    cout << "\nCount of values: " << count
         << "\nSmallest value is " << minValue
         << " at position " << minPos
         << "\nLargest value is " << maxValue
         << " at position " << maxPos << endl;

    return 0;
}
```

12 & 13.

```
/* prog6-12+13.cpp is a driver program converts English currency to U.S.
 * and conversly.
 *
 * Input:   English-to-US exchange rate
 *          amounts in English currency
 *          amounts in U.S. currency and
 * Output: equivalent amounts in U.S. / English currency
 ********************************************************************/

#include <iostream.h>                 // cin, cout, >>, <<

double EnglishToUS(double EnglishDollars, double EnglandUSExchangeRate);
double USToEnglish(double USDollars, double EnglandUSExchangeRate);

int main()
{
    double exchRate,
           amount;

    cout << "Enter the US-to-English exchange rate: ";
    cin >> exchRate;

    for (;;)
    {
        cout << "\nEnter an amount in English currency (0 to stop):";
        cin >> amount;
        if (amount == 0) break;

        cout << "Equivalent amount in US currency = $"
             << EnglishToUS(amount, exchRate) << endl;
    }

    cout << endl;
    for (;;)
    {
        cout << "\nEnter an amount in U.S. currency (0 to stop):";
        cin >> amount;
        if (amount == 0) break;

        cout << "Equivalent amount in English currency = $"
             << USToEnglish(amount, exchRate) << endl;
    }

    return 0;
}
```

```
/* EnglishToUS receives a number of English dollars and the English-to-US
 * exchange rate and returns the equivalent number of U.S. dollars.
 *
 * Receive: amount, a number of English dollars
 *          EnglandUSExchangeRate, the number of U.S. dollars equal to
 *             one English dollar
 * Return:  the equivalent number of US dollars
 ************************************************************************/

double EnglishToUS(double amount, double EnglandUSExchangeRate)
{
   return amount * EnglandUSExchangeRate;
}

/* USToEnglish receives a number of US dollars and the English-to-US
 * exchange rate and returns the equivalent number of English dollars.
 *
 * Receive: amount, a number of US dollars
 *          EnglandUSExchangeRate, the number of U.S. dollars equal to
 *             one English dollar
 * Return:  the equivalent number of English dollars
 ************************************************************************/

double USToEnglish(double amount, double EnglandUSExchangeRate)
{
   return amount / EnglandUSExchangeRate;
}
```

14.

```
/* This program accepts various integers and bases and displays the digits
 * of the base-b representation (in reverse order) for each integer.
 *
 * Input:  various integers
 * Output: the digits of the base-b representation (in reverse order)
 ************************************************************************/

#include <iostream.h>              // cin, cout, >>, <<

int main()
{
   unsigned base10,
            b;

   cout << "Enter a number in base-10: ";
   cin >> base10;

   if (base10 < 0)
   {
     cout << "\nNumber should be non-negative!\n";
     return 1;
   }

   cout << "Enter the base you wish to convert to: ";
   cin >> b;

   if (b < 2)
   {
      cout << "\nBase must be greater than 1!\n";
      return 1;
   }
```

```
   cout << "\nDigits of the base-" << b
        << " representation (in reverse order): ";

   do
   {
      cout << base10 % n;
      base10 /= n;
   }
   while (base10 != 0);

   cout << endl;

   return 0;
}
```

15.

```
/* This program accepts various integers and bases and displays the digits of
 * the base-16 (hexadecimal) representation (in reverse order) for each integer.
 *
 * Input:  various integers
 * Output: the hexadecimal digits (in reverse order)
 ***************************************************************************/

#include <iostream.h>                    // cin, cout, >>, <<

int main()
{
   unsigned base10,
            digit;
   const unsigned B = 16;

   cout << "Enter a number in base-10: ";
   cin >> base10;

   if (base10 < 0)
   {
     cout << "\nNumber should be non-negative!\n";
     return 1;
   }

   cout << "\nDigits of the base-" << B
        << " representation (in reverse order): ";

   do
   {
      digit = base10 % B;
      switch (digit)
      {
         case 10:
                 cout << 'A'; break;
         case 11:
                 cout << 'B'; break;
         case 12:
                 cout << 'C'; break;
         case 13:
                 cout << 'D'; break;
         case 14:
                 cout << 'E'; break;
         case 15:
                 cout << 'F'; break;
```

```
            default:
                        cout << digit; break;
        }

        base10 /= B;
    }
    while (base10 != 0);

    cout << endl;

    return 0;
}
```

16.

```
/* This program reads the amount of a loan, an annual interest rate, and a
 * monthly payment and then displays in a table with appropriate headings
 * the payment number, the interest for that month, the balance remaining
 * after that payment, and the total interest paid to date.
 *
 * Input:  balance, annualIntRate, monthlyPayment
 * Output: table of information
 ********************************************************************************/

#include <iostream.h>                 // cin, cout, >>, <<
#include <iomanip.h>                  // setw(), setiosflags(), setprecison()

int main()
{
    char answer;
    int payment;
    double balance,
           annualIntRate,
           monthPayment,
           totalInt,
           monthIntRate,
           monthInt;

    do
    {
        cout << "\nEnter amount of loan: $";
        cin >> balance;

        cout << "Enter annual interest rate: ";
        cin >> annualIntRate;

        cout << "Enter amount of monthly payments: ";
        cin >> monthPayment;

        payment = 0;
        totalInt = 0.00;
        monthIntRate = annualIntRate / 100.0 / 12.0;

        cout << "\nPayment #  Interest  Balance  Interest to date  Payment Due"
                "\n========================================================="
                "\n";

        cout << setiosflags(ios::showpoint | ios::fixed)
             << setprecision(2);
```

```
      do
      {
         payment++;
         balance -= monthPayment;
         monthInt = monthIntRate * balance;
         balance += monthInt;
         if (monthPayment > balance)
            monthPayment = balance;
         totalInt += monthInt;

         cout << setw(5) << payment
              << setw(12) << monthInt
              << setw(12) << balance
              << setw(13) << totalInt
              << setw(17) << monthPayment << '\n';
      }
      while (balance >= 0.005);

      cout << "\nExecute again (y/n)? ";
      cin >> answer;

   }
   while ( (answer == 'y') || (answer == 'Y') );

   return 0;
}
```

17 & 18. These are straightforward and similar to the previous problem.

19. The folowing function implements the double-declining method.

```
/* DoubleDecliningBalance displays the depreciation of amount over numYears,
 * using the double-declining balance method.
 *
 * Receive: a (double) amount, (int) numYears, and (int) currYear
 * Output:  a depreciation table
 **********************************************************************/

void DoubleDecliningBalance(double amount, int numYears, int currYear)
{
   double depreciation;

   cout << "\nYear -  Depreciation"
        << "\n--------------------\n";

   cout << fixed << showpoint << right         // set up format for $$
        << setprecision(2);

   for (int year = 1; year <= numYears - 1; year++)
   {
      depreciation = amount * 2.0 / numYears;
      amount = amount - depreciation;
      cout << setw(3) << (currYear + year - 1)
           << setw(11) << depreciation << endl;
   }

   depreciation = amount;

   cout << setw(3) << (currYear + year - 1)
        << setw(11) << depreciation << endl;
}
```

Chapter 7: Functions in Depth

Exercises 7.3

1. OK if `two` is changed to `TWO` as was intended.   (Otherwise not.)

2. No: `v` is a `double`, `n` is an `int` reference parameter. The fifth argument must be an `int` variable. (Also not valid becuse of the typo — `two` should be `TWO`.)

3. No: `PI` is a constant `double` being sent to a `double` reference. The second argument must be a `double` variable.

4. No: `13` (fourth argument) is a constant `int` being sent to a `int` reference. The second argument must be a `double` variable.

5. No: `PI` is a constant `double` being sent to a `double` reference. The second argument must be a `double` variable.

6. No: `PI * hours` is a `double` expression being sent to a `double` reference. The second argument must be a `double` variable.

7. OK, but not recommended, since `u` will never be changed by the function call.

8. OK if there is a semicolon at the end of the statement as was intended.   (Otherwise not.)

9. No: `INITIAL` is a constant `char` being sent to a `char` reference. The sixth argument must be an `char` variable.

10. No: `p + q` is an `int` expression being sent to an `int` reference. The second argument must be an `int` variable.

11. No: `Calculate()` returns no value for `cout` to process.

12.
```
/* ConvertLbsOz_To_Grams converts a weight in pounds and ounces to grams.
 *
 * Receive: pounds and ounces
 * Return:  grams
 ********************************************************************/

double ConvertLbsOz_to_Grams(int pounds, double ounces)
{
   return (16.0 * pounds + ounces) * 28.349527;
}
```

13.
```
/* ConvertGrams_To_LbsOz converts a weight in grams to pounds and ounces.
 *
 * Receive:   grams
 * Pass back: pounds and ounces
 ********************************************************************/
```

```
void ConvertGrams_To_LbsOz(double grams, int & pounds, double & ounces)
{
   ounces = 0.35274 * grams;
   pounds = int(ounces / 16.0);
   ounces -= 16.0 * pounds
}
```

14
```
/* Convert_YFtIn_To_Cm converts a measurement in yards, feet, and inches
 * to centimeters.
 *
 * Receive: yards, feet, and inches
 * Return:  centimeters
 ********************************************************************/

double Convert_YFtIn_To_Cm(int yards, int feet, double inches)
{
   return (36.0 * yards + 12.0 * feet + inches) * 2.54001;
}
```

15.
```
/* Convert_Cm_To_YFtIn converts a weight in grams to pounds and ounces.
 *
 * Receive:   centimeters
 * Pass back: yards, feet, and inches
 ********************************************************************/

void Convert_Cm_To_YFtIn(double cm, int & yards, int & feet, double & inches)
{
   inches = 0.3937 * cm;
   feet = int(inches / 12.0);
   inches -= 12.0 * feet;
   yards = feet / 3;
   feet %= 3;
}
```

16.
```
/* ConvertNormal_To_Military converts "normal" time to military time.
 *
 * Receive:  hours, the number of hours in "normal" time
 *           minutes, the number of minutes in "normal" time
 *           ampm, 'A' if AM, 'P' if PM
 * Return:   The time in military format
 ********************************************************************/

int ConvertNormal_To_Military(int hours, int minutes, char ampm)
{
   if (hours == 12)
      hours = 0;

   return hours * 100 + minutes + (ampm == 'P' ? 1200 : 0);
}
```

17.

```
/* ConvertMilitary_To_Normal converts military time to "normal" time.
 *
 * Receive:     military, a decimal military time
 * Pass back:   hours, the hours in "normal" time
 *              minutes, the minutes in "normal" time
 *              ampm, 'A' if AM, 'P' if PM
 ******************************************************************/

void ConvertMilitary_To_Normal(int military,
                               int & hours, int & minutes, char & ampm)
{
   hours = (military / 100) % 12;
   if (hours == 0)
      hours = 12;
   minutes = military % 100;
   ampm = (military / 100) / 12 == 0 ? 'A' : 'P';
}
```

Exercises 7.6

1.   123

2.   1234567

3.   (only a newline)

4.   876543

5.   87

6.   (only a newline)

7.   321
     123

8.   7654321
     1234567

9.   (only a newline)

10. 321

11. 7654321

12. (only a newline)

13. `F(1, 5)` evaluates to 6.

14. `F(8, 3)` evaluates immediately to 0.

15.
```
11
12
13
13
13
14
15
14
13
14
15
15
15
16
17
```

16. 1023 numbers are output.

17.
```
14131211

13

1413

15

151413

15

1615

17
```

18. Always calculates 0

19. Calculates `n * x`.

20. Calculates the integer part of $\log_2 n$

21. Calculates the sum of the digits of `n`

22. Calculates the first digit of `n`

For Exercises 23-27, replace the function body with the given statements.

23. `return 0;`

24. `return n * x;`

25.
```
unsigned x = 0;
while (n >= 2)
{
    n /= 2;
    x++;
}
return x;
```

26.
```
unsigned x = 0;
while (n != 0)
{
   x += n % 10;
   n /= 10;
}
return x;
```

27.
```
if (n < 0)
    n = -n;
while (n >= 10)
    n /= 10;
return n;
```

28.
```
/* RecNumDigits recursively calculates the number of digits
 * in an integer.
 *
 * Receive:  number
 * Return:   the number of digits in number
 ***********************************************************/

unsigned RecNumDigits(unsigned number)
{
   if (number < 10)
      return 1;
   else
      return 1 + RecNumDigits(number / 10);
}
```

29.
```
/* NonrecNumDigits nonrecursively calculates the number of digits
 * in an integer.
 *
 * Receive:  number
 * Return:   the number of digits in number
 ***********************************************************/

unsigned NonrecNumDigits(unsigned number)
{
   unsigned count = 1;
   while (number >= 10)
   {
      count++;
      number /= 10;
   }
   return count;
}
```

30.
```
/* NonrecPrintReverse recursively displays a number's digits
 * in reverse order.
 *
 * Receive:  An integer number >= 0
 * Output:   The digits of number in reverse order
 ***************************************************************/

void RecPrintReverse(unsigned number)
{
   cout << number % 10;                    // output the rightmost digit

   unsigned leftDigits = number / 10;   // leftmost part of Number

   if (leftDigits != 0)                 // inductive step:
      RecPrintReverse(leftDigits);      // ... output the rest recursively
   else                                 // anchor case:
      cout << endl;                     // ... generate a new line
}
```

31.
```
/* NonrecPrintReverse nonrecursively displays a number's digits
 * in reverse order.
 *
 * Receive:  An integer number >= 0
 * Output:   The digits of Number in reverse order
 ***************************************************************/

void NonrecPrintReverse(unsigned number)
{
   do
    {
       cout << number% 10;
       number/= 10;
    }
   while (number != 0);
}
```

32.
```
/* Power computes x raised to the power n recursively.
 *
 * Receive: x, a real value, and
 *          n, an integer
 * Return:  x raised to the power n
 ***************************************************************/

double Power(double x, int n)
{
   if (n == 0)
      return 1.0;                     // anchor case
   else if (n > 0)
      return Power(x, n - 1) * x;   // inductive step (n > 0)
   else
      return Power(x, n + 1) / x;   // inductive step (n < 0)
}
```

33. <u>Function calls</u>   <u>Output</u>
```
Move(4, 'A', 'B', 'C');
  Move(3, 'A', 'C', 'B');
    Move(2, 'A', 'B', 'C');
      Move(1, 'A', 'C', 'B');      Move the top disk from A to C
      Move(1, 'A', 'B', 'C');      Move the top disk from A to B
      Move(1, 'C', 'B', 'A');      Move the top disk from C to B
    Move(1, 'A', 'C', 'B');        Move the top disk from A to C
    Move(2, 'B', 'C', 'A');
      Move(1, 'B', 'A', 'C');      Move the top disk from B to A
```

34. <u>Function calls</u>   <u>Output</u>
```
Move(5, 'A', 'B', 'C');
  Move(4, 'A', 'C', 'B');
    Move(3, 'A', 'B', 'C');
      Move(2, 'A', 'C', 'B');
        Move(1, 'A', 'B', 'C');    Move the top disk from A to B
        Move(1, 'A', 'C', 'B');    Move the top disk from A to C
        Move(1, 'B', 'C', 'A');    Move the top disk from B to C
      Move(1, 'A', 'C', 'B');      Move the top disk from A to B
      Move(2, 'C', 'B', 'A');
        Move(1, 'C', 'A', 'B');    Move the top disk from C to A
```

Programming Problems

Section 7.3

1.
```
/* prog7-1.cpp is a driver program to test the weight-conversion
 * function from Exercises 12 & 13.
 *
 * Input:  pounds and ounces  or  grams
 * Output: grams  or  pounds and ounces
 **************************************************************/

#include <iostream.h>                  // cin, cout, >>, <<

double ConvertLbsOz_to_Grams(double pounds, double ounces);
void ConvertGrams_To_LbsOz(double grams, double & pounds, double & ounces);


int main()
{
    int lbs;
    double oz, g;

    for (;;)
    {
        cout << "\nEnter pounds and ounces (negative to stop): ";
        cin >> lbs >> oz;
        if (lbs < 0) break;

        g = ConvertLbsOz_to_Grams(lbs, oz);
        cout << "This is equivalent to " << g << " g\n";
    }

    for (;;)
    {
        cout << "\nEnter grams (negative  to stop): ";
        cin >> g;

        if (g < 0) break;

        ConvertGrams_To_LbsOz(g, lbs, oz);
        cout << "This is equivalent to " << lbs << " lbs " << oz << " oz\n";
    }

    return 0;
}

/* Insert definitions of ConvertLbsOz_to_Grams() and
   ConvertGrams_To_LbsOz() from Exercises 12 & 13 here */
```

2.
```
/* prog7-2.cpp is a driver program to test the length-conversion
 * function from Exercises 14 & 15.
 *
 * Input:  yards, feet, & inches  or  centimeters
 * Output: centimeters  or  yards, feet, & inches
 **************************************************************/
```

```
#include <iostream.h>                    // cin, cout, >>, <<

double Convert_YFtIn_To_Cm(int yards, int feet, double inches);
void Convert_Cm_To_YFtIn(double cm, int & yards, int & feet, double & inches);

int main()
{
   int yds, ft;
   double in, cm;

   for (;;)
   {
      cout << "\nEnter yards, feet, inches (negative to stop): ";
      cin >> yds >> ft >> in;
      if (yds < 0) break;

      cm = Convert_YFtIn_To_Cm(yds, ft, in);
      cout << "This is equivalent to " << cm << " cm\n";
   }

   for (;;)
   {
      cout << "\nEnter centimeters(negative  to stop): ";
      cin >> cm;

      if (cm < 0) break;

      Convert_Cm_To_YFtIn(cm, yds, ft, in);
      cout << "This is equivalent to " << yds << " yds " << ft << " ft "
           << in << " in\n";
   }

   return 0;
}

/* Insert definitions of Convert_YFtIn_To_Cm() and
   Convert_Cm_To_YFtIn() from Exercises 14 & 15 here */
```

3.
```
/* prog7-3.cpp is a driver program to test the time-conversion
 * functions from Exercises 16 & 17.
 *
 * Input:  hours, minutes, & AM/PM  or  military time
 * Output: military time  or  hours, minutes, & AM/PM
 ********************************************************************/

#include <iostream.h>                    // cin, cout, >>, <<

int ConvertNormal_To_Military(int hours, int minutes, char ampm);
void ConvertMilitary_To_Normal(int military,
                               int & hours, int & minutes, char & ampm);

int main()
{
   int hours, min, milTime;
   char ampm;
```

```
    for (;;)
    {
        cout << "\nEnter hours, minutes, and A (for AM) or "
                "P (for PM) (0 0 0 to stop): ";
        cin >> hours >> min >> ampm;
        if (hours == 0) break;

        milTime = ConvertNormal_To_Military(hours, min, ampm);
        cout << "In military time this is " << milTime << endl;
    }

    for (;;)
    {
        cout << "\nEnter military time (negative  to stop): ";
        cin >> milTime;

        if (milTime < 0) break;

        ConvertMilitary_To_Normal(milTime, hours, min, ampm);
        cout << "This is equivalent to "
            << (hours < 12 ? 0 : "") << hours << " :"
            << (min < 12 ? 0 : "") << min << " :"
            << ampm << ".M.\n";
    }

    return 0;
}

/* Insert definitions of ConvertNormal_To_Military() and
   ConvertMilitary_To_Normal() from Exercises 16 & 17 here */
```

4.

```
/* prog7-4.cpp converts polar coordinates to rectangular.
 *
 * Input:  polar coordinates of points
 * Output: polar and rectangular coordinates of points
 *********************************************************************/
#include <iostream.h>               // cin, cout, >>, <<

void Convert(double r, double t, double& x, double& y);

int main()
{
    double r, theta,               // polar coordinates
           x, y;                   // rectangular coordinates
    char response;                 // user response to "More points?" query
    do
    {
        cout << "Enter polar coordinates of a point: ";
        cin >> r >> theta;

        Convert(r, theta, x, y);
        cout << "Polar coordinates:  (" << r << ", " << theta << ")\n";
        cout << "Rectangular coordinates:  (" << x << ", " << y << ")\n";

        cout << "\nMore points (Y or N)? ";
        cin >> response;
    }
    while (response == 'Y' || response == 'y');

    return 0;
}
```

```
/* Convert converts polar coordinates to rectangular coordinates.
 *
 * Receive:  r, t, the rho and Theta of the polar coordinates
 * Return:   x, y, the x and y of the rectangular coordinates
 *******************************************************************/

void Convert(double r, double t, double& x, double& y)
{
   x = r * cos(t);
   y = r * sin(t);
}
```

5.

```
/* prog7-5.cpp reads employee information and calculates gross wages,
 * taxes withheld, and net wages.
 *
 * Input:  empNum, hoursWorked, hourlyRate, numDependents, cityTaxToDate,
 *         fedTaxToDate
 * Output: wages
 *********************************************************************/

#include <iostream.h>                  // cin, cout, >>, <<
#include <iomanip.h>                   // setprecision(), setiosflags()

double Wages(double hours, double rate);
void CalculateTaxes(double grossWages, int numDeps,
                    double & cityTax, double & cityToDate,
                    double & fedTax, double & fedToDate);

int main()
{
   long int empNum;                   // employee number
   int numDependents;                 // # of dependents
   double hoursWorked,                // hours worked
          hourlyRate,                 // hourly rate
          grossPay, netPay,           // gross and net pay
          cityTax, fedTax,            // city and federal tax withheld
          cityTaxToDate, fedTaxToDate; // city & fed. tax withheld to date
   for (;;)
   {
      cout << "\nEnter employee number (0 to stop): ";
      cin >> empNum;
      if (empNum <= 0) break;

      cout << "Enter hours worked and hourly rate: ";
      cin >> hoursWorked >> hourlyRate;

      cout << "Enter # dependents, city tax withheld to date, and\n"
              "federal tax withheld to date: ";
      cin >> numDependents >> cityTaxToDate >> fedTaxToDate;

      grossPay = Wages(hoursWorked, hourlyRate);
      CalculateTaxes(grossPay, numDependents, cityTax, cityTaxToDate,
                     fedTax, fedTaxToDate);
      netPay = grossPay - (cityTax + fedTax);
```

```
      cout << setprecision(2) << setiosflags(ios::fixed | ios::showpoint)
           << "\nFor employee #" << empNum << ":\n"
           << "Gross wages: $" << grossPay << endl
           << "Net wages:    $" << netPay << endl
           << "City tax withheld: $" << cityTax
           << "  Federal tax withheld: $" << fedTax << endl
           << "City tax to date:    $" << cityTaxToDate
           << "  Federal tax to date:  $" << fedTaxToDate << endl;
   }

   return 0;
}

/* Wages computes an employee's wages.  Hours over 40 are paid
 * at 1.5 times the regular hourly rate.
 *
 * Receive: hours worked and hourly rate
 * Output:  wages.
 ****************************************************************/

double Wages(double hours, double rate)
{
   if (hours <= 40.0)
      return hours * rate;
   else
      return hours * rate + ((hours - 40) * (rate * 0.5));
}

/* CalculateTaxes computes an employee's taxe withheld.
 *
 * Receive:   gross wages, number of dependents, city tax
 *            withheld to date, and federal tax withheld to date
 * Pass gack: city tax and federal tax withheld and updated
 *            city and federal tax withheld to date
 ****************************************************************/

void CalculateTaxes(double grossPay, int numDeps,
                    double & cityTax, double & cityToDate,
                    double & fedTax, double & fedToDate)
{
   const double CITY_RATE = 0.0115,
                MAX_CITY_TAX = CITY_RATE * 40000,
                FED_RATE = 0.30,
                DEP_ALLOWANCE = 40.00;

   cityTax = CITY_RATE * grossPay;
   if (cityTax + cityToDate > MAX_CITY_TAX)
      cityTax = MAX_CITY_TAX - cityToDate;
   cityToDate += cityTax;

   fedTax = FED_RATE * (grossPay - DEP_ALLOWANCE * numDeps);
   if (fedTax < 0)
      fedTax = 0;
   fedToDate += fedTax;
}
```

6.

```cpp
/* prog7-6.cpp finds the GCD and LCM of pairs of numbers.
 *
 * Input:  integers a and b
 * Output: GCD and LCM of a and b
 ********************************************************/

#include <iostream.h>                 // cin, cout, >>, <<

void FindGCDandLCM(int a, int b, int & gcd, int & lcm);

int main()
{
   int a, b, gcd, lcm;

   for (;;)
   {
      cout << "\nEnter 2 integers (0 0) to stop: ";
      cin >> a >> b;

      FindGCDandLCM(a, b, gcd, lcm);
      cout << "GCD = " << gcd << "\nLCM = " << lcm << endl;
   }

   return 0;
}

/* FindGCDandLCM returns the greatest common divisor and least
 * common multiple of a and b.
 *
 * Receive:  a, b, two integers
 * Return:   gcd, greatest common divisor of a and b
 *           lcm, least common multiple of a and b
 ********************************************************/

#include <stdlib.h>       // abs()

void FindGCDandLCM(int a, int b, int & gcd, int & lcm)
{
   int r = a % b;

   lcm = abs(a * b);

   while (r != 0)
   {
      a = b;
      b = r;
      r = a % b;
   }

   gcd = b;
   lcm /= b;
}
```

7.
```
/* prog7-7.cpp accepts the current date and a person's birthdate
 * and then calculates the biorhythm index for that person.
 *
 * Input:  Month, day, and year of current date and birthdate
 * Output: The biorhythm indexx
 *********************************************************************/

#include <iostream.h>              // cin, cout, >>, <<
#include <iomanip.h>               // setw(), setiosflags()
#include <math.h>                  // sin

int DaysIn(int month, int year);
int NDays(int fromMonth, int fromDay, int fromYear,
          int toMonth, int toDay, int toYear);
bool IsLeapYear(int year);
double BiorhythmIndex(int days);

int main()
{
    int  birthMonth,
         birthDay,
         birthYear,
         currentMonth,
         currentDay,
         currentYear;

    cout << "\nWhat is your birthdate (month day year)? ";
    cin >> birthMonth >> birthDay >> birthYear;

    cout << "\nWhat is the current date (month day year)? ";
    cin >> currentMonth >> currentDay >> currentYear;

    int days = NDays(birthMonth,birthDay,birthYear,
                     currentMonth,currentDay,currentYear);

    double index = BiorhythmIndex(days);

    cout << setiosflags(ios::showpoint | ios::fixed)
         << setprecision(6)
         << "\nYour biorhythm index is: " << index << endl;

    return 0;
}

/* DaysIn returns the number of days in the specified month.
 *
 * Receive:  month, the month
 *           year, the year
 * Return:   the number of days in the month of that year
 *********************************************************************/

int DaysIn(int month, int year)
{
    if (month == 2)
        if (IsLeapYear(year))
            return 29;
        else
            return 28;
```

```
        else if ( (month == 4) || (month == 6) ||
                  (month == 9) || (month == 11) )
            return 30;
        else
            return 31;
}

/* NDays returns the number of days between two dates.
 *
 * Receive:  fromMonth, fromDay, fromYear,
 *           toMonth, toDay, toYear
 * Return:   the number of days between the "from" date
 *           and the "to" date
 *****************************************************************/

int NDays(int fromMonth, int fromDay, int fromYear,
          int toMonth, int toDay, int toYear)
{
    int days = 0;

    while ( (fromYear != toYear) ||
            (fromMonth != toMonth) ||
            (fromDay != toDay) )
    {
        fromDay++;

        if (fromDay > DaysIn(fromMonth,fromYear))
        {
            fromDay = 1;
            fromMonth++;

            if (fromMonth > 12)
            {
                fromMonth = 1;
                fromYear++;
            }
        }

        days++;
    }

    return days;
}

/* IsLeapYear returns true if the specified year is a leap year.
 *
 * Receive:  year
 * Return:   true if year is a leap year; false if not
 *****************************************************************/

bool IsLeapYear(int Year)
{
    return (Year % 4 == 0) &&
           (!(Year % 100 == 0) || (Year % 400 == 0));
}

/* BiorhythmIndex returns the biorhythm index for a person of
 * the specified age.
 *
 * Receive:  days, the age of a person in days
 * Return:   the biorhythm index
 *****************************************************************/
```

```
double BiorhythmIndex(int days)
{
    const double PI = 3.14159265358979323846;

    return sin( (double(days) / 23.0) * (2 * PI) ) +
           sin( (double(days) / 33.0) * (2 * PI) ) +
           sin( (double(days) / 28.0) * (2 * PI) );
}
```

Section 7.6

8.
```
/* prog7-8.cpp is a driver program to test the digit-counting
 * functions from Exercises 28 & 29.
 *
 * Input:  an integer
 * Output: the number of digits in the integer
 ***************************************************************/

#include <iostream.h>                    // cin, cout, >>, <<

unsigned RecNumDigits(unsigned number);
unsigned NonrecNumDigits(unsigned number);


int main()
{
    int n;

    for (;;)
    {
        cout << "\nEnter a nonnegative integer (negative to stop): ";
        cin >> n;
        if (n < 0) break;

        cout << "This number has:\n"
             << RecNumDigits(n) << " digits as computed recursively\n"
             << NonrecNumDigits(n) << " digits as computed monrecursively\n";
    }

    return 0;
}

/* Insert definitions of RecNumDigits() and
   NonrecNumDigits() from Exercises 28 & 29 here */
```

9.
```
/* prog7-9.cpp is a driver program to test the reverse-printing
 * functions from Exercises 30 & 31.
 *
 * Input:  an integer
 * Output: the integer reversed
 ***************************************************************/
```

```
#include <iostream.h>                    // cin, cout, >>, <<

void RecPrintReverse(unsigned number);
void NonrecPrintReverse(unsigned number);


int main()
{
   int n;

   for (;;)
   {
      cout << "\nEnter a nonnegative integer (negative to stop): ";
      cin >> n;
      if (n < 0) break;

      cout << "This number reversed recursively is: ";
      RecPrintReverse(n);
      cout << "This number reversed nonrecursively is: ";
      NonrecPrintReverse(n);
      cout << endl;
   }

   return 0;
}

/* Insert definitions of RecPrintReverse() and
   NonrecPrintReverse() from Exercises 28 & 29 here */
```

10.
```
/* prog7-10.cpp is a driver program to test the recursive power
 * function from Exercise 32.
 *
 * Input:  a real x an integer n
 * Output: x to the n-th power
 ***************************************************************/

#include <iostream.h>                    // cin, cout, >>, <<

double Power(double x, int n);

int main()
{
   double x;
   int n;

   for (;;)
   {
      cout << "\nEnter a real x and an integer n (0 0 to stop): ";
      cin >> x >> n;
      if (x == 0 && n == 0) break;

      cout << "x to the n-th power is " << Power(x, n) << endl;
   }

   return 0;
}

/* Insert definitions of Power() from Exercise 32 here */
```

11.

```
/* prob7-11.cpp is a test driver for the function F() of Exercise 20.
 *
 * Output:  Test drive of F(number)
 **********************************************************************/

#include <iostream.h>                 // cin, cout, >>, <<

int level = 0;                        // global variable to control indentation

void Indent(int spaces)
{
   while (spaces--)
      cout << "   ";
}

unsigned F(unsigned n)
{
   if (n < 2)
   {
      Indent(level);
      cout << "F(" << n << ") returns 0\n";
      return 0;
   }
   else
   {
      Indent(level);
      cout << "F(" << n << ") = 1 + F(" << (n / 2) << ")\n";
      level++;
      unsigned value = 1 + F(n / 2);
      level--;
      Indent(level);
      cout << "F(" << n << ") returns " << value << '\n';
      return value;
   }
}

int main()
{
   int number;

   cout << "Enter a positive integer: ";
   cin >> number;
   F(number);

   return 0;
}
```

12.

```
/* prog7-12.cpp is a test driver for the function PrintReverse()
 *
 * Output:  Test drive of PrintReverse(number)
 ********************************************************************/

#include <iostream.h>                 // cin, cout, >>, <<

int level = 0;                        // global variable to control indentation
```

```
void Indent(int spaces)
{
   while (spaces--)
      cout << "   ";
}

/* PrintReverse displays a number's digits in reverse order.
 *
 * Receive:  an integer number >= 0
 * Output:   the digits of number in reverse order
 ***************************************************************/

void PrintReverse(int number)
{
   Indent(level);
   cout << "PrintReverse(" << number << "): Output ";
   cout << number % 10;                 // output the rightmost digit

   int leftDigits = number / 10;     // leftmost part of Number

   if (leftDigits)                   // inductive step:
   {
      cout << ", then call PrintReverse(" << leftDigits << ").\n";
      level++;
      PrintReverse(leftDigits);       // ... output the rest recursively
      level--;
   }
   else                              // anchor case:
   {
      cout << " and \\n.";
      cout << endl;                   // ... generate a new line
   }

   Indent(level);
   cout << "PrintReverse(" << number << ") returns.\n";
}

int main()
{
   int number;

   cout << "Enter a positive integer: ";
   cin >> number;
   PrintReverse(number);

   return 0;
}
```

13.

```
/* prog7-13.cpp displays the lyrics of the song "Bingo."
 *
 * Output: lyrics of "Bingo"
 ***************************************************************/

#include <iostream.h>                      // cin, cout, <<, >>

void PrintSong(int verse);

int main()
{
   PrintSong(1);
}
```

```
/* PrintSong displays the lyrics of the song "BINGO" beginning
 * with a given verse.
 *
 * Receive: number of the verse
 * Output:  the song beginning with that verse
 *******************************************************************/

void PrintSong(int verse)
{
   const char BINGO[] = "BINGO";

   cout << "There was a farmer had a dog;\n"
           "And Bingo was his name-o.\n";

   if (verse > 1)
   {
      cout << "(Clap";
      for (int i = 2; i < verse; i++)
        cout << ", clap";
      cout << (verse < 6 ? ")-" : ")\n");

   }

   for (int i = verse; i <= 5; i++)
      cout << BINGO[i-1] << (i < 5 ? "-" : "!\n");

   cout << "And Bingo was his name-o!\n\n";

   if (verse < 6)
      PrintSong(verse + 1);
}
```


14.
```
/* prog7-14.cpp is a driver program to test the a recursive
 * function to display a number with commas.
 *
 * Input:  an integer n
 * Output: n with commas in correct locations
 *************************************************************/

#include <iostream.h>              // cin, cout, >>, <<

void PrintNumberWithCommas(long int Number);

int main()
{
   long int n;

   for (;;)
   {
      cout << "\nEnter an integer n (negative to stop): ";
      cin >> n;
      if (n < 0) break;

      PrintNumberWithCommas(n);
   }

   return 0;
}
```

```
/* PrintNumberWithCommas prints a number with commas in the appropriate
 * locations.
 *
 * Receive:  number
 * Output:   number, with commas
 *****************************************************************/

void PrintNumberWithCommas(long int number)
{
   if (number < 1000)
      cout << number;
   else
   {
      PrintNumberWithCommas(number / 1000);
      cout << ','
           << (number % 1000) / 100
           << (number % 100) / 10
           << (number % 10);
   }
}
```

15.
```
/* prog7-15.cpp finds the GCD of pairs of numbres.
 *
 * Input:  integers a and b
 * Output: GCD of a and b
 *******************************************************/

#include <iostream.h>                 // cin, cout, >>, <<

long int GCD(long int a, long int b);

int main()
{
   int a, b;

   for (;;)
   {
      cout << "\nEnter 2 integers (0 0) to stop: ";
      cin >> a >> b;

      if (a == 0 && b == 0) break;

      cout << "GCD = " << GCD(a,b) << endl;
   }

   return 0;
}
```

```
/* GCD returns the greatest common divisor of a and b.
 *
 * Receive:  a, b, two integers
 * Return:   greatest common divisor of a and b
 ***************************************************************/

long int GCD(long int a, long int b)
{
   long int r = a % b;

   if (r != 0)
      return GCD(b,r);

   return b;
}
```

16. *Note*: **The anchor step in the definition should read**
$$f_1 = f_2 = 1 \qquad \text{(anchor)}$$

```
/* prog7-16.cpp calculates Fibonacci numbers recursively
 * (which is horribly inefficient).
 *
 * Input:  integer n
 * Output: n-th Fibonacci number
 ***************************************************************/

#include <iostream.h>                    // cin, cout, >>, <<

unsigned Fibonacci(int n);

int main()
{
   int n;

   for (;;)
   {
      cout << "\nWhich Fibonacci number do you want (0 to stop> ";
      cin >> n;

      if (n == 0) break;

      cout << n << "-th Fibonacci number is " << Fibonacci(n) << endl;
   }

   return 0;
}

/* Fibonacci finds the n-th Fibonacci number recursively
 * (and very inefficiently).
 * Receive:  n
 * Return:   n-th Fibonacci number
 ***************************************************************/

unsigned Fibonacci(int n)
{
   if (n <= 2)
      return 1;
   else
      return Fibonacci(n-1) + Fibonacci(n-2);
}
```

17.

```cpp
/* prog7-17.cpp displays the prime factorization of a number and
 * indicates if it is prime.
 *
 * Input:  a number
 * Output: its prime factorization
 ***********************************************************************/

#include <iostream.h>                // cin, cout, >>, <<

bool PrintPrimeFactorizationOf(long int mumber);

int main()
{
   long number;

   cout << "\nPlease enter the number to be factored: ";
   cin >> number;

   if (number< 2)
   {
      cout << "\nNumber must be 2 or more!\n";
      return 1;
   }

   cout << "\nFactorization:\n";

   if (PrintPrimeFactorizationOf(number))
      cout << " is a prime!";

   cout << endl;

   return 0;
}

/* PrintPrimeFactorizationOf displays the prime factorization of
 * a number in descending order and returns true if it is a prime.
 *
 * Receive:  number, an integer
 * Output:   the prime factorization in descending order
 * Return:   true if number is prime, false if not
 ***********************************************************/

bool PrintPrimeFactorizationOf(long int number)
{
   long int divisor = 2;

   while (number % divisor != 0)
      divisor++;

   if (number != divisor)
   {
      PrintPrimeFactorizationOf(number / divisor);
      cout << " * " << divisor;
      return false;
   }
   else
   {
      cout << divisor;
      return true;
   }
}
```

18.

```
/* prog7-18.cpp uses a recursive function to count the number of
 * northeast paths from one point to another in a rectangular
 * grid.
 *
 * Input:   location of B relative to A
 * Output: the number of northeast paths from A to B
 *****************************************************************/

#include <iostream.h>

int NortheastPaths(int pointsNorth, int pointsEast);

int main()
{
    int pointsNorth,
        pointsEast;

    cout << "\nHow many points north of A is B? ";
    cin >> pointsNorth;

    cout << "How many points east of A is B? ";
    cin >> pointsEast;

    cout << "\nThere are " << NortheastPaths(pointsNorth, pointsEast)
         << " northeast paths between A and B.\n";

    return 0;
}

/* NortheastPaths returns the number of northeast paths from the current
 * point to the point pointsNorth north and pointsEast east of the
 * current point.
 *
 * Receive:  pointsNorth, the points north to the destination
 *           pointsEast, the point east to the destination
 * Return:   the number of northeast paths
 *****************************************************************/

int NortheastPaths(int pointsNorth, int pointsEast)
{
    if ( (pointsNorth < 0) || (pointsEast < 0) )
        return 0;
    else if ( (pointsNorth == 0) && (pointsEast == 0) )
        return 1;
    else
        return NortheastPaths(pointsNorth - 1, pointsEast) +
               NortheastPaths(pointsNorth , pointsEast - 1);
}
```

19. This problem requires an array or list for a general solution. Here we present a solution that generates permutations of characters in a string.

```
/* prog7-19.cpp generates permutations recursively.
 *
 * Input:   number of elements to permute
 * Output: list of permutations
 *****************************************************************/

#include <iostream.h>            // cin, cout, >>, <<
#include <string>                // string
```

```
string Permutation(string source, int number);

int main()
{
   int n;
   string basis = "1234567890ABCDEF";

   cout << "Enter number of characters (at most 16) to permute: ";
   cin >> n;

   basis.remove(n, basis.length() - n);
   string source = basis;

   int number = 0;
   string nextPerm;

   cout << "\nPermutations:\n";

   for (;;)
   {
      nextPerm = Permutation(source, number);

      if (nextPerm.length() == 0)
         break;

      cout << nextPerm << endl;
      number++;
   }

   return 0;
}

/* Permutation generates the m-th permutation in the sequence
 * of permutations.  The current permutation is stored in source
 * and the next permutation is returned.
 *
 * Receive: source and number
 * Return:  dest
 **************************************************************/

string Permutation(string source, int number)
{
   if (source.length() == 0)
      return "";

   if (source.length() == 1)
   {
      if (number == 0)
         return source;
      else
         return "";
   }

   string newSource = source;
   int len = newSource.length();

   newSource.remove(len-1, 1);
   string perm = Permutation(newSource, number / len);
```

```
    if (perm.length() != 0)
        perm.insert((len-1) - int(number % len), source.substr(len-1, 1));

    return perm;
}
```

20.

```
/* prog7-20.cpp uses Simpson's rule to find the volume of dirt
 * that must be removed to construct a road through a hill.
 *
 * Input:  the length of roadway through the hill,
 *         the width of the roadway
 * Output: the approximate volume of dirt removed
 ****************************************************************/

#include <iostream.h>               // cin, cout. >>, <<

double SimpsonArea(int n, double totalLength);

int main()
{

    cout << "Enter the length of roadway through the hill: ";
    double roadLength;                          // get the road length
    cin >> roadLength;

    cout << "Enter the number of points at which hill elevation "
            "was measured: ";
    int numPoints;
    cin >> numPoints;

    cout << "Enter the hill elevations (y values) at the " << numPoints
         << " equally-spaced points.\n  The amount of dirt to be removed"
            " from the hill will be computed.\n\n";

                                                // compute X-sectional area
    double hillCrossSectionalArea = SimpsonArea(numPoints-1, roadLength);

    cout << "Enter the width of the roadway: ";
    double roadWidth;                           // get the road width
    cin >> roadWidth;
                                                // compute volume
    double dirtVolume = roadWidth * hillCrossSectionalArea;
                                                // display volume
    cout << "\n--> The volume of dirt to be removed is approximately "
         << dirtVolume << " cubic units." << endl;

    return 0;
}

/* SimpsonArea computes the approximate area under a curve for
 * which a collection of y values at equally spaced x values are
 * entered from the keyboard.
 *
 *   Receive:       n, number of subintervals along the x axis
 *                  intLength, the length of the interval on the x axis
 *   Preconditions: 1. n is even.
 *                  2. the y values correspond to equally-spaced x
 *                     values in the interval on the x axis.
 *   Return:        the approximate area under the curve
 ****************************************************************/
```

```
double SimpsonArea(int n, double intLength)
{
   double yValue;
   cout << "First y value? ";
   cin >> yValue;                         // the first y value
   double sum = yValue;                   // initialize sum to it

   for (int i = 1; i <= n - 1; i++)
   {
      cout >> "Next y value?  ";;
      cin >> yValue;                      // i-th y value
      if (i % 2 == 0)                     // even-numbered term in formula
         sum += 2.0 * yValue;            //   multiplier is 2
      else                               // odd-numbered term in formula
         sum += 4.0 * yValue;            //   multiplier is 4
   }

   cout << "Last y value?  ";
   cin >> yValue;                         // the last y value
   sum += yValue;                         // add it to sum

   double deltaX = intLength / double(n);

   return (deltaX / 3.0) * sum;           // final approximation
}
```

21.

```
/* prog7-21 uses the trapezoidal method to find the work done
 * by a force appied at a constant angle theta in moving an
 * an object along the x axis from a to b.
 *
 *  Input:  a, b
 *  Output: the approximate amount of work done
 ***************************************************************/

#include <iostream.h>              // cin, cout. >>, <<
#include <math.h>                  // cos()

double TrapezoidalArea(int n, double totalLength);

int main()
{
   double a, b;
   cout << "Enter the interval endpoints: ";
   cin >> a >> b;
   double distance = b - a;

   double theta;
   cout << "Enter the angle theta at which the force was applied: ";
   cin >> theta;

   cout << "Enter the number of points at which the force was measured: ";
   int numPoints;
   cin >> numPoints;

   cout << "Enter the force values (newtons) at the " << numPoints
        << " equally-spaced points.\nThe work done by the force in"
           " moving an object from a to b will be computed.\n\n";
```

```
    double work = cos(theta) *
                 TrapezoidalArea(numPoints-1, distance);

    cout << "\n--> The work done by the force in moving an object over"
            " the interval\nis approximately "
        << work << " joules." << endl;

    return 0;
}

/* TrapezoidalArea computes the approximate area under a curve for
 * which a collection of y values at equally spaced x values are
 * entered from the keyboard.
 *
 *    Receive:      n, number of subintervals along the x axis
 *                  intLength, the length of the interval on the x axis
 *    Precondition: the y values correspond to equally-spaced x values
 *                  in the interval on the x axis.
 *    Return:       the approximate area under the curve
 *******************************************************************/

double TrapezoidalArea(int n, double intLength)
{
    double yValue;
    cout << "First y value? ";
    cin >> yValue;                       // the first y value
    double sum = yValue / 2.0;           // initialize sum to 1/2 of it

    for (int i = 1; i <= n - 1; i++)
    {
        cout << "Next y value?  ";
        cin >> yValue;                   // i-th y value
        sum += yValue;                   // add it to sum
    }

    cout << "Last y value?  ";
    cin >> yValue;                       // the last y value
    sum += yValue/ 2.0;                  // add 1/2 of it to sum

    double deltaX = intLength / double(n);

    return deltaX * sum;                 // total area of trapezoids
}
```

22. Replace the function `TrapezoidalArea()` in Problem 21 with the function `SimpsonArea()` from Problem 20.

23.
```
/* prog7-23 is a driver program to test the function TrapezoidalArea().
 *
 *  Input:  a, b
 *  Output: the approximate area under y = F(x) from x = a to x = b
 *******************************************************************/

#include <iostream.h>            // cin, cout. >>, <<

inline double F(double x)
{
    return x*x;                  // the function F for which the
}                                // area is being approximated

double TrapezoidalArea(int n, double a, double b);
```

```cpp
int main()
{
    double a, b;
    cout << "Enter the interval endpoints: ";
    cin >> a >> b;

    cout << "Enter the number of subintervals to use: ";
    int n;
    cin >> n;

    cout << "The approximate area under y = F(x) from x = a to x = b"
            "\nis approximately " << TrapezoidalArea(n, a, b) << endl;

    return 0;
}

/* TrapezoidalArea computes the approximate area under the graph
 * of a function y = F(x).
 *
 * Receive:      n, number of subintervals along the x axis
 *               a, b, the length of the interval on the x axis
 * Return:       the approximate area under the curve
 *******************************************************************/

double TrapezoidalArea(int n, double a, double b)
{
    double deltaX = (b - a) double(n),  // the length of a subinterval
           x = a,                       // a point in interval [a, b]
           sum = F(a)/ 2.0;             // initialize sum to 1/2 of first y value

    for (int i = 1; i <= n - 1; i++)
    {
        x += deltaX;                    // i-th x value in [a, b]
        sum += F(x);                    // add corresponding y value to sum
    }
    sum += F(b)/ 2.0;                   // add 1/2 of last y value to sum

    return deltaX * sum;                // total area of trapezoids
}
```

24.
```cpp
/* prog7-24.cpp finds an approximate solution of the equation
 * F(x) = 0 in a given interval, using the bisection method.
 *
 * Input:   desired accuracy of approximation, endpoints of an
 *          interval containing a solution
 * Output:  the approximate solution
 *******************************************************************/

#include <iostream.h>          // cin, cout. >>, <<

inline double F(double x)
{
    return x*x*x + x - 5;       // the function F for which the
}                               // equation F(x) = 0 is being solved


double Bisector(double left, double right, double accuracy);
```

```
int main()
{
    cout << "This program uses the bisection method to find an\n"
         << "approximate solution to the equation F(x) = 0.\n";

    double desiredAccuracy;     // the accuracy desired
    cout << "\nEnter the accuracy desired (e.g. .001): ";
    cin >> desiredAccuracy;

    double left, right;
    do                          // get the interval containing a solution
    {
        cout << "Enter the x-values of interval containing solution: ";
        cin >> left >> right;
    }
    while (F(left) * F(right) >= 0.0);


    double solution = Bisector(left, right, desiredAccuracy);

    cout << Bisector(left, right, desiredAccuracy)
         << " is an approximate solution of F(x) = 0, to within "
         << desiredAccuracy << endl;

    return 0;
}

/* Bisector implements the bisection algorithm.
 *
 * Receive:  left, the left endpoint of the original interval
 *           right, the right endpoint of the original interval
 *           accuracy, the desired accuracy of the approximation
 * Return:   midPoint, the middle of the final interval
 ********************************************************************/

double Bisector(double left, double right, double accuracy)
{
    double width = right - left,        // the interval width
           midPoint,                    // the midpoint of the interval
           F_mid;                       // value of F at midpoint

    while (width/2.0 > accuracy)        // while loop
    {
        midPoint= (left + right) / 2.0;  //    compute midpoint
        F_mid= F(midPoint);              //    compute function at midpoint

        if (F(left) * F_mid< 0.0 )       //    solution is in left half
            right = midPoint;
        else                             //    solution is in right half
            left = midPoint;

        width /= 2.0;                    //    split the interval
    }                                    // end while loop

    return midPoint;
}
```

Chapter 8: Files and Streams

Exercises 8.2

1. (a)
```
istream inputStream;
inputStream.open("InData");
```
   (b) `istream inputStream("InData");`

2. (a)
```
ostream outputStream;
outputStream.open("OutData");
```
   (b) `ostream outputStream("OutData");`

3. (a)
```
string inputFileName;
cout << "Enter name of input file: ";
getline(cin, inputFileName);
istream inputStream;
inputStream.open(inputFileName.data());
```

   (b)
```
string inputFileName;
cout << "Enter name of input file: ";
getline(cin, inputFileName);
istream inputStream(inputFileName.data());
```

4. (a)
```
stroutg outputFileName;
cout << "Enter name of output file: ";
getline(cin, outputFileName);
ostream outputStream;
outputStream.open(outputFileName.data());
```

   (b)
```
stroutg outputFileName;
cout << "Enter name of output file: ";
getline(cin, outputFileName);
ostream outputStream(outputFileName.data());
```

5. num1 = 1   num2 = -2 num3 = 3   num4 = 4

6. num1 = 1   num2 = -2   num3 = 3   num4 = 4

7. num1 = -8 num2 = 7   num3 = 6   num4 = -5

8.
```
n1 = 123        r1 = 45.6      c1 = 'X'       n2 = 78
r2 = -909.8     c2 = '7'       n3 = -65       c3 = '$'
c4 = '4'        r3 = 32.1
```

9. `n1 = 123`   `c1 = '4'`   `c2 = '5'`   `r1 = 0.6`
   r2 = **error -- real numbers cannot contain letters (i.e., 'X')**

10.
```
n1 = 123        r1 = 45.6      c1 = 'X'       c2 = '7'
c3 = '8'        n2 = -909      r2 = 0.8       c4 = '7'
r3 = -65        n3 = 432
```

11. `c1 = '1'`   `n1 = 23`   `r1 = 45.6`
   r2 = **error -- real numbers cannot contain letters (i.e., 'X')**

12.
```
n1 = 123        r1 = 45.6      c1 = 'X'       c2 = '7'
c3 = '8'        n2 = -909      c4 = '.'
```

13. n1 = 54   r1 = 32E1   r2 = -6.78   c1 = '$'
    n2 = 90   n3 = 1
    (read position is at the last newline)

14. n1 = 54   r1 = 32E1   r2 = -6.78   c1 = '$'
    c2 = '9'   n2 = 0   n3 = 1
    n3 = error -- end-of-file hit
    (read position is at the end-of-file marker)

15. n1 = 54   n2 = 32   c1 = 'E'   c2 = '1'   c3 = '-'
    r1 = 6.78   c4 = '$'   n2 = 90   r2 = 1.0

16. r1 = 54   r2 = 32E1   r3 = -6.78   c1 = '$'
    n1 = 90   n2 = 1
    (read position is at the last newline)

17. n1 = 54   n2 = 32   c1 = 'E'   n3 = 1
    c2 = '-'   r1 = 6.78   c3 = '$'   n3 = 90
    r2 = 1
    (read position is at the last newline)

Programming Problems

Sections 8.1 - 8.3

1.
```
/* prog8-1.cpp appends one file to the end of the other.
 *
 * Input(keyboard): names of the files
 * Input(file):     integers in file2.
 * Output(file):    integers in file2 to the end of file1.
 ******************************************************************/

#include <iostream.h>                    // cin, cout
#include <fstream.h>                     // ifstream, ofstream
#include <string>                        // string, getline()
#include <assert.h>                      // assert()

int main()
{
    cout << "This program appends file2 to file1.\n"
            "Enter the name of file1: ";
    string file1Name;
    getline(cin, file1Name);
    cout << "Enter the name of file2: ";
    string file2Name;
    getline(cin, file2Name);

    ofstream                             // output stream to file1
      file1(file1Name.data(), ios::app); // open it for appending
    assert(file1.is_open());
    ifstream file2(file2Name.data());    // open input stream to file2
    assert(file2.is_open());

    int number;                          // element of file1 and file2
```

```
    for (;;)                              // loop:
    {
        file2 >> number;                  //    read a value from file2
        if (file2.eof()) break;           //    if eof, quit
        file1 << number << endl;          //    write it to file1
    }                                     // end loop

    file1.close();                        // close the connections
    file2.close();

    cout << "Processing complete.\n";
}
```

2.
```
/* prog8-2.cpp reads a text file and counts the vowels in the file.
 *
 * Input(keyboard): name of the file
 * Input(InFile):   text
 * Output(screen):  the number of vowels in the text
 *****************************************************************/

#include <iostream.h>                     // cin, cout
#include <fstream.h>                      // ifstream, ofstream
#include <string>                         // string
#include <assert.h>                       // assert()

int main()
{
    string fileName;
    cout << "Enter name of file: ";
    getline(cin, fileName);

    ifstream inFile(fileName.data());
    assert(inFile.is_open());

    unsigned vowelCount = 0;
    char ch;

    while (!inFile.eof())
    {
        inFile >> ch;
        if (islower(ch))
            ch = toupper(ch);

        switch (ch)
        {
            case 'A': case 'E': case 'I':
            case 'O': case 'U':
                                            vowelCount++;
        }
    }

    cout << "\nThere are " << vowelCount << " vowel(s) in the file "
        << fileName << endl;

    return 0;
}
```

3.

```cpp
/* prog8-3.cpp reads a text file and counts occurrences of a
 * specified string in the file.
 *
 * Input(keyboard): name of the file and string to search for
 * Input(InFile):   text
 * Output(screen):  number of occurrences of the string in the text
 *******************************************************************/

#include <iostream.h>              // cin, cout
#include <fstream.h>               // ifstream, ofstream
#include <string>                  // string
#include <assert.h>                // assert()

int main()
{
    string fileName;
    cout << "Enter name of file: ";
    getline(cin, fileName);

    int numStudents,
        numScores;

    Table scores;
    Load(fileName, scores);


    string str;
    cout << "Enter string to search for: ";
    getline(cin, str);

    unsigned strCount = 0;
    string line;

    while (!inFile.eof())
    {
        getline(inFile, line);

        int pos = 0;
        while (pos >= 0)
        {
            pos = line.find(str, pos);
            if (pos > 0)
            {
                strCount++;
                pos++;
            }
        }

    }
    cout << "\nThere are " << strCount << " occurrences of " << str
         << " in the file " << fileName << endl;

    return 0;
}
```

4.

```
/* prog8-4.cpp reads a text file and counts the characters in each
 * line.  It displays the line number and the length of the shortest
 * and longest lines in the file, as well as the average number of
 * characters per line.
 *
 * Input(inFile):  text
 * Output(screen): information
 ******************************************************************/

#include <iostream.h>               // cin, cout
#include <fstream.h>                // ifstream, ofstream
#include <string>                   // string
#include <assert.h>                 // assert()
#include <limits.h>                 // INT_MAX

int main()
{
   string fileName;
   cout << "Enter name of file: ";
   getline(cin, fileName);

   ifstream inFile(fileName.data());
   assert(inFile.is_open());

   int lineCount = 1,
       totalChars = 0,
       shortestLine = 0,
       longestLine = 0,
       shortestChars = INT_MAX,
       longestChars = 0,
       lineChars;
   char ch;

   while (!inFile.eof())
   {
      lineChars = 0;

      for (;;)
      {
         inFile.get(ch);
         if (inFile.eof() || (ch == '\n'))
            break;
         lineChars ++;
      }

      if (lineChars < shortestChars)
      {
         shortestLine = lineCount;
         shortestChars = lineChars;
      }
      if (lineChars > longestChars)
      {
         longestLine = lineCount;
         longestChars = lineChars;
      }

      lineCount++;
      totalChars += lineChars;
   }
```

```
   if (lineCount == 0)
      cout << "\nNo lines to count!\n";
   else
      cout << "\nShortest line (#" << shortestLine
           << ") has " << shortestChars << " chars."
           << "\nLongest line (#" << longestLine
           << ") has " << longestChars << " chars."
           << "\nAverage chars per line: " << totalChars / lineCount
           << endl;

   return 0;
}
```

5.
```
/* This program copies one text file into another text file in which the
 * lines are numbered 1, 2, 3, . . . with a number at the left of each line.
 *
 * Input(InFile):    text
 * Output(OutFile): text with numbered lines
 *****************************************************************/

#include <iostream.h>              // cin, cout
#include <fstream.h>               // ifstream, ofstream
#include <string>                  // string, getline()
#include <assert.h>                // assert()

int main()
{
   cout << "Enter the name of the file to be numbered: ";
   string inFileName;
   getline(cin, inFileName);
   cout << "Enter the name of the output file: ";
   string outFileName;
   getline(cin, outFileName);

   ifstream inFile(inFileName.data());   // open input stream to inFile
   assert(inFile.is_open());
   ofstream outFile(outFileName.data()); // open output stream to outFile
   assert(outFile.is_open());

   unsigned lineNumber = 1;
   char ch;

   outFile << lineNumber << ' ';
   lineNumber++;

   while (!inFile.eof())
   {
      inFile.get(ch);

      if (ch == '\n')
      {
         outFile << ch << lineNumber << ' ';
         lineNumber++;
      }
      else
         outFile << ch;
   }

   return 0;
}
```

6.
```
/* prog8-6.cpp reads a text file and writes it to another text file, but
 * with leading blanks and blank lines removed.
 *
 * Input(InFile):    text
 * Output(OutFile): text with leading blanks and blank lines removed
 ************************************************************************/

#include <iostream.h>              // cin, cout
#include <fstream.h>               // ifstream, ofstream
#include <string>                  // string, getline()
#include <assert.h>                // assert()
#include <ctype.h>                 // isspace()

int main()
{
   cout << "Enter the name of the file to be cleaned: ";
   string inFileName;
   getline(cin, inFileName);
   cout << "Enter the name of the output file: ";
   string outFileName;
   getline(cin, outFileName);

   ifstream inFile(inFileName.data());   // open input stream to inFile
   assert(inFile.is_open());
   ofstream outFile(outFileName.data()); // open output stream to outFile
   assert(outFile.is_open());

   char ch;

   do
   {
      do
         inFile.get(ch);
      while (inFile.good() && isspace(ch));

      while (inFile.good() && (ch != '\n'))
      {
         outFile << ch;

         inFile.get(ch);
      }

      outFile << '\n';
   }
   while (inFile.good());

   return 0;
}
```

7.
```
/* prog8-7.cpp reads a text file and prints it in blocks of 20 lines.
 * If there are still lines left after a block of lines is printed,
 * it allows the user to indicate whether more output is desired.
 *
 * Input(InFile):   text
 * Output(screen): the text, 20 lines at a time
 ************************************************************************/
```

```cpp
#include <iostream.h>              // cin, cout
#include <fstream.h>               // ifstream, ofstream
#include <string>                  // string, getline()
#include <assert.h>                // assert()

int main()
{
   const int LINES_PER_PAGE = 20;

   cout << "Enter the name of the file to be displayed: ";
   string inFileName;
   getline(cin, inFileName);

   ifstream inFile(inFileName.data());   // open input stream to inFile
   assert(inFile.is_open());

   int lineCount = 0;
   char ch,
        answer;

   for (;;)
   {
      inFile.get(ch);

      if (inFile.eof()) break;

      cout << ch;

      if (ch == '\n')
      {
         lineCount++;

         if (lineCount == LINES_PER_PAGE )
         {
            cout << "More (Y/N)? ";
            cin >> answer;

            if ( (answer == 'n') || (answer == 'N') )  break;

            lineCount = 0;
         }
      }
   }

   return 0;
}
```

8.
```cpp
/* prog8-8.cpp reads information from a file in the format specified
 * in the text and calculates, for each income bracket, the average
 * rating for Product 1.
 *
 * Input(InFile):    Information
 * Output(screen):  The average rating for Product 1
 ******************************************************************/

#include <iostream.h>              // cin, cout
#include <fstream.h>               // ifstream, ofstream
#include <string>                  // string, getline()
#include <assert.h>                // assert()
```

```cpp
int main()
{
    cout << "Enter the name of the file containing the ratings: ";
    string inFileName;
    getline(cin, inFileName);

    ifstream inFile(inFileName.data());   // open input stream to inFile
    assert(inFile.is_open());

    char incomeLevel;
    int product1, product2,
        ARatings = 0, ACount = 0,
        BRatings = 0, BCount = 0,
        CRatings = 0, CCount = 0,
        fiveOrHigher = 0,
        lowerThan3OnTwo = 0;

    for (;;)
    {
        infile >> incomelevel >> product1 >> product2;

        if (InFile.fail()) break;

        switch (incomeLevel)
        {
            case 'A':
                        ARatings += Product1;
                        ACount++;
                        break;
            case 'B':
                        BRatings += Product1;
                        BCount++;
                        if (product1 >= 5 && product2 >= 5)
                            fiveOrHigher++;
                        break;
            case 'C':
                        CRatings += Product1;
                        CCount++;
                        break;
            default:
                        cerr << "\nInvalid income bracket '"
                            << incomeLevel << "'!\n";
                        return -1;
        }

        if (product1 < 3)
            lowerThan3OnTwo += product2;
    }

    cout << "\nProduct 1 average ratings:"
        << "\n\tIncome A: " << double(ARatings) / double(ACount)
        << "\n\tIncome B: " << double(BRatings) / double(BCount)
        << "\n\tIncome C: " << double(CRatings) / double(CCount)
        << "\n\n << fiveOrHigher << " in bracket B rated both products 5 "
            "or better\n\m"
        << "Average rating on Product 2 by people rating Product 1 "
            "lower than 3 "
        << double(lowerThan3OnTwo) / double(ACount + BCount + CCount)
        << endl;

    return 0;
}
```

9.

```
/* prog8-9.cpp searches the file Users to find and display the
 * resources used to date for specified users whose identification
 * numbers are entered during execution of the program.
 *
 * Input(keyboard):  id numbers for which to search
 * Input(inFile):    data
 * Output(screen):   resouces used to date
 *****************************************************************/

#include <iostream.h>                  // cin, cout
#include <fstream.h>                   // ifstream, ofstream
#include <assert.h>                    // assert()

int main()
{
    const char INFILE_NAME[] = "Users";

    ifstream inFile(INFILE_NAME);
    assert(inFile.is_open());

    int id,
        searchId;
    double resources,
           limit;
    char ch,
         answer;
    do
    {
        inFile.seekg(0, ios::beg);
        inFile.clear();

        cout << "\nEnter id number to search for: ";
        cin >> searchId;

        do
        {
            inFile >> id;

            do
                inFile.get(ch);
            while (inFile.good() && (ch != '\n'));
            do
                inFile.get(ch);
            while (inFile.good() && (ch != '\n'));

            inFile >> limit >> resources;
        }
        while ( (id != searchId) && !(inFile.fail()) );

        if (inFile.fail())
            cout << "\nId number not found!\n";
        else
            cout << "\nThat user has used " << resources
                 << " resources to date.\n";

        cout << "\nAnother search (Y/N)? ";
        cin >> answer;
    }
    while ( (answer == 'y') || (answer == 'Y') );

    return 0;
}
```

10. This is very similar to Problem 9.

11.

```
/* prog8-11.cpp accepts the current date and produces a report based
 * on data in User and according to the specifications in the text.
 *
 * Input(InFile):  data
 * Output(screen): report
 *****************************************************************/

#include <iostream.h>         // cin, cout
#include <iomanip.h>          // setw(), setprecision(), setiosflags()
#include <fstream.h>          // ifstream, ofstream
#include <assert.h>           // assert()

int main()
{
   const char INFILE_NAME[] = "Users";
   const double PERC_USED = .90;

   ifstream inFile(INFILE_NAME);
   assert(inFile.is_open());

   int month, day, year,
       id;
   double resources,
          limit;
   char ch;

   cout << "\nPlease enter the date in the format mm dd yy: ";
   cin >> month >> day >> year;

   cout << "\n            USER ACCOUNTS--"
        << month
        << (day < 10 ? "/0" : "/") << day
        << (year < 10 ? "/0" : "/") << year << "\n\n"
        << "USER-ID          RESOURCE             RESOURCES\n"
        << "                 LIMIT                USED\n"
        << "--------------------------------------------------\n";

   for (;;)
   {
      inFile >> id;

      do
         inFile.get(ch);
      while (inFile.good() && (ch != '\n'));
      do
         inFile.get(ch);
      while (inFile.good() && (ch != '\n'));

      inFile >> limit >> resources;

      if (inFile.fail()) break;
```

```
        cout << setiosflags(ios::fixed)
             << setprecision(0)
             << setw(6) << id
             << "             $" << setw(3) << limit
             << "               $" << setw(3) << resources;

        if (resources >= limit * PERC_USED)
            cout << "***";

        cout << endl;
    }

    return 0;
}
```

12. This problem is intended as a mini-project. It is straightforward (albeit long), and is an extension of Problems 2, 3, and 4.

13. This is a project.

Section 8.4

14 & 15.
```
/* prog8-14+15.cpp reads a set of names and exam scores from a file,
 * counts them, calculates and displays the mean, variance, and
 * standard deviation of the scores, and assigns letter grades,
 * using grading on the curve.
 *
 * Input(keyboard): the name of the file
 * Input(inFile):   a set of student names and test scores
 * Output(screen):  the count, mean, variance, standard deviation,
 * Output(outFile): student names with exam scores and letter grades
 *******************************************************************/

#include <iostream.h>          // cin, cout
#include <string>              // string

void ReadAndCalculateStats(istream & inFile, int & n, double & mean,
                           double & variance, double & stdDev);
void AssignLetterGrades(istream & inFile, ostream & outFile,
                        double mean, double stdDev);

int main()
{
    string fileName;
    cout << "Enter name of student info file: ";
    getline(cin, fileName);

    ifstream inFile(fileName.data());  // open an istream to file
    assert(inFile.is_open());

    int count = 0;
    double mean = 0,
           variance = 0,
           stdDeviation = 0;

    ReadAndCalculateStats(inFile, count, mean, variance, stdDeviation);
```

```
   if (n == 0)
      cout << "\nNo student information read!\n";
      return 1;

   cout << "\nMean: " << mean
        << "\nVariance: " << variance
        << "\nStandard Deviation: " << stdDeviation << '\n';

   cout << "Enter name of grade report file to be generated: ";
   getline(cin, fileName);

   ofstream outFile(fileName.data()); // open an ostream to file
   assert(outFile.is_open());

   AssignLetterGrades(inFile, outFile, count, mean, stdDeviation);

   return 0;
}

#include <fstream.h>              // ifstream, ofstream
#include <assert.h>               // assert()
#include <math.h>                 // sqrt()

/* ReadAndCalculateStats reads and counts student names and exam scores
 * from a file and calculates the mean, variance, and standard deviation.
 *
 * Receive:   inFile
 * Pass back: count, mean, variance, and standard deviation
 ********************************************************************/

void ReadAndCalculateStats(istream & inFile, int & n, double & mean,
                           double & variance, double & stdDev)
{
   string firstName, lastName;      // a student's name
   double score,                    // exam score
          sum = 0.0,                // the sum of all the numbers
          squaresSum = 0.0;         // the sum of squares of the numbers

   for (;;)
   {
      inFile >> firstName >> lastName >> score;
      if (inFile.eof()) break;

      n++;
      sum += number;
      squaresSum += number * number;
   }

   if (n != 0)
      double mean = sum / double(n),
             variance = (squaresSum - (sum * sum) / (double(n) * double(n))),
             stdDev = sqrt(variance);
}
```

```
/* LetterGrade assigns a letter grade to a score using grading
 * on the curve.
 *
 * Receive: score, mean, standard deviation
 * Return:  letter grade
 ********************************************************************/

char LetterGrade(double Score, mean, stdDev)
{
   if (score < mean - 1.5 * stdDev)
      return 'F';
   if (score < mean - 0.5 * stdDev)
      return 'D';
   if (score < mean + 0.5 * stdDev)
      return 'C';
   if (score < mean + 1.5 * stdDev)
      return 'B';
   // else
      return 'A';
}


/* AssignLetterGrades reads student names and exam scores from a file
 * calculates letter grades using grading on the curve, and displays
 * the names, scores, and grades.
 *
 * Receive: fileName, count, mean, variance, and standard deviation
 * Output:  student names, exam scores, and letter grades
 ********************************************************************/

void AssignLetterGrades(istream & inFile, ostream & outFile,
                        double mean, double stdDev)
{
   inFile.seekg(0, ios::beg);
   inFile.clear();

   for (;;)
   {
      inFile >> firstName >> lastName >> score;
      if (inFile.eof()) break;

      outFile >> firstName >> ' ' >> lastName >> "  Exam: " >> score
              >> "  Grade: " >> LetterGrade(score, mean, stdDev)
              >> endl;
   }
}
```

16, 17, & 18.
```
/* prog8-16+17+18.cpp reads a number of a terminal, retrieves the record
 * for that file from a file and displays it on the screen.
 * Problem 18: It reads the date that terminal was last serviced and
 * writes the terminal number and new service date to an output file.
 * Problem 19: It reopens both files for input and uses the information
 * in the new-service file to update the records in the original file
 * and writes this information to a new output file.
 *
 * Input (keyboard): fileNames, terminal numbers, service dates, and
 *                   user responses to query
 * Input (file #1):  computer terminal records
 * Output (screen):  computer terminal records
 * Output (file #2): terminal number and date of service
 * Input (file #2):  terminal number and date of service
 * Output (file #3): updated computer terminal records
 **********************************************************************/

#include <iostream.h>              // cin, cout
#include <fstream.h>               // ifstream, ofstream
#include <string>                  // string, getline()
#include <assert.h>                // assert()
#include <iomanip.h>               // setw()

int main()
{
    const int MAX_TERMINAL_NUMBER = 10,
              RECORD_LENGTH = 43;

    // information in record for a terminal --------------------------
    string terminal,                        // type
           building;                        // location
    int transmissionRate;                   // trans. rate
    char accessCode;                        // access code
    int serviceMonth, serviceDay, serviceYear; // date of last service
    //---------------------------------------------------------------

    cout << "Enter the name of the file containing the terminal info: ";
    string inFileName;
    cin >> inFileName;

    ifstream inFile(inFileName.data());    // open input stream to inFile
    assert(inFile.is_open());

    cout << "Enter the name of the file to contain new service information: ";
    string outFileName;
    cin >> outFileName;

    ofstream outFile(outFileName.data()); // open output stream to outFile
    assert(outFile.is_open());

    cout << "Enter the name of the file to contain updated terminal info: ";
    string newOutFileName;
    cin >> newOutFileName;
                                            // open output stream to newOutFile
    ofstream newOutFile(newOutFileName.data());
    assert(newOutFile.is_open());

    int terminalNumber,                     // # of terminal to be retrieved
        newMonth, newDay, newYear;          // date of new service
    char response;                          // user response to query
```

```
do
{
   cout << "\nTerminal number (1 - " << MAX_TERMINAL_NUMBER << ")? ";
   cin >> terminalNumber;
   if (terminalNumber < 1 || terminalNumber > MAX_TERMINAL_NUMBER)
      cout << "Illegal terminal number\n";
   else
   {
      inFile.seekg((terminalNumber-1)*RECORD_LENGTH, ios::beg);
      inFile >> terminal >> building
             >> transmissionRate >> accessCode
             >> serviceMonth >> serviceDay >> serviceYear;
      cout << "Terminal type = "<< terminal
           << "\nLocated in " << building
           << "\nTransmission rate: " << transmissionRate
           << "\nAccess code is " << accessCode
           << "\nLast serviced " << serviceMonth << '/'
           << serviceDay << '/' << serviceYear << endl;
   }

   // --- PROBLEM 18 -----
   cout << "\nDate of service for this terminal? ";
   cin >> newMonth >> newDay >> newYear;
   outFile << terminalNumber
           << (newMonth < 10 ? "   0" : "   ") << newMonth
           << (newDay < 10 ? " 0" : " ") << newDay
           << (newYear< 10 ? " 0" : " ") << newYear<< endl;
   //--------------------

   cout << "\nMore terminals (Y or N)? ";
   cin >> response;
}
while (response == 'Y' || response == 'y');

outFile.close();

// --- PROBLEM 19 -----

                                 // open input stream to output file
ifstream newInFile(outFileName.data());
assert(newInFile.is_open());
                                 // process each record in original file
inFile.seekg(0, ios::beg);
for(int termNum = 1; termNum <= MAX_TERMINAL_NUMBER; termNum++)
{
   inFile >> terminal >> building
          >> transmissionRate >> accessCode
          >> serviceMonth >> serviceDay >> serviceYear;

   newInFile.seekg(0, ios::beg);
   newInFile.clear();
   for (;;)                      // search for update info for terminal
   {
      newInFile >> terminalNumber >> newMonth >> newDay >> newYear;
      if (termNum == terminalNumber || newInFile.eof()) break;
   }
   newOutFile << terminal << '\t'<< building << '\t'
              << setw(4) << transmissionRate << ' ' << accessCode;
```

```
        if (termNum == terminalNumber)// terminal has been serviced
        {                             // output updated information
            serviceMonth = newMonth;
            serviceDay = newDay;
            serviceYear = newYear;
        }
        newOutFile << (serviceMonth < 10 ? " 0" : " ") << serviceMonth
                   << (serviceDay < 10 ? " 0" : " ") << serviceDay
                   << (serviceYear< 10 ? " 0" : " ") << serviceYear << endl;
    }

    inFile.close();
    newInFile.close();
    newOutFile.close();

    return 0;
}
```

A sample file:

```
VT100      SCIENCE_CENTER     9600 A 11 29 96
PC         VANDERVAN_HALL     2400 B 12 15 96
ESPRIT     COLLEGE_UNION      9600 B 01 05 97
VT100      LIBRARY_DESK       1200 C 10 10 96
PC         COMPUTER_CENTER    1200 A 11 20 96
MAC        BUSINESS_OFFICE    1200 B 03 17 97
VT100      PHY._ED._OFFICE    2400 C 12 19 95
DAEWOO     SWAZINSKI_DORM     2400 B 04 04 96
VT100      ADAMS_ANNEX        1200 B 04 05 97
VT100      NYHOFF_NOOK        1200 B 04 01 97
```

Chapter 9:

Exercises 9.2

1. `number[0] = 0,`   `number[1] = 0,`   `number[2] = 1,`   `number[3] = 1,`   `number[4] = 2,`
   `number[5] = 2,`   `number[6] = 3,`   `number[7] = 3,`   `number[8] = 4,`   `number[9] = 4`

2. `number[0] = 0,`   `number[1] = 1,`   `number[2] = 4,`   `number[3] = 9,`   `number[4] = 16,`
   `number[5] = 25,`   `number[6] = 1,`   `number[7] = 4,`   `number[8] = 9,`   `number[9] = 16`

3. **Error** — `LittleDouble` **is a type, not an array.**

4. `value[0] = 0.0,`   `value[1] = 0.0,`   `value[2] = 1.0,`
   `value[3] = 10.0,`   `value[4] = 2.0,`   `value[5] = 20.0`

5. `number[0] = 0,`   `number[1] = 1,`   `number[2] = 2,`   `number[3] = 0,`   `number[4] = 4,`
   `number[5] = 5,`   `number[6] = 0,`   `number[7] = 7,`   `number[8] = 8,`   `number[9] = 0`

6. `number[0] = 1,`   `number[1] = 2,`   `number[2] = 4,`   `number[3] = 8,`   `number[4] = 16,`
   `number[5] = 32,`   `number[6] = 64,`   `number[7] = 128,`   `number[8] = 256,`   `number[9] = 512`

7. `letterCount['A'] = 1,`   `letterCount['B'] = 2,`   `letterCount['C'] = 3,`
   `letterCount['D'] = 4,`   `letterCount['E'] = 5,`   `letterCount['F'] = 6`

8. **Assuming** `n = 9` **and** `j` **is** `int` **(as intended):**
   `number[0] = 0,`   `number[1] = 11,`   `number[2] = 22,`   `number[3] = 33,`   `number[4] = 44,`
   `number[5] = 55,`   `number[6] = 66,`   `number[7] = 77,`   `number[8] = 77,`   `number[9] = 99`

9. (a) `int array[10];`
   (b) `typedef int IntArray[10];`
   `IntArray array;`

10. (a) `double array[11];`
    (b) `typedef double RealArray[11];`
    `RealArray array;`

11. (a) `int array[10] = {0};`
    (b) `typedef int IntArray[10];`
    `IntArray array = {0};`

12. (a) `string array[5];`
    (b) `typedef string StringArray[5];`
    `StringArray array;`

13 (a) `char array[5] = "aeiou";     // or = {'a','e','i','o','u');`
   (b) `typedef char CharArray[5];`
   `CharArray array = "aeiou";   // or = {'a','e','i','o','u');`

14. (a) `bool array[100];`
    (b) `typedef bool BooleanArray[10];`
    `BooleanArray array;`

15. (a) `bool array[128];`
    (b) `typedef bool BooleanArray[128];`
    `BooleanArray array;`

16.
```
int array1[100];
for (int i = 0; i < 100; i++)
   array1[i] = i;
```

17.
```
int array1[100];
for (int i = 0; i < 100; i++)
   array1[i] = 99 - i;
```

18.
```
bool array[50];
for (int i = 0; i < 50; i++)
   array[i] = (i % 2 == 0);
```

19.
```
const int CAP = 100;
typedef int IntArray[CAP];

/* MinElement finds the least of n values stored in an int
 * array x.
 *
 * Receive: x and n
 * Return:  least value among x[0], x[1], . . ., x[n-1]
 ****************************************************************/

int MinElement(IntArray x, int n)
{
   int min = x[0];
   for (int i = 1; i < n; i++)
      if (x[i] < min)
         min = x[i];

   return min;
}
```

20.
```
const int CAP = 100;
typedef int IntArray[CAP];

/* MaxElement finds the greatest of n values stored in an int
 * array x.
 *
 * Receive: x and n
 * Return:  largest value among x[0], x[1], . . ., x[n-1]
 ****************************************************************/

int MaxElement(IntArray x, int n)
{
   int max = x[0];
   for (int i = 1; i < n; i++)
      if (x[i] > max)
         max = x[i];

   return max;
}
```

21.

```
const int CAP = 100;
typedef int IntArray[CAP];

/* Range finds the range of n values stored in an int
 * array x.
 *
 * Receive: x and n
 * Return:  range of values among x[0], x[1], . . ., x[n-1]
 ***************************************************************/

int Range(IntArray x, int n)
{
  int min = x[0],
      max = x[0];
    for (int i = 1; i < n; i++)
    {
        if (x[i] > max)
            max = x[i];
        if (x[i] < min)
            min = x[i];
    }

    return max - min;
}
```

22.

```
const int CAP = 100;
typedef int IntArray[CAP];

/* IsAscending determines if n values stored in an int
 * array x are in ascending order.
 *
 * Receive: x and n
 * Return:  true if x[0], x[1], . . ., x[n-1] are in ascending
 *          order, false otherwise
 ***************************************************************/

bool IsAscending(IntArray x, int n)
{
    for (int i = 0; i < n - 1; i++)
        if (x[i] > x[i+1])
            return false;

    return true;
}
```

23.

```
/* Insert inserts an item at a specified location loc in the
 * n elements of an int array x.
 *
 * Receive:    x, n, item, loc
 * Pass back: x with item inserted at location loc and n
 ***************************************************************/
```

```
void Insert(IntArray x, int & n, int item, int loc)
{
   if (n == CAP)
   {
      cerr << "\n*** Insert fails -- array is full!\n";
      return;
   }

   if (loc < 0 || loc > CAP)
   {
      cerr << "\n*** Insert fails -- invalid location received: "
             << loc << "!\n";
      return;
   }

   // Shift array elements right to make room
   n++;
   for (int i = n; i > loc; i--)
      x[i] = x[i-1];

   x[loc] = item;
}
```

24.

```
/* Delete removes an item at a specified location loc from the
 * n elements of an int array x.
 *
 * Receive:   x, n, loc
 * Pass back: x with item removed from location loc and n
 ***************************************************************/

void Delete (IntArray x, int & n, int loc)
{
   if (loc < 0 || loc >= n)
   {
      cerr << "\n*** Delete fails -- invalid location received: "
             << loc << "!\n";
      return;
   }

   // Shift array elements left to close gap
   for (int i = loc; i < n; i++)
      x[i] = x[i+1];

   n--;
}
```

25.

```
const int CAP = 100;
typedef int IntArray[CAP];

/* LinearSearch searches a list of n values stored in an int
 * array x for an item.
 *
 * Receive: x, n, and item
 * Return:  location of item iffound in x[0], x[1], . . ., x[n-1],
 *          -1 otherwise
 ***************************************************************/
```

```
int LinearSearch(IntArray x, int n, int item)
{
    for (int i = 0; i < n; i++)
        if (x[i] == item)
            return i;

    return -1;
}
```

Exercises 9.5

1. number[0] = 0   number[1] = 0   number[2] = 1   number[3] = 1   number[4] = 2
    number[5] = 2   number[6] = 3   number[7] = 3   number[8] = 4   number[9] = 4

2. w[0] = 0   w[1] = 0   w[2] = 0   w[3] = 0   w[4] = 0
    w[5] = 0   w[6] = 0   w[7] = 0   w[8] = 0   w[9] = 0
    w[10] = 0   w[11] = 0   w[12] = 1   w[13] = 1   w[14] = 2
    w[15] = 2

3. number[0] = 99   number[1] = 33   number[2] = 44   number[3] = 88   number[4] = 22
    number[5] = 11   number[6] = 55   number[7] = 66   number[8] = 77

4. number[0] = 0   number[1] = 1   number[2] = 2   number[3] = 3   number[4] = 0
    number[5] = 1   number[6] = 2   number[7] = 3   number[8] = 4   number[9] = 5

5. number[0] = 33   number[1] = 33   number[2] = 88   number[3] = 88   number[4] = 11
    number[5] = 11   number[6] = 66   number[7] = 66   number[8] = 77

6. number[0] = 99   number[1] = 33   number[2] = 44   number[3] = 88   number[4] = 22
    number[5] = 11   number[6] = 55   number[7] = 66   number[8] = 99

7. number[0] = 77   number[1] = 33   number[2] = 44   number[3] = 88   number[4] = 22
    number[5] = 11   number[6] = 55   number[7] = 66   number[8] = 99

8. number[0] = 11   number[1] = 22   number[2] = 33   number[3] = 44   number[4] = 55
    number[5] = 66   number[6] = 77   number[7] = 88   number[8] = 99

9. w[0] = 0   w[1] = 0   w[2] = 0   w[3] = 0   w[4] = 0
    w[5] = 0   w[6] = 0   w[7] = 0   w[8] = 0   w[9] = 0
    w[10] = 119   w[11] = 53   w[12] = 64   w[13] = 108   w[14] = 42
    w[15] = 31   w[16] = 75   w[17] = 86   w[18] = 97

10. v[0] = 20   v[1] = 20   v[2] = 20   v[3] = 20   v[4] = 20

    number[0] = 11   number[1] = 55   number[2] = 66   number[3] = 77

11. number[0] = 33   number[1] = 88   number[2] = 22   number[3] = 11   number[4] = 55
    number[5] = 66   number[6] = 77

12. w[0] = 0   w[1] = 0   w[2] = 0   w[3] = 0   w[4] = 0
    w[5] = 0   w[6] = 0   w[7] = 0   w[8] = 0   w[9] = 0
    w[10] = 100   w[11] = 34   w[12] = 45   w[13] = 89   w[14] = 23
    w[15] = 12   w[16] = 56   w[17] = 67   w[18] = 78
```
```

13. `vector<long int> v;`

14. `vector<long int> v(10);`

15. `vector<long int> v(10, 0);`

16. `vector<string> v(5, "xxx");`

17. `vector<bool> v(100);`

18.
```
vector<int> v;
   for (int i = 0; i < 100; i++)
      v.push_back(i);
```

19.
```
vector<int> v;
   for (int i = 99; i >=0; i--)
      v.push_back(i);
```

20.
```
vector<bool> v(50);
      . . .
   for (int i = 0; i < 50; i++)
      v[i] = (i % 2 == 0);
```

21.
```
/* IsAscending determines if the values stored in a
 * vector<double> v are in ascending order.
 *
 * Receive: v
 * Return:  true if v[0], v[1], . . ., are in ascending
 *          order, false otherwise
 ************************************************************/

bool IsAscending(vector<double> v)
{
   for (int i = 0; i < v.size() - 1; i++)
      if (v[i] > v[i+1])
         return false;

   return true;
}
```

22.
```
/* Range finds the range of n values stored in a vector<double> v.
 *
 * Receive: v
 * Return:  range of values stored in v
 ****************************************************************/

double Range(vector<double> v)
{
   double min = v[0],
          max = v[0];
   for (int i = 1; i < v.size(); i++)
   {
      if (v[i] > max)
         max = v[i];
      if (v[i] < min)
         min = v[i];
   }
```

```
   return max - min;
}
```

23.
```
/* Sum finds the sum of two vectors a and b.
 *
 * Receive: a and b
 * Return:  a + b
 ***********************************************/

vector<double> Sum(vector<double> a, vector<double> b)
{
   int n = a.size();
   vector<double> c(n, 0);
   if (a.size() != b.size())
   {
      cerr << "Sum:  vectors don't have the same size\n";
      return c;
   }

   for (int i = 0; i < n; i++)
      c[i] = a[i] + b[i];

   return c;
}
```

24.
```
/* Difference finds the difference of two vectors a and b.
 *
 * Receive: a and b
 * Return:  a - b
 *****************************************************************/

vector<double> Difference(vector<double> a, vector<double> b)
{
   int n = a.size();
   vector<double> c(n, 0);if (a.size() != b.size())
   {
      cerr << "Difference:  vectors don't have the same size\n";
      return c;
   }

   for (int i = 0; i < n; i++)
      c[i] = a[i] - b[i];

   return c;
}
```

25.
```
/* ScalarMultiple finds the product of a scalar c and a vector a.
 *
 * Receive: c and a
 * Return:  ca
 *****************************************************************/
```

```
vector<double> ScalarMultiple(double c, vector<double> a)
{
   int n = a.size();
   vector<double> x(n, 0);
   for (int i = 0; i < n; i++)
    x[i] = c * a[i];

  return x;
}
```

26.
```
/* Magnitude finds the magnitude of a vector a.
 *
 * Receive: a
 * Return:  |a|
 ********************************************************/

#include <math.h>
double Magnitude(vector<double> a)
{
   int n = a.size();

   double sum = 0;
   for (int i = 0; i < a.size(); i++)
      sum += a[i] * a[i];

   return sqrt(sum);
}
```

27.
```
/* DotProduct finds the dot product of two vectors a and b.
 *
 * Receive: a and b
 * Return:  dot product of a and b
 ********************************************************/

double DotProduct(vector<double> a, vector<double> b)
{
   if (a.size() != b.size())
   {
      cerr << "DotProduct:  vectors don't have the same size\n";
      return 0;
   }

   int n = a.size();
   double prod = 0;
   for (int i = 0; i < n; i++)
      prod += a[i] * b[i];

   return prod;
}
```

Programming Problems

1.
```
/* prog9-1.cpp is a driver program to test the functions
 * MinElement() and MaxElement() from Exercises 19 & 20.
 *
 * Input:  an integer n and an array of n integers
 * Output: least and greatest of the n values
 ***************************************************************/

#include <iostream.h>                // cin, cout, >>, <<

const int CAP = 100;
typedef int IntArray[CAP];
int MinElement(IntArray x, int n);
int MaxElement(IntArray x, int n);

int main()
{
   cout << "How many integers do you want to enter (at most "
        << CAP << ")? ";
   int numInts;
   cin >> numInts;

   IntArray number;
   cout << "Enter the integers: ";
   for (int i = 0; i < numInts; i++)
      cin >> number[i];

   cout << "Least integer is " << MinElement(number, numInts) << endl;
   cout << "Greatest integer is " << MaxElement(number, numInts) << endl;

   return 0;
}

/* Insert definitions of functions minElement()
   and maxElement() from Exercises 19 & 20 here */
```

2.
```
/* prog9-2.cpp is a driver program to test the functions
 * Range() from Exercise 21.
 *
 * Input:  an integer n and an array of n integers
 * Output: range of the n values
 ***************************************************************/

#include <iostream.h>                // cin, cout, >>, <<

const int CAP = 100;
typedef int IntArray[CAP];
int Range(IntArray x, int n);

int main()
{
   cout << "How many integers do you want to enter (at most "
        << CAP << ")? ";
   int numInts;
   cin >> numInts;
```

```
    IntArray number;
    cout << "Enter the integers: ";
    for (int i = 0; i < numInts; i++)
       cin >> number[i];

    cout << "Range is " << Range(number, numInts) << endl;

    return 0;
}

/* Insert definition of function Range()
   from Exercise 21 here */
```

3.

```
/* prog9-3.cpp is a driver program to test the function
 * IsAscending() from Exercise 21.
 *
 * Input:  an integer n and an array of n integers
 * Output: true if values are ascending, else false
 *************************************************************/

#include <iostream.h>                    // cin, cout, >>, <<

const int CAP = 100;
typedef int IntArray[CAP];
bool IsAscending(IntArray x, int n);

int main()
{
    cout << "How many integers do you want to enter (at most "
         << CAP << ")? ";
    int numInts;
    cin >> numInts;

    IntArray number;
    cout << "Enter the integers: ";
    for (int i = 0; i < numInts; i++)
       cin >> number[i];

    cout << "Values are "
         << (IsAscending(number, numInts) ? "in " : "not in ") << "order\n";

    return 0;
}

/* Insert definition of function IsAscending()
   from Exercise 22 here */
```

4.

```
/* prog9-4.cpp is a driver program to test the function
 * Insert() from Exercise 22.
 *
 * Input:  an integer n, an array of n integers, an integer
 *         to insert, and a location where it is to be inserted
 * Output: the list of n + 1 values
 *************************************************************/

#include <iostream.h>                    // cin, cout, >>, <<
```

```
const int CAP = 100;
typedef int IntArray[CAP];
void Insert(IntArray x, int & n, int item, int loc);

int main()
{
   cout << "How many integers do you want to enter (at most "
        << CAP << ")? ";
   int numInts;
   cin >> numInts;

   IntArray number;
   cout << "Enter the integers: ";
   for (int i = 0; i < numInts; i++)
      cin >> number[i];

   int item,
       location;

   cout << "Enter integer to insert and location: ";
   cin >> item >> location;

   Insert(number, numInts, item, location);
   cout << "New list of values:\n";
   for (int i = 0; i < numInts; i++)
      cout << number[i] << endl;

   return 0;
}

/* Insert definition of function Insert()
   from Exercise 23 here */
```

5.
```
/* prog9-5.cpp is a driver program to test the function
 * Delete() from Exercise 23.
 *
 * Input:  an integer n, an array of n integers, and a
 *         location where item is to be removed
 * Output: the list of n - 1 values
 *************************************************************/

#include <iostream.h>                 // cin, cout, >>, <<

const int CAP = 100;
typedef int IntArray[CAP];
void Delete (IntArray x, int & n, int loc);

int main()
{
   cout << "How many integers do you want to enter (at most "
        << CAP << ")? ";
   int numInts;
   cin >> numInts;

   IntArray number;
   cout << "Enter the integers: ";
   for (int i = 0; i < numInts; i++)
      cin >> number[i];
```

```
    int item,
        location;

    cout << "Enter location to remove item: ";
    cin >> location;

    Delete(number, numInts, location);
    cout << "New list of values:\n";
    for (int i = 0; i < numInts; i++)
       cout << number[i] << endl;

    return 0;
}

/* Insert definition of function Delete()
   from Exercise 24 here */
```

6.
```
/* prog9-6.cpp is a driver program to test the function
 * LinearSearch() from Exercise 26.
 *
 * Input:  an integer n, an array of n integers, and item to
 *         search for
 * Output: location of item
 ******************************************************************/

#include <iostream.h>                  // cin, cout, >>, <<

const int CAP = 100;
typedef int IntArray[CAP];
int LinearSearch(IntArray x, int n, int item);

int main()
{
    cout << "How many integers do you want to enter (at most "
         << CAP << ")? ";
    int numInts;
    cin >> numInts;

    IntArray number;
    cout << "Enter the integers: ";
    for (int i = 0; i < numInts; i++)
       cin >> number[i];

    cout << "Enter value to search for: ";
    int value;
    cin >> value;
    int location = LinearSearch(number, numInts, value);
    if (location > 0)
       cout << "Value found at location " << location << endl;
    else
       cout << "Value not found.\n";

    return 0;
}

/* Insert definition of function LinearSearch()
   from Exercise 26 here */
```

7.

```
/* prog9-7.cpp reads and stores production levels for dooflingies and
 * then retrieves these for a given day of a given week.
 *
 * Input:  production levels, week and day numbers
 * Output: production levels
 **********************************************************************/

#include <iostream.h>              // cin, cout, >>, <<

const int CAP = 60;
typedef int IntArray[CAP];

int main()
{
    cout << "How many weeks of production levels do you want to enter "
            "(at most " << CAP / 4 << ")? ";
    int numWeeks;
    cin >> numWeeks;

    IntArray productionLevel;
    for (int week = 0; week < numWeeks; week++)
    {
        cout << "Enter the 5 production levels for week " << week + 1 << ": ";
        for (int i = 0; i < 5; i++)
            cin >> productionLevel[5*week + i];
    }

    int week, day;
    for (;;)
    {
        cout << "\nEnter a week # and a day # in that week (0 0 to stop): ";
        cin >> week >> day;

        if (week == 0) break;

        if (week > numWeeks)
            cerr << "Illegal week number -- must be <= " << numWeeks << endl;
        else
            cout << "Production level was "
                    << productionLevel[5*(week - 1) + day - 1] << endl;;
    }
    return 0;
}
```

8 & 9.

```
/* prog9-8+9.cpp reads product numbers of products stocked in two different
 * warehouses, storing these in arrays, and then finds the intersection
 * and the union of these two lists of numbers.
 *
 * Input:  production levels, week and day numbers
 * Output: production levels
 **********************************************************************/

#include <iostream.h>              // cin, cout, >>, <<

const int CAP = 60;
typedef int IntArray[CAP];
```

```
void ReadProductNumbers(IntArray prodNumber, int & prodCount);

void DisplayProductNumbers(IntArray prodNumber, int prodCount);

void FindIntersection(IntArray list1, int numList1,
                      IntArray list2, int numList2,
                      IntArray intersect, int & numIntersect);

void FindUnion(IntArray list1, int numList1,
               IntArray list2, int numList2,
               IntArray setUnion, int & numUnion);

int main()
{
    IntArray prodChicago,
             prodDetroit,
             intersection,
             setUnion;
    int numChicago,
        numDetroit,
        numIntersection,
        numUnion;

    cout << "Enter production numbers for Chicago "
         << "(-1 when done):\n";
    ReadProductNumbers(prodChicago, numChicago);

    cout << "\nEnter production numbers for Detroit "
         << "(-1 when done):\n";
    ReadProductNumbers(prodDetroit, numDetroit);

    FindIntersection(prodChicago, numChicago,
                     prodDetroit, numDetroit,
                     intersection, numIntersection);

    cout << "\nProduct numbers in "
            "both Chicago and Detroit:\n";
    DisplayProductNumbers(intersection, numIntersection);

    FindUnion(prodChicago, numChicago,
              prodDetroit, numDetroit,
              setUnion, numUnion);

    cout << "\nProduct numbers in "
            "either Chicago or Detroit (or both):\n";
    DisplayProductNumbers(setUnion, numUnion);

    return 0;
}

/* ReadProductNumbers reads and stores production numbers.
 *
 * Receive:   production numbers
 * Pass back: array ProdNumber and count of production numbers
 ***********************************************************************/

void ReadProductNumbers(IntArray prodNumber, int & count)
{
    const ARRAY_CAP = 25;
    int product;
```

```
    for (count = 0; count <= ARRAY_CAP; count++)
    {
        cin >> product;

        if (product < 0)
            break;

        prodNumber[count] = product;
    }
}

/* DisplayProductNumbers displays a list of production numbers.
 *
 * Receive: array and count of production numbers
 * Output:  list of production numbers
 ************************************************************************/

void DisplayProductNumbers(IntArray prodNumber, int prodCount)
{
    for (int i = 0; i < prodCount; i++)
        cout << prodNumber[i] << endl;
}

/* FindIntersection finds the intersection of two lists.
 *
 * Receive:    arrays storing two lists and number of elements in each
 * Pass back: intersection of the lists and number of elements in it
 ************************************************************************/

void FindIntersection(IntArray list1, int numList1,
                      IntArray list2, int numList2,
                      IntArray intersect, int & numIntersect)
{
    numIntersect = 0;

    for (int i = 0; i < numList1; i++)
    {
        for (int j = 0; j < numList2; j++)
        {
            if (list1[i] == list2[j])
            {
                intersect[numIntersect] = list1[i];
                numIntersect++;
                break;
            }
        }
    }
}

/* FindUnion finds the union of two lists.
 *
 * Receive:    arrays storing two lists and number of elements in each
 * Pass back: union of the lists and number of elements in it
 ************************************************************************/

void FindUnion(IntArray list1, int numList1,
               IntArray list2, int numList2,
               IntArray setUnion, int & numUnion)
{
    for (int k = 0; k < numList1; k++)
        setUnion[k] = list1[k];
    numUnion= numList1;
```

```
      for (int i = 0; i < numList2; i++)
      {
         int j;
         for (j = 0; j < numList1; j++)
         {
            if (list2[i] == list1[j])
               break;
         }

         if (j == numList1)
         {
            setUnion[numUnion] = list2[i];
            numUnion++;
         }
      }
}
```

10. This is a simple application of setting and retrieving the elements of arrays. You may also want to try solving this problem by writing a class Item with attributes Number and Price and using array of Items.

```
/* prog9-10.cpp reads and stores product numbers and prices of items in
 * parallel arrays -- number and price --  and then searches number for
 * input product numbers and retrieves the item's price.
 *
 * Input:  number of products, arrays of product numbers and prices,
 *         product numbers to search for
 * Output: prices
 ********************************************************************/

#include <iostream.h>              // cin, cout, >>, <<
#include <iomanip.h>               // setiosflags(), setprecision()

const int CAP = 60;
typedef int IntArray[CAP];
typedef double DoubleArray[CAP];

int LinearSearch(IntArray x, int n, int item);

int main()
{
   cout << "How many products are there (at most " << CAP << ")? ";
   int numProducts;
   cin >> numProducts;

   IntArray number;
   DoubleArray price;
   for (int i = 0; i < numProducts; i++)
   {
      cout << "Enter product number and price for item " << i + 1 << ": ";
      cin >> number[i] >> price[i];
   }

   int itemSought,
       location;
```

```
    for (;;)
    {
        cout << "\nEnter product number of item to search for (0 to stop): ";
        cin >> itemSought;

        if (itemSought == 0) break;

        location = LinearSearch(number, numProducts, itemSought);

        if (location >= 0)
          cout << "Price of item is " << price[location] << endl;
        else
          cout << "Item not found.\n";
    }

    cout << "\n\nProduct Number    Price"
            "\n---------------------\n"
        << setiosflags(ios::fixed | ios::showpoint) << setprecision(2);
    for (int i = 0; i <y numProducts; i++)
        cout << setw(11) << number[i] << setw(13) << price[i] << endl;

    return 0;
}

/* Insert definition of function LinearSearch()
   from Problem 6 (Exercise 26) here */

/* LinearSearch searches a list of n values stored in an int
 * array x for an item.
 *
 * Receive: x, n, and item
 * Return:  location of item iffound in x[0], x[1], . . ., x[n-1],
 *          -1 otherwise
 ****************************************************************/

int LinearSearch(IntArray x, int n, int item)
{
    for (int i = 0; i < n; i++)
        if (x[i] == item)
            return i;

    return -1;
}
```

11. Note: The open boxes are those whose numbers are perfect squares: 1, 4, 9, 16, 25, . . .

```
/* prog9-11.cpp illustrates the results of Peter the Postman.
 *
 * Output: A list of zeros and ones, where a zero represents
 *         a closed mailbox, and a one represents
 *         an open mailbox
 ****************************************************************/

#include <iostream.h>              // cin, cout, >>, <<

const int CAP = 200;
typedef bool BooleanArray[CAP];
const int NUM_BOXES = 150;
```

```
int main()
{
   BooleanArray mailbox = {false};

   for (int x = 2; x <= NUM_BOXES; x++)
      for (int y = x; y <= NUM_BOXES; y += x)
         mailbox[y] = !mailbox[y];

   cout << "Closed mailboxes: ";

   for (int y = 1; y <= NUM_BOXES; y++)
      if (mailbox[y]) cout << y << endl;

   return 0;
}
```

12 & 13.

```
/* prog9-12+13.cpp reads a set of names and exam scores and stores,
 * them in an array, calculates and displays the mean, variance, and
 * standard deviation of the scores, and assigns letter grades,
 * using grading on the curve.
 *
 * Input:   a set of test scores
 * Output:  the count, mean, variance, standard deviation, and a
 *          list of scores and letter grades
 ********************************************************************/

#include <iostream.h>           // cin, const int CAP = 60;

const int CAP = 60;
typedef double DoubleArray[CAP];

void ReadAndCalculateStats(DoubleArray score, int & numScores, double & mean,
                        double & variance, double & stdDev);
char LetterGrade(double score, double mean, double stdDev);

int main()
{

   DoubleArray score;
   int numScores = 0;
   double mean = 0,
          variance = 0,
          stdDeviation = 0;

   ReadAndCalculateStats(score, numScores , mean, variance, stdDeviation);

   if (numScores == 0)
   {
      cout << "\nNo scores read!\n";
      return 1;
   }

   cout << "\nMean: " << mean
        << "\nVariance: " << variance
        << "\nStandard Deviation: " << stdDeviation << endl;
```

```
      cout << "\nLetter grades for scores:\n";
      for (int i = 0; i < numScores; i++)
         cout << score[i] << '\t'
              << LetterGrade(score[i], mean, stdDeviation) << endl;

      return 0;
}

/* ReadAndCalculateStats reads and counts test scores and calculates
 * and passes back theor mean, variance, and standard deviation.
 *
 * Receive:   inFile
 * Pass back: count, mean, variance, and standard deviation
 ***********************************************************************/

#include <math.h>                        // pow(), sqrt()
void ReadAndCalculateStats(DoubleArray score, int & n, double & mean,
                           double & variance, double & stdDev)
{
   double number,                  // a nonnegative real number
          sum = 0.0;               // the sum of all the numbers

   n = 0;
   for (;;)
   {
      cout << "Score (-1 to stop)? ";
      cin >> number;
      if (number < 0) break;

      n++;
      score[n-1] = number;
      sum += number;
   }

   if (n == 0) return;

   mean = sum / double(n);

   sum = 0;
   for (int i = 0; i < n; i ++)
      sum += pow(score[i] - mean, 2);

   variance = sum / double(n);
   stdDev = sqrt(variance);
}

/* LetterGrade assigns a letter grade to a score using grading
 * on the curve.
 *
 * Receive: score, mean, standard deviation
 * Return:  letter grade
 ***********************************************************************/

char LetterGrade(double score, double mean, double stdDev)
{
   if (score < mean - 1.5 * stdDev)
      return 'F';
   if (score < mean - 0.5 * stdDev)
      return 'D';
   if (score < mean + 0.5 * stdDev)
      return 'C';
```

```
    if (score < mean + 1.5 * stdDev)
       return 'B';
    // else
       return 'A';
}
```

14.

```cpp
/* prog9-14.cpp uses the Sieve Method of Eratosthenes to find all
 * primt numbers < some given number.
 *
 * Input:  an integer >= 2
 * Output: all prime numbers <= that integer
 ********************************************************************/

#include <iostream.h>                    // cin, cout, >>, <<

const int CAP = 1000;
typedef bool BooleanArray[CAP];

int main()
{
    int max;

    cout << "\nGenerate all primes less than: ";
    cin >> max;

    BooleanArray sieve;
    for (int i = 2; i <= max; i++)
       sieve[i] = true;

    int prime = 2;

    while (prime * prime < max)
    {
       for (int i = prime*2; i <= max; i += prime)
          sieve[i] = false;

       do
          prime++;
       while (!sieve[prime]);
    }

    cout << "\nPrimes:";

    for (int i = 2; i <= max; i++)
       if (sieve[i])
          cout << ' ' << i;

    cout << endl;

    return 0;
}
```

15.

```
/* prog9-15.cpp reads and stores integers and then sorts them
 * using selection sort.
 *
 * Input:  number of integers and an array of integers,
 * Output: sorted array of integers
 ***********************************************************************/

#include <iostream.h>              // cin, cout, >>, <<

const int CAP = 100;
typedef int IntArray[CAP];

void SelectionSort(IntArray array, int n);

int main()
{
   cout << "How many integers are there (at most " << CAP << ")? ";
   int numInts;
   cin >> numInts;

   IntArray number;
   cout << "Enter the " << numInts << " integers:\n";

   for (int i = 0; i < numInts; i++)
      cin >> number[i];

   SelectionSort(number, numInts);

   cout << "\nSorted Array:\n";
   for (int i = 0; i < numInts; i++)
      cout << number[i] << endl;

   return 0;
}

/* SelectionSort sorts a list into ascending order using simple
 * selection sort.
 *
 * Receive: an array of n integers
 * Return:  the sorted array
 *********************************************************************/

void SelectionSort(IntArray array, int n)
{
   int minValue,
       minPos;

   for (int i = 0; i < n - 1; i++)
   {
      int minValue = array[i];
         minPos = i;

      // find min value among array[i], . . ., array[n]
      for (int j = i; j < n; j++)
         if (array[j] < minValue)
         {
            minValue = array[j];
            minPos = j;
         }
```

```
        // swap min value with array[i]
        array[minPos] = array[i];
        array[i] = minValue;
    }
}
```

16.
```
/* prog9-16.cpp reads and stores integers and then sorts them
 * `sing insertion sort.
 *
 * Input:  number of integers and an array of integers,
 * Output: sorted array of integers
 ********************************************************************/

#include <iostream.h>                    // cin, cout, >>, <<

const int CAP = 100;
typedef int IntArray[CAP];

void InsertionSort(IntArray array, int n);

int main()
{
    cout << "How many integers are there (at most " << CAP << ")? ";
    int numInts;
    cin >> numInts;

    IntArray number;
    cout << "Enter the " << numInts << " integers:\n";

    for (int i = 0; i < numInts; i++)
        cin >> number[i];

    InsertionSort(number, numInts);

    cout << "\nSorted Array:\n";
    for (int i = 0; i < numInts; i++)
        cout << number[i] << endl;

    return 0;
}

/* InsertionSort sorts a List into ascending order using
 * insertion sort.
 *
 * Receive: an array of n integers
 * Return:  the sorted array
 ************************************************************/

void InsertionSort(IntArray array, int n)
{
    int item,       // item to insert
        i, j;       // indices
```

```
   for (i = 1; i < n ; i++)
   {
      item = array[i];
      j = i-1;
      while (j >= 0 && item < array[j])
      {
         array[j+1] = array[j];
         j--;
      }

      array[j+1] = item;
   }
}
```

17.

```
/* prog9-17.cpp reads and stores stock prices and then sorts them
 * using insertion sort.  It then displays the trading range.
 *
 * Input:  number of prices and an array of prices
 * Output: trading range (highest - lowest price)
 ********************************************************************/

#include <iostream.h>              // cin, cout, >>, <<

const int CAP = 100;
typedef double DoubleArray[CAP];

void InsertionSort(DoubleArray array, int n);

int main()
{
   cout << "How many prices are there (at most " << CAP << ")? ";
   int numPrices;
   cin >> numPrices;

   DoubleArray price;
   cout << "Enter the " << numPrices << " prices:\n";

   for (int i = 0; i < numPrices; i++)
      cin >> price[i];

   InsertionSort(price, numPrices);

   cout << "\nTrading range = " << price[numPrices - 1] - price[0] << endl;

   return 0;
}

/* InsertionSort sorts a List into ascending order using
 * insertion sort.
 *
 * Receive: an array of n doubles
 * Return:  the sorted array
 ************************************************************/

void InsertionSort(DoubleArray array, int n)
{
   double item;       // item to insert
   int i, j;          // indices
```

```
    for (i = 1; i < n ; i++)
    {
        item = array[i];
        j = i-1;
        while (j >= 0 && item < array[j])
        {
            array[j+1] = array[j];
            j--;
        }

        array[j+1] = item;
    }
}
```

Sections 9.3-9.5

18.
```
/* prog9-18.cpp is a driver program to test the function
 * IsAscending() from Exercise 21.
 *
 * Input:  a vector of double values
 * Output: true if values are ascending, else false
 ****************************************************************/

#include <iostream.h>              // cin, cout, >>, <<
#include <vector>                  // vector

bool IsAscending(vector<double> v);

int main()
{
    vector<double> dub;
    double number;
    cout << "Enter a list of positive doubles (0 to stop): ";
    for (;;)
    {
        cin >> number;
        if (number == 0) break;
        dub.push_back(number);
    }

    cout << "Values are "
         << (IsAscending(dub) ? "in " : "not in ") << "order\n";

    return 0;
}

/* Insert definition of function IsAscending()
   from Exercise 21 here */
```

19.
```
/* prog9-19.cpp is a driver program to test the functions
 * Range() from Exercise 22.
 *
 * Input:  a vector of double values
 * Output: range of the values
 ****************************************************************/
```

```
#include <iostream.h>              // cin, cout, >>, <<
#include <vector>                  // vector

double Range(vector<double> v);

int main()
{
   vector<double> dub;
   double number;

   cout << "Enter a list of positive doubles (0 to stop): ";
   for (;;)
   {
      cin >> number;
      if (number == 0) break;
      dub.push_back(number);
   }

   cout << "Range is " << Range(dub) << endl;

   return 0;
}

/* Insert definition of function Range()
   from Exercise 21 here */
```

20.

```
/* prog9-20.cpp is a menu-driven program for carrying out
 *   n-dimensional vector  operations using the functions \
 * from Exercises 23-27.
 *
 * Input:  a menu option, vectors of double values,
 *         a scalar (double)
 * Output: menu of options,
 *         sum, difference, scalar product, magnitude, dot
 *         product of vectors
 ****************************************************************/

#include <iostream.h>            // cin, const int CAP = 60;
#include <vector>                // vector<T>
#include <ctype.h>               // islower(), toupper()

vector<double> Sum(vector<double> a, vector<double> b);
vector<double> Difference(vector<double> a, vector<double> b);
vector<double> ScalarMultiple(double c, vector<double> a);
double Magnitude(vector<double> a);
double DotProduct(vector<double> a, vector<double> b);
void ReadVector(int n, vector<double> & a);
void PrintVector(const vector<double> & a);

int main()
{
   const char MENU[] =
               "\nEnter: \n"
                  "  A -- to add 2 vectors\n"
                  "  S -- to subtract 2 vectors\n"
                  "  M -- to find a scalar multiple of a vector\n"
                  "  N -- to find the norm (magnitude) of a vector\n"
                  "  D -- to find the dot product of 2 vectors\n"
                  "  Q -- to quit\n";
   int n;
```

```
cout << "What dimension vectors are you processing? ";
cin >> n;

char option;
vector<double> a(n,0), b(n,0);
for (;;)
{
   cout << MENU;
   cout << "Option? ";
   cin >> option;
   if (islower(option))
     option = toupper(option);
   if (option == 'Q') break;

   cout << "\nEnter a(n) " << n << "-dimensional vector a: ";
   ReadVector(n, a);

   switch (option)
   {
      case 'A' : cout << "Enter a(n) " << n
                      << "-dimensional vector b: ";
                 ReadVector(n, b);
                 cout << "a + b is:\n";
                 PrintVector(Sum(a, b));
                 break;

      case 'S' : cout << "Enter another " << n
                      << "-dimensional vector b:\n";
                 ReadVector(n, b);
                 cout << "a - b is:\n";
                 PrintVector(Difference(a, b));
                 break;

      case 'M' : cout << "Enter a scalar: ";
                 double m;
                 cin >> m;
                 cout << m <<"*a is:\n";
                 PrintVector(ScalarMultiple(m, a));
                 break;

      case 'N' : cout << "Magnitude of vector a is "
                      << Magnitude(a) << endl;
                 break;

      case 'D' : cout << "Enter a(n) " << n
                      << "-dimensional vector b: ";
                 ReadVector(n, b);
                 cout << "Dot product of a and b is:\n"
                      << DotProduct(a, b) << endl;
                 break;

      default  :
                 cout << "Illegal option -- " << option << endl;
   }
}
}
```

```
/* ReadVector reads an n-dimensional vector v.
 *
 * Receive:    n and v
 * Input:      components of v
 * Pass back:  v
 ********************************************/

void ReadVector(int n, vector<double> & v)
{
  for (int i = 0; i < n; i++)
    cin >> v[i];
}

/* PrintVector displays a vector v.
 *
 * Receive:  v
 * Output:   components of v
 ********************************************/

void PrintVector(const vector<double> & v)
{
  for (int i = 0; i < v.size(); i++)
    cout << v[i] << "  ";
  cout << endl;
}

/* Insert function Sum(), Difference(), ScalarMultiple(),
   Magnitude, and DotProduct from Exercises 23-27 here. */
```

21.

```
/* prog9-21.cpp reads and stores production levels for dooflingies in a
 * vector<int> and then retrieves these for a given day of a given week.
 *
 * Input:  production levels, response, week and day numbers
 * Output: production levels
 ************************************************************************/

#include <iostream.h>              // cin, cout, >>, <<
#include <vector>                  // vector<T>

int main()
{
   int numWeeks = 0,               // number of weeks
       oneDayProdLevel;            // production level for one day
   vector<int> productionLevel;    // vector of production levels
   char response;                  // user response to query

   do
   {
     numWeeks++;
     cout << "Enter the 5 production levels for week " << numWeeks << ": ";
     for (int i = 0; i < 5; i++)
     {
        cin >> oneDayProdLevel;
        productionLevel.push_back(oneDayProdLevel);
     }
     cout << "\nMore weeks? ";
     cin >> response;
   }
   while (response == 'Y' || response == 'y');
```

```
      int week, day;
      for (;;)
      {
         cout << "\nEnter a week # and a day # in that week (0 0 to stop): ";
         cin >> week >> day;

         if (week == 0) break;

         if (week > numWeeks)
            cerr << "Illegal week number -- must be <= " << numWeeks << endl;
         else
            cout << "Production level was "
                 << productionLevel[5*(week - 1) + day - 1] << endl;;
      }
      return 0;
}
```

22 & 23.

```
/* prog9-22+23.cpp reads product numbers of products stocked in two different
 * warehouses, storing these in vector<int>s, and then finds the intersection
 * and the union of these two lists of numbers.
 *
 * Input:  production levels, week and day numbers
 * Output: production levels
 ***************************************************************************/

#include <iostream.h>             // cin, cout, >>, <<
#include <vector>                 // vector<T>
#include <algorithm>              // find()


void ReadProductNumbers(vector<int> & prodNumber);
void DisplayProductNumbers(const vector<int> & prodNumber);
void FindIntersection(const vector<int> & list1, const vector<int> & list2,
                      vector<int> & intersect);
void FindUnion(const vector<int> & list1, const vector<int> & list2,

                      vector<int> & setUnion);

int main()
{
   vector<int> prodChicago,
               prodDetroit,
               intersection,
               setUnion;

   cout << "For Chicago: ";
   ReadProductNumbers(prodChicago);

   cout << "For Detroit: ";
   ReadProductNumbers(prodDetroit);

   FindIntersection(prodChicago, prodDetroit, intersection);

   cout << "\nProduct numbers in "
           "both Chicago and Detroit:\n";
   DisplayProductNumbers(intersection);

   FindUnion(prodChicago, prodDetroit, setUnion);
```

```
      cout << "\nProduct numbers in "
              "either Chicago or Detroit (or both):\n";
      DisplayProductNumbers(setUnion);

      return 0;
   }

   /* ReadProductNumbers reads and stores production numbers.
    *
    * Receive:   production numbers
    * Pass back: vector<int> prodNumber
    ***********************************************************************/

   void ReadProductNumbers(vector<int> & prodNumber)
   {
      cout << "Enter product numbers (-1 to stop):\n";
      int product;

      for (;;)
      {
         cin >> product;

         if (product < 0) return;

         prodNumber
           .push_back(product);
      }
   }

   /* DisplayProductNumbers displays a list of production numbers.
    *
    * Receive: vector<int> of production numbers
    * Output:  list of production numbers
    ***********************************************************************/

   void DisplayProductNumbers(const vector<int> & prodNumber)
   {
      for (int i = 0; i < prodNumber.size(); i++)
         cout << prodNumber[i] << endl;
   }

   /* FindIntersection finds the intersection of two lists.
    *
    * Receive:   vector<int>s storing two lists
    * Pass back: vector<int> storing the intersection of the lists
    ***********************************************************************/

   void FindIntersection(const vector<int> & list1, const vector<int> & list2,
                         vector<int> & intersect)
   {
      for (int i = 0; i < list1.size(); i++)
         if ( find(list2.begin(), list2.end(), list1[i]) != list2.end() )
            intersect.push_back(list1[i]);
   }

   /* FindUnion finds the union of two lists.
    *
    * Receive:   vector<int>s storing two lists
    * Pass back: vector<int> storing the union of the lists
    ***********************************************************************/
```

```cpp
void FindUnion(const vector<int> & list1, const vector<int> & list2,
               vector<int> & setUnion)
{
   setUnion = list1;

   for (int i = 0; i < list2.size(); i++)
      if ( find(list1.begin(), list1.end(), list2[i]) == list1.end() )
         setUnion.push_back(list2[i]);
}
```

24.
```cpp
/* prog9-24.cpp reads and stores product numbers in a vector<int> number
 * and prices of items in a vector<double> price and then searches number
 * for input product numbers and retrieves the item's price.
 *
 * Input:  vectors of product numbers and prices,
 *         product numbers to search for
 * Output: prices
 ********************************************************************/

#include <iostream.h>              // cin, cout, >>, <<
#include <iomanip.h>               // setiosflags(), setprecision()
#include <vector>                  // vector<T>

int LinearSearch(const vector<int> & x, int item);

int main()
{
   vector<int> number;
   vector<double> price;
   int prodNumber;
   double prodPrice;
   for (;;)
   {
      cout << "Enter product number and price (0 0 to stop): ";
      cin >> prodNumber >> prodPrice;
      if (prodNumber == 0) break;
      number.push_back(prodNumber);
      price.push_back(prodPrice);
   }

   int itemSought,
       location;
   for (;;)
   {
      cout << "\nEnter product number of item to search for (0 to stop): ";
      cin >> itemSought;

      if (itemSought == 0) break;

      location = LinearSearch(number, itemSought);

      if (location >= 0)
         cout << "Price of item is " << price[location] << endl;
      else
         cout << "Item not found.\n";
   }
```

```
        cout << "\n\nProduct Number    Price"
                 "\n----------------------\n"
            << setiosflags(ios::fixed | ios::showpoint) << setprecision(2);
        for (int i = 0; i < number.size(); i++)
            cout << setw(11) << number[i] << setw(13) << price[i] << endl;

        return 0;
}

/* LinearSearch searches a list of n values stored in a
 * vector<int> x for an item.
 *
 * Receive: x, n, and item
 * Return:  location of item if found, -1 otherwise
 ***************************************************************/

int LinearSearch(const vector<int> & x, int item)
{
        for (int i = 0; i < x.size(); i++)
            if (x[i] == item)
                return i;

        return -1;
}
```

25. Note: The open boxes are those whose numbers are perfect squares: 1, 4, 9, 16, 25, . . .

```
/* prog9-25.cpp illustrates the results of Peter the Postman.
 *
 * Output: a list of zeros and ones, where a zero represents
 *         a closed mailbox, and a one represents
 *         an open mailbox
 ***************************************************************/

#include <iostream.h>              // cin, cout, >>, <<
#include <vector>                  // vector<T>

const int NUM_BOXES = 150;
int main()
{
        vector<bool> mailbox(NUM_BOXES + 1, false);

        for (int x = 2; x <= NUM_BOXES; x++)
            for (int y = x; y <= NUM_BOXES; y += x)
                mailbox[y] = !mailbox[y];

        cout << "Closed mailboxes:\n";

        for (int y = 1; y <= NUM_BOXES; y++)
        {
            cout << mailbox[y];
            if (y % 50 == 0) cout << endl;
        }
        cout << endl;

        return 0;
}
```

26 & 27.

```
/* prog9-26+27.cpp reads a set of names and stores them in a vector<string>,
 * and exam scores which are stored in a vector<double>,  calculates and
 * displays the mean, variance, and standard deviation of the scores,
 * and assigns letter grades, using grading on the curve.
 *
 * Input:   a set of test scores
 * Output:  the count, mean, variance, standard deviation, and a
 *          list of scores and letter grades
 **********************************************************************/

#include <iostream.h>                // cin, cout, >>, <<
#include <vector>                    // vector<T>

const int CAP = 60;
typedef double DoubleArray[CAP];

void ReadAndCalculateStats(vector<double> & score, double & mean,
                           double & variance, double & stdDev);
char LetterGrade(double score, double mean, double stdDev);

int main()
{

   vector<double> score;
   double mean = 0,
          variance = 0,
          stdDeviation = 0;

   ReadAndCalculateStats(score, mean, variance, stdDeviation);

   int numScores = score.size();
   if (numScores == 0)
   {
      cout << "\nNo scores read!\n";
      return 1;
   }

   cout << "\nMean: " << mean
        << "\nVariance: " << variance
        << "\nStandard Deviation: " << stdDeviation << endl;

   cout << "\nLetter grades for scores:\n";
   for (int i = 0; i < numScores; i++)
      cout << score[i] << '\t'
           << LetterGrade(score[i], mean, stdDeviation) << endl;

   return 0;
}

/* ReadAndCalculateStats reads test scores and calculates
 * and passes back theor mean, variance, and standard deviation.
 *
 * Receive:   inFile
 * Pass back: count, mean, variance, and standard deviation
 **********************************************************************/

#include <math.h>                    // pow(), sqrt()
```

```
void ReadAndCalculateStats(vector<double> &  score, double & mean,
                           double & variance, double & stdDev)
{
   double number,                    // a nonnegative real number
          sum = 0.0;                 // the sum of all the numbers

   for (;;)
   {
      cout << "Score (-1 to stop)? ";
      cin >> number;
      if (number < 0) break;

      score.push_back(number);
      sum += number;
   }

   int n = score.size();
   if (n == 0) return;

   mean = sum / double(n);

   sum = 0;
   for (int i = 0; i < n; i ++)
      sum += pow(score[i] - mean, 2);

   variance = sum / double(n);
   stdDev = sqrt(variance);
}

/* LetterGrade assigns a letter grade to a score using grading
 * on the curve.
 *
 * Receive: score, mean, standard deviation
 * Return:  letter grade
 ******************************************************************/

char LetterGrade(double score, double mean, double stdDev)
{
   if (score < mean - 1.5 * stdDev)
      return 'F';
   if (score < mean - 0.5 * stdDev)
      return 'D';
   if (score < mean + 0.5 * stdDev)
      return 'C';
   if (score < mean + 1.5 * stdDev)
      return 'B';
   // else
      return 'A';
}
```

28.
```
/* prog9-28.cpp uses the Sieve Method of Eratosthenes to find all
 * primt numbers < some given number.
 *
 * Input:  an integer >= 2
 * Output: all prime numbers <= that integer
 ******************************************************************/

#include <iostream.h>                // cin, cout, >>, <<
#include <vector>                    // vector<T>
```

```cpp
int main()
{
   int max;

   cout << "\nGenerate all primes less than: ";
   cin >> max;

   vector<bool> sieve(max, true);

   int prime = 2;

   while (prime * prime < max)
   {
      for (int i = prime*2; i <= max; i += prime)
         sieve[i] = false;

      do
         prime++;
      while (!sieve[prime]);
   }

   cout << "\nPrimes:";

   for (int i = 2; i <= max; i++)
      if (sieve[i])
         cout << ' ' << i;

   cout << endl;

   return 0;
}
```

29.

```cpp
/* prog9-29.cpp reads and stores stock prices in a vector<double> and
 * then sorts them using them using the sort algorithm in STL.
 * It then displays the trading range.
 *
 * Input:  a vector<double> of prices
 * Output: trading range (highest - lowest price)
 ********************************************************************/

#include <iostream.h>              // cin, cout, >>, <<
#include <vector>                  // vector<T>
#include <algorithm>               // sort()

int main()
{
   vector<double> price;
   cout << "Enter the prices (0 to stop):\n";

   double aPrice;
   for (;;)
   {
      cin >> aPrice;
      if (aPrice == 0) break;
      price.push_back(aPrice);
   }

   sort(price.begin(), price.end());
```

```
    int numPrices = price.size();
    cout << "\nTrading range = " << price[numPrices - 1] - price[0] << endl;

    return 0;
}
```

30-34. These problems constitute a significant project. It is best assigned after chapter 10 where a `BigInt` class can
be constructed with operations defined for it.For simplicity we will assume the big integers are all
nonnegative. The following program shows a non-class solution for + and *. It assumes for simplicity that
the integers are all nonnegative.

```
/* prog9-30-34.cpp does big-integer arithmetic
 *
 * Input:  menu option, big integers
 * Output: menu, big integers
 ********************************************************************/

#include <iostream.h>              // cin, cout, >>, <<
#include <iomanip.h>               // setfill()
#include <vector>                  // vector<T>
#include <algorithm>               // sort()

typedef vector<short int> BigInt;
void ReadBig(BigInt & x);
void PrintBig(const BigInt & x);
void Add(BigInt int1, BigInt int2, BigInt & answer);
void Multiply(BigInt int1, BigInt int2, BigInt & answer);

int main()
{
    cout << "Enter BigInts in blocks of 3 digits (-1 to stop).\n";

    char option;
    for (;;)
    {
        cout << "\nEnter +, -, *, /; or Q (to quit): ";
        cin >> option;

        if (option == 'Q' || option == 'q') break;

        BigInt int1, int2, answer;
        cout << "Enter first BigInt:  ";
        ReadBig(int1);
        cout << "Enter second BigInt: ";
        ReadBig(int2);

        switch (option)
        {
            case '+' : Add(int1, int2, answer);
                       break;
            case '*' : Multiply(int1, int2, answer);
                       break;
            default  : cerr << "Illegal operation\n";
                       }
        cout << "Answer: ";
        PrintBig(answer);
    }
}
```

```
/* ReadBig reads a BigInt.
 *
 * Receive:   BigInt x
 * Pass back: x with a value input for it
 *************************************************************/

void ReadBig(BigInt & x)
{
   short int block;
   for (;;)
   {
      cin >> block;
      if (block < 0) return;
      x.push_back(block);
   }

}

/* PrintBig displays a BigInt.
 *
 * Receive: BigInt x
 * Output:  x
 *************************************************************/

void PrintBig(const BigInt & x)
{
  cout << setfill('0');
   for (int i = 0; i < x.size(); i++)
   {
      cout << setw(3) << x[i] << ' ';
      if (i > 0 && i % 20 == 0) cout << endl;
   }
   cout << endl;
}

/* Add adds two BigInts.
 *
 * Receive:    BigInts int1 and int2
 * Pass back : int1 + int2
 *************************************************************/

void Add(BigInt int1, BigInt int2, BigInt & answer)
{
   short int first,        // a block of int1
             second,       // a block of int2
             result,       // a block in their sum
             carry = 0;     // the carry in adding two blocks

   int size1 = int1.size(),
       size2 = int2.size(),
       maxSize = (size1 < size2 ? size2 : size1);

   reverse(int1.begin(), int1.end());
   reverse(int2.begin(), int2.end());

   for (int i = 0; i < maxSize; i++)
   {
      if (i < size1)
         first = int1[i];
      else
         first = 0;
```

```
        if (i < size2)
            second = int2[i];
        else
            second = 0;

        short int temp = first + second + carry;
        result = temp % 1000;
        carry = temp / 1000;
        answer.push_back(result);
    }

    if (carry > 0)
        answer.push_back(carry);

    reverse(answer.begin(), answer.end());
}


/* Multiply multiplies two BigInts.
 *
 * Receive:    BigInts int1 and int2
 * Pass back : int1 * int2
 ********************************************************/

void Multiply(BigInt int1, BigInt int2, BigInt & answer)
{
    int first,          // a block of int1
        second,         // a block of int2
        result,         // a block in their product
        carry = 0;      // the carry in multiplying two blocks

    reverse(int1.begin(), int1.end());
    reverse(int2.begin(), int2.end());

    BigInt emptyVec,
           aResult;

    for (int i = 0; i < int2.size(); i++)
    {
        second = int2[i];
        carry = 0;
        aResult = emptyVec;
        for (int k = 0; k < i; k++)
            aResult.push_back(0);

        for (int j = 0; j < int1.size(); j++)
        {
            first = int1[j];

            int temp = first * second + carry;
            result = temp % 1000;
            carry = temp / 1000;

            aResult.push_back(result);
        }
        if (carry > 0)
            aResult.push_back(carry);

        reverse(aResult.begin(), aResult.end());
```

```
        BigInt tempAns;
        if (i == 0)
            answer = aResult;
        else
        {
            Add(answer, aResult, tempAns);
            answer = tempAns;
        }
    }
}
```

Chapter 10: Building Classes

Exercises 10.5

1. Add the following to `Temperature.h`:

```
Temperature Celsius() const;
Temperature Kelvin() const;
```

Add the following to `Temperature.h`:

```
// -------- The equivalent Celsius temperature -----------------------

Temperature Temperature::Celsius() const
{
    switch (myScale)
    {
        case 'C':
            return Temperature(myDegrees, 'C');
        case 'F':
            return Temperature((myDegrees - 32.0) / 1.8, 'C');
        case 'K':
            return Temperature(myDegrees - 273.15, 'C');
    }
}


// -------- The equivalent Kelvin temperature -----------------------

Temperature Temperature::Kelvin() const
{
    switch (myScale)
    {
        case 'K':
            return Temperature(myDegrees, 'K');
        case 'F':
            return Temperature((myDegrees - 32.0) / 1.8 + 273.15, 'K');
        case 'K':
            return Temperature(myDegrees + 273.15, 'K');
    }
}
```

2. Add the following to `Temperature.h`:

```
Temperature operator-(double rightOperand);
```

Add the following to `Temperature.cpp`:

```
// -------- The equivalent Celsius temperature -----------------------

inline Temperature Temperature::operator-(double rightOperand)
{
    return Temperature(myDegrees - rightOperand, myScale);
}
```

3. class PlayingCard
   {
       char myValue,
            mySuit;
      // ...
   };

4. class Time
   {
       int myHours,
           myMinutes,
           mySeconds;
      // ...
   };

5. class PhoneNumber
   {
       int myAreaCode,
           myLocalExchange,
           myNumber;
      // ...
   };

6. class Checker
   {
        int myRow,
            myColumn;
      // ...
   };

7. class RectPoint
   {
       double myX,
              myY;
      // ...
   };

8. class PolarPoint
   {
       double myR,
              myTheta;
      // ...
   };

9-17. There are obviously many different ways that these classes can be implemented.   They are all
      straightforward but require quite a lot of code. For that reason, only one implementation is given here — for
      Problem 9, an implementation of the class `PlayingCard` in Exercise 3. The others are similar — choose
      appropriate types for the members of each class and supply member functions to set and retrieve those
      members, in addition to member functions for I/O, etc.

PlayingCard.doc

```
/* PlayingCard.doc contains the documentation for class PlayingCard.
 *
 *******************************************************************/

#ifndef PLAYINGCARD
#define PLAYINGCARD

#include <iostream.h>
```

```
class PlayingCard
{
 public:

    /* This constructor initializes the instance with an
     * invalid card (IsValid() returns 0).
     ********************************************************/
    -----------------------------------------------------*/
    PlayingCard() { myValue = mySuit = ' '; }

    /* This constructor specifies the value and suit of
     * the desired card.
     ********************************************************/
    PlayingCard(char value, char suit)
    { SetCard(value,suit); }

    /* SetCard changes the value and suit of this card.
     ********************************************************/
    void SetCard(char value, char suit);

    /* Value returns the card value of the PlayingCard
     * (A, 2-9, T, J, Q, or K, or space if invalid).
     ********************************************************/
    char Value() const { return myValue; }

    /* Suit returns the card suit of the PlayingCard
     * (H, D, S, or C, or space if invalid).
     ********************************************************/
    char Suit() const { return mySuit; }

    /* IsValid returns 1 if the card is valid, and 0 if it
     * is not (if Value or Suit are empty).
     ********************************************************/
    bool IsValid() const
    { return (myValue != ' ') && (mySuit != ' '); }

    /* ToRandom sets the card to a random card.
     ********************************************************/
    void ToRandom();

    /* Print outputs a PlayingCard to an output stream.
     *
     * Receive: out, an ostream reference
     *          card, a PlayingCard
     * Output:  a string corresponding to card
     ********************************************************/
    void Print(ostream & out);

    /* Read inputs a PlayingCard from an input stream.
     *
     * Receive: in, an istream reference
     * Input:   a string
     * Return:  card, with the proper value,
     *                or on error
     ********************************************************/
    void Read(istream & in);

 private:
    char myValue,
         mySuit;
};
```

```
/* operator<< calls Print() to output a PlayingCard to an
 * output stream.
 *
 * Receive: out, an ostream reference
 *          card, a PlayingCard
 * Output:  a string corresponding to card
 * Return:  out
 ********************************************************/
inline ostream & operator<<(ostream & out, PlayingCard card)
{
   card.Print(out);
   return out;
}

/* operator>> calls Read() to input a PlayingCard from an
 * input stream.
 *
 * Receive:  in, an istream reference
 *           card, a PlayingCard
 * Input:    a string
 * Pass bak: card, with a proper value
 * Return:   in
 ********************************************************/
inline istream & operator>>(istream & in, PlayingCard & card)
{
   card.Read(in);
   return in;
}

#endif
```

PlayingCard.h
```
/* PlayingCard.h contains the interface for class PlayingCard.
 *
 ************************************************************/

#ifndef PLAYINGCARD
#define PLAYINGCARD

#include <iostream.h>

class PlayingCard
{
 public:

   PlayingCard() { myValue = mySuit = ' '; }

   PlayingCard(char value, char suit)
   { SetCard(value, suit); }

   void SetCard(char value, char suit);

   char Value() const { return myValue; }

   char Suit() const { return mySuit; }

   bool IsValid() const
   { return (myValue != ' ') && (mySuit != ' '); }
```

```
    void ToRandom();

    void Print(ostream & out);

    void Read(istream & in);

 private:
    char myValue,
         mySuit;

};

inline ostream & operator<<(ostream & out, PlayingCard card)
{
   card.Print(out);
   return out;
}

inline istream & operator>>(istream & in, PlayingCard & card)
{
   card.Read(in);
   return in;
}

#endif
```

PlayingCard.cpp
```
/* PlayingCard.cpp contains the implementation for class PlayingCard.
 *
 ********************************************************************/

#include "PlayingCard.h"

#include "RandomInt.h"            // RandomInt
#include <string>                 // string
#include <ctype.h>                // islower(), // toupper()

//-------------------------------------------------------------

void PlayingCard::SetCard(char value, char suit)
{
   if (islower(value))            // force uppercase
      value = toupper(value);

   if ( (value == 'A') ||                     // ace
        ( ('2' <= value) && (value <= '9') ) ||    // 2 - 9
        (value == 'T') ||                     // 10
        (value == 'J') ||                     // jack
        (value == 'Q') ||                     // queen
        (value == 'K') )                      // king
      myValue = value;
   else
      myValue = ' ';              // space on error


   if (islower(suit))            // force uppercase
      suit = toupper(suit);

   if ( (suit == 'H') ||                      // hearts
        (suit == 'D') ||                      // diamonds
        (suit == 'S') ||                      // spades
```

```
              (suit == 'C') )                              // clubs
         mySuit = suit;
      else
         mySuit = ' ';                      // space on error
}

//----------------------------------------------------------------

RandomInt cardNumber(0,51);
// Declared  outside all functions so random number
// generator is initialized only once.

void PlayingCard::ToRandom()
{
   cardNumber.Generate();

   switch ( int(cardNumber) % 13 )        // set random value
   {
      case 0:  myValue = 'A'; break;
      case 1:  myValue = '2'; break;
      case 2:  myValue = '3'; break;
      case 3:  myValue = '4'; break;
      case 4:  myValue = '5'; break;
      case 5:  myValue = '6'; break;
      case 6:  myValue = '7'; break;
      case 7:  myValue = '8'; break;
      case 8:  myValue = '9'; break;
      case 9:  myValue = 'T'; break;
      case 10: myValue = 'J'; break;
      case 11: myValue = 'Q'; break;
      case 12: myValue = 'K'; break;
      default: myValue = ' ';
   }

   switch ( int(cardNumber) / 13 )        // set random suit
   {
      case 0:  mySuit = 'H'; break;
      case 1:  mySuit = 'D'; break;
      case 2:  mySuit = 'S'; break;
      case 3:  mySuit = 'C'; break;
      default: mySuit = ' ';
   }
}

//----------------------------------------------------------------

void PlayingCard::Print(ostream & out)
{
   switch(myValue)
   {
      case 'A':  out << "Ace";    break;
      case '2':  out << "2";      break;
      case '3':  out << "3";      break;
      case '4':  out << "4";      break;
      case '5':  out << "5";      break;
      case '6':  out << "6";      break;
      case '7':  out << "7";      break;
      case '8':  out << "8";      break;
      case '9':  out << "9";      break;
      case 'T':  out << "10";     break;
      case 'J':  out << "Jack";   break;
      case 'Q':  out << "Queen";  break;
```

```
      case 'K':  out << "King";  break;
      default:   out << "ERROR"; break;
   }

   out << ' ';

   switch(mySuit)
   {
      case 'H':  out << "Hearts";   break;
      case 'D':  out << "Diamonds"; break;
      case 'S':  out << "Spades";   break;
      case 'C':  out << "Clubs";    break;
      default:   out << "ERROR";    break;
   }
}

//------------------------------------------------------------

void PlayingCard::Read(istream & in)
{
   string inStr;
   char firstChar;

   in >> inStr;
   firstChar = inStr[0];

   if (islower(firstChar))
      firstChar = toupper(firstChar);

   switch (firstChar)
   {
      case 'A': case 'J':
      case 'Q': case 'K':
      case '2': case '3':
      case '4': case '5':
      case '6': case '7':
      case '8': case '9':  myValue = firstChar; break;

      case '1':            if ( (inStr.length() > 1) &&
                                (inStr[1] == '0') )
                             myValue = 'T';
                           else
                             myValue = ' ';
                           break;

      default:             myValue = ' '; break;
   }

   in >> inStr;
   firstChar = inStr[0];

   if (islower(firstChar))
      firstChar = toupper(firstChar);

   switch (firstChar)
   {
      case 'H': case 'D':
      case 'S': case 'C':  mySuit = firstChar; break;

      default:             mySuit = ' '; break;
   }
}
```

18.
```
class Student
{
  public:
    // ... operations ...

  private:
    int myStudentNumber;
    string myLastName;
    string myFirstName;
    char myMiddleInitial;
    string myCity;
    string myState;
    string myPhoneNumber;
    char myGender;
    short int myYear;
    int myCreditsToDate;
    double myGPA;
    string myMajor;
};
```

19.
```
class Inventory
{
  public:
    // ... operations ...

  private:
    int myItemNumber;
    int myInStock;
    double myUnitPrice;
    int myMinumumInventory;
    string myItemName;
};
```

20.
```
class UserId
{
  public:
    // ... operations ...

  private:
    int myIDNumber;
    string myLastName;
    string myFirstName;
    string myPassword;
    int myResourceLimit;
    double myResourcesUsed;
};
```

Exercises 10.6

1.
```
bool Student::operator<(const Student & left, const Student & right)
{
    return (left.myLastName < right.myLastName) ||
            ( (left.myLastName == right.myLastName)  & &
              (left.myFirstName < right.myFirstName) );
}
```

```
2.  bool Student::operator==(const Student & left, const Student & right)
    {
        return (left.myLastName == right.myLastName)  & &
               (left.myFirstName == right.myFirstName);
    }

3.  bool Student::operator==(const Student & left, const Student & right)
    {
        return left.myIDNumber == right.myIDNumber;
    }

4.  bool Student::operator<=(const Student & left, const Student & right)
    {
        return (left == right) || (left < right);
    }

    bool Student::operator>=(const Student & left, const Student & right)
    {
        return (left == right) || (left > right);
    }
```

Programming Problems
Section 10.5

1-9. Driver programs to test the classes developed are straightforward. Here is one for Problem 1, the playing-card class of Exercise 9.

```
/* prog10-1.cpp tests the PlayingCard class
 *
 * Input:  a card
 * Output: the card and a few random cards.
 ************************************************************/

#include <iostream.h>              // cin, cout, >>, <<

#include "PlayingCard.h"           // PlayingCard

int main()
{
   PlayingCard card ('A','S');

   do
   {
      cout << "\nEnter a " << (card.IsValid() ? "" : "VALID ")
           << "playing card (e.g., Q H, Queen Hearts, 10 D, etc.)\n";
      cin >> card;
   }
   while (!card.IsValid());

   cout << "\nGuess what?  You entered: " << card << endl;

   cout << "\nHere's a few random cards for you:\n";
```

```
    for (int i = 0; i < 5; i++)
    {
       card.ToRandom();

       cout << card << endl;
    }

    return 0;
}
```

10. To save space, no documentation files (*.doc) are included here.

(a)

//CartesianPoint.h   (All operations are inline, so there is no Cartesian.cpp)

```
#ifndef CARTESIANPOINT
#define CARTESIANPOINT

#include <iostream.h>

class CartesianPoint
{
 public:
   CartesianPoint();
   CartesianPoint(double xVal, double yVal);
   double X() const;
   double Y() const;
   void SetX(double xVal);
   void SetY(double yVal);

 private:
   double myX, myY;
};

inline CartesianPoint::CartesianPoint()
{ myX = 0;  myY = 0;}

inline CartesianPoint::CartesianPoint(double xVal, double yVal)
{ myX = xVal;  myY = yVal;}

inline double CartesianPoint::X() const { return myX;}

inline double CartesianPoint::Y()  const { return myY;}

inline void CartesianPoint::SetX(double xVal) {myX = xVal;}

inline void CartesianPoint::SetY(double yVal) {myY = yVal;}

inline ostream & operator<<(ostream & out, CartesianPoint & point)
{
   out << "(" << point.X() << ", " << point.Y() << ')';
   return out;
}
```

```
inline istream & operator>>(istream & in, CartesianPoint & point)
{
    char punc;
    double x, y;
    in >> punc >> x >> punc >> y >> punc;
    point.SetX(x);
    point.SetY(y);
    return in;
}

#endif
```

(b)
//LineSegment.h

```
#ifndef LINESEGMENT
#define LINESEGMENT

#include "CartesianPoint.h"
#include <iostream.h>

class LineSegment
{
 public:
    double Slope();

    void Print(ostream & out);
    void Read(istream & in);
    void FindPerpBisector();

 private:
    CartesianPoint first, last;
    double slope;
};

inline double LineSegment::Slope()
{
    if (first.X() == last.X())
      {
        cerr << "No slope -- line segment is vertical\n";
        return 1E38;
      }
    return (last.Y() - first.Y()) / (last.X() - first.X());
}

inline void LineSegment::Read(istream & in)
{
    in >> first >> last;
}


inline ostream & operator<<(ostream & out, LineSegment & seg)
{
    seg.Print(out);
    return out;
}
```

```
inline istream & operator>>(istream & in, LineSegment & seg)
{
   seg.Read(in);
   return in;
}

#endif
```

//LineSegment.cpp

```
#include "LineSegment.h"

void LineSegment::Print(ostream & out)
{
   if (first.X() == last.X())
      cout << "x = " << first.X();
   else
   {
      out << "y - " << first.Y() << " = "
          << Slope() << "(x - " << first.X() << ")";
   }
}

void LineSegment::FindPerpBisector()
{
   LineSegment perpBis;
   CartesianPoint
      midPt(first.X() + last.X())/2.0), (first.Y() + last.Y())/2.0);

   perpBis.first = midPt;

   perpBis.last.SetX(1 + midPt.X());
   perpBis.last.SetY(-1.0 / Slope() + midPt.Y());

   cout << perpBis;
}
```

(c)

//Line.h   (All operations are inline, so there is no Line.cpp)

```
#ifndef LINE
#define LINE

#include "CartesianPoint.h"
#include "LineSegment.h"

#include <iostream.h>

class Line
{
 public:
   Line(CartesianPoint p, double m);
   void PointSlope(ostream & out);
   void SlopeIntercept(ostream & out);

 private:
   CartesianPoint point;
   double slope;
 };
```

```
inline Line::Line(CartesianPoint p, double m)
{
   point.SetX(p.X());
   point.SetY(p.Y());
   slope = m;
 }

inline void Line::PointSlope(ostream & out)
{
   out << "y - " << point.Y() << " = "
         << slope << "(x - " << point.X() << ")" << endl;
 }

inline void Line::SlopeIntercept(ostream & out)
{
   out << "y = " << slope << "*x + "
       << -slope*point.X() + point.Y() << endl;
 }

#endif
```

(d)
```
/* prog10-10.cpp reads point-slope information for two lines and
 * determines whether they intersect or are parallel.  If they
 * intersect, the point of intersection is found and perpendicularity
 * is also checked.
 *
 * Input:  CartesianPoints p1, p2,  doubles slope1, slope2
 * Output: Message indicating if lines intersect or are parallel
 *         point of intersection, message about perpendicularity
 ***********************************************************************/
#include <iostream.h>                       // cin, cout, >>, <<
#include "CartesianPoint.h"
#include "Line.h"

int main()
{
  CartesianPoint p1, p2;
  double slope1, slope2;

  cout << "Enter point and slope info. for line 1: ";
  cin >> p1 >> slope1;
  cout << "Enter point and slope info. for line 2: ";
  cin >> p2 >> slope2;

  Line line1(p1, slope1),
       line2(p2, slope2);

  cout << "\nline 1: ";
  line1.PointSlope(cout);
  cout << "\nline 2: ";
  line2.PointSlope(cout);

  if (slope1 == slope2)
     cout << "Lines are parallel\n";
  else
  {
     double xInt = (slope1 * p1.X() - slope2*p2.X() + p2.Y() - p1.Y())
                    / (slope1 - slope2),
            yInt = slope1 * (xInt - p1.X()) + p1.Y();
```

```
        CartesianPoint pInt(xInt, yInt);
        cout << "Lines intersect at " << pInt << " and they "
             << (slope1 * slope2 == -1 ? "are " : "are not ")
             << "perpendicular\n";
    }
}
```

11. This program is straightforward and similar to Problem 3 in Chapter 7 (see `prog7-3.cpp`) except that all functions are now to be encapsulated into a class.

12.
```
/* prog10-12.cpp is a rational number calculator.
 *
 * Input:  rational numbers and operators
 * Output: messages and results of operations on
 *         rational numbers
 ****************************************************************/

#include "Rational.h"            // Rational

#include <iostream.h>            // cin, cout, >>, <<

int main()
{
  const char HELP_INFO[] =
                  "\nA rational number x can be entered in the form"
                  "\na or a/b.  (e.g. 4, 3/4, 5/2)"
                  "\n"
                  "\nValid inputs:"
                  "\n x + y     addition (lowest terms)"
                  "\n x - y     subtraction (lowest terms)"
                  "\n x * y     multiplication (lowest terms)"
                  "\n x / y     division (lowest terms)"
                  "\n x I       inverse of x"
                  "\n x M       x as a mixed number"
                  "\n x R       x reduced to lowest terms"
                  "\n x G       greatest common divisor"
                  "\n x L y     lowest common denominator"
                  "\n x < y     true if x is less than y"
                  "\n x <= y    true if x is less than or equal to y"
                  "\n x > y     true if x is greater than y"
                  "\n x >= y    true if x is greater than or equal to y"
                  "\n x = y     true if x is equal to y";

  const char BAD_INPUT[] = "*** Bad input! Type 'h' for help. ***\n";

  cout << "\nThis program is a rational number calculator.\n";

  for (;;)
  {
    cout << "\nInput (h=help,q=quit): ";

    if (cin.peek() == 'h')
    {
      cin.get();
      cout << HELP_INFO << endl;
    }
```

```
else if (cin.peek() == 'q')
{
  cin.get();
  return 0;
}

else
{
  Rational x, y;
  char op;

  cin >> x >> op;

  switch (op)
  {
    case '+':
            cin >> y;
            cout << x + y << endl;
            break;

    case '-':
            cin >> y;
            cout << x - y << endl;
            break;

    case '*':
            cin >> y;
            cout << x * y  << endl;
            break;

    case '/':
            cin >> y;
            cout << x / y << endl;
            break;

    case 'i': case 'I':
            cout << x.Inverse() << endl;
            break;

    case 'm': case 'M':
            long i;
            x.MixedNumber(i,y);
            if (i > 0)
              cout << i << " + ";
            cout << y << endl;
            break;

    case 'r': case 'R':
            x.Reduce();
            cout << x << endl;
            break;

    case 'g': case 'G':
            cout << x.GCD() << endl;
            break;

    case 'l': case 'L':
            cin >> y;
            cout << LCD(x,y) << endl;
            break;
```

```
        case '<':
                if (cin.peek() == '=')
                {
                  cin >> op >> y;
                  cout << ( x<= y ? "True" : "False" ) << endl;
                }
                else
                {
                  cin >> y;
                  cout << ( (x<y) ? "True" : "False" ) << endl;
                }
                break;

        case '>':
                if (cin.peek() == '=')
                {
                  cin >> op >> y;
                  cout << ( (x>=y) ? "True" : "False" ) << endl;
                }
                else
                {
                  cin >> y;
                  cout << ( (x>y) ? "True" : "False" ) << endl;
                }
                break;

        case '=':
                cin >> y;
                cout << ( (x==y) ? "True" : "False" ) << endl;
                break;

        case 'x': case 'X':
                cin >> op;
                if (op == '+')
                {
                  cin >> y >> op;
                  if (op == '=')
                  {
                    Rational z;
                    cin >> z;
                    cout << (z-y)/x << endl;
                  }
                  else
                    cout << BAD_INPUT;
                }
                else
                  cout << BAD_INPUT;
                break;

      default:
                cout << BAD_INPUT;
    }
  }

  if (cin.fail())
  {
    cout << BAD_INPUT;
    cin.clear();
  }
  cin.ignore(9999,'\n');
  }
}
```

```
//Rational.h
// This file defines the class Rational.  Note that to save space we have
// defined inline functions right within the class declaration.

#ifndef RATIONAL
#define RATIONAL

#include <iostream.h>

class Rational
{
 public:

    // constructor -- default (no initialization)
    //
    Rational()
        {}

    // constructor -- whole number
    //
    Rational(long Integer)
        { myNumerator = Integer; myDenominator = 1; }

    // constructor -- numerator and denominator
    //
    Rational(long numer, long denom)
        { myNumerator = numer; myDenominator = denom; }

    // Inverse -- the inverse rational
    //
    Rational Inverse() const
        { return Rational(myDenominator,myNumerator); }

    // Numerator -- return the numerator
    //
    long Numerator() const
        { return myNumerator; }

    // Denominator -- return the denominator
    //
    long Denominator() const
        { return myDenominator; }

    // Reduce -- reduce to lowest terms
    //
    void Reduce();

    // MixedNumber -- return whole number and fraction
    //
    void MixedNumber(long & whole, Rational & fraction) const;

    // GCD -- greatest common divisor of numerator and denominator
    //
    long GCD() const;

    // LCD -- least common denominator of two rationals
    //
    friend long LCD(const Rational & x, const Rational & y);

    // operator+=, operator+ -- addition
    //
    Rational & operator+=(const Rational & x);
```

```
        friend Rational operator+ (const Rational & x, const Rational & y);

        // operator-=, operator- -- subtraction
        //
        Rational & operator-=(const Rational & x);
        friend Rational operator- (const Rational & x, const Rational & y);

        // operator*=, operator* -- multiplication
        //
        Rational & operator*=(const Rational & x);
        friend Rational operator* (const Rational & x, const Rational & y);

        // operator/=, operator/ -- division
        //
        Rational & operator/=(const Rational & x);
        friend Rational operator/ (const Rational & x, const Rational & y);

        // operator== -- equality
        //
        friend int operator==(const Rational & x, const Rational & y);

        // operator!= -- inequality
        //
        friend int operator!=(const Rational & x, const Rational & y);

        // operator< -- less than
        //
        friend int operator< (const Rational & x, const Rational & y);

        // operator> -- greater than
        //
        friend int operator> (const Rational & x, const Rational & y);

        // operator<= -- less than or equal to
        //
        friend int operator<=(const Rational & x, const Rational & y);

        // operator>= -- greater than or equal to
        //
        friend int operator>=(const Rational & x, const Rational & y);

        // operator<< -- stream output
        //
        friend ostream & operator<<(ostream & out, const Rational & x)

        // operator>> -- stream input
        //
        friend istream & operator>>(istream & in, Rational & x)
private:
    long myNumerator,
        myDenominator;
};

#endif
```

```
//Rational.cpp:

// This file defines the class Rational.
//

#include "Rational.h"

void Rational::Reduce()
{
   int negative = 0;

   if (myNumerator < 0)
   {
      negative = !negative;
      myNumerator = -myNumerator;
   }

   if (myDenominator < 0)
   {
      negative = !negative;
      myDenominator = -myDenominator;
   }

   long gcd = GCD();

   myNumerator /= gcd;
   myDenominator /= gcd;

   if (negative)
      myNumerator = -myNumerator;
}

void Rational::MixedNumber(long & whole, Rational & fraction) const
{
   whole = myNumerator / myDenominator;

   fraction = Rational(myNumerator % myDenominator, myDenominator);
}

long Rational::GCD() const
{
  long a = myNumerator,
       b = myDenominator,
       r = a % b;

  while (r != 0)
  {
    a = b;
    b = r;
    r = a % b;
  }

  return b;
}

long LCD(const Rational & x, const Rational & y)
{
  long a = x.myDenominator,
       b = y.myDenominator,
       x1 = a,
       y1 = b;
```

```
   while (x1 != y1)
   {
      if (x1 > y1)
        y1 += b;
      else
        x1 += a;
   }

   return x1;
}

Rational & Rational::operator+=(const Rational & x)
{
   myNumerator = myNumerator * x.myDenominator + myDenominator * x.myNumerator;
   myDenominator *= x.myDenominator;
   Reduce();
   return *this;
}

Rational operator+ (const Rational & x, const Rational & y)
{
   Rational answer = x;
   answer += y;
   return answer;
}

Rational & Rational::operator-=(const Rational & x)
{
   myNumerator = myNumerator * x.myDenominator - myDenominator * x.myNumerator;
   myDenominator *= x.myDenominator;
   Reduce();
   return *this;
}

Rational operator- (const Rational & x, const Rational & y)
{
   Rational answer = x;
   answer -= y;
   return answer;
}

Rational & Rational::operator*=(const Rational & x)
{
   myNumerator *= x.myNumerator;
   myDenominator *= x.myDenominator;
   Reduce();
   return *this;
}

Rational operator* (const Rational & x, const Rational & y)
{
   Rational answer = x;
   answer *= y;
   return answer;
}
```

```
Rational & Rational::operator/=(const Rational & x)
{
    myNumerator *= x.myDenominator;
    myDenominator *= x.myNumerator;
    Reduce();
    return *this;
}

Rational operator/ (const Rational & x, const Rational & y)
{
    Rational answer = x;
    answer /= y;
    return answer;
}

int operator==(const Rational & x, const Rational & y)
{
    Rational xRed = x,
             yRed = y;

    xRed.Reduce();
    yRed.Reduce();

    return (xRed.myNumerator == yRed.myNumerator) &&
           (xRed.myDenominator == yRed.myDenominator);
}

int operator!=(const Rational & x, const Rational & y)
{
    Rational xRed = x,
             yRed = y;

    xRed.Reduce();
    yRed.Reduce();

    return (xRed.myNumerator != yRed.myNumerator) &&
           (xRed.myDenominator != yRed.myDenominator);
}

int operator< (const Rational & x, const Rational & y)
{
    long left = x.myNumerator * y.myDenominator,
         right = x.myDenominator * y.myNumerator;

    return left < right;
}

int operator> (const Rational & x, const Rational & y)
{
    long left = x.myNumerator * y.myDenominator,
         right = x.myDenominator * y.myNumerator;

    return left > right;
}

int operator<=(const Rational & x, const Rational & y)
{
    long left = x.myNumerator * y.myDenominator,
         right = x.myDenominator * y.myNumerator;

    return left <= right;
}
```

```
int operator>=(const Rational & x, const Rational & y)
{
   long left = x.myNumerator * y.myDenominator,
        right = x.myDenominator * y.myNumerator;

   return left >= right;
}

ostream & operator<<(ostream & out, const Rational & x)
{
   out << x.myNumerator;

   if (x.myDenominator != 1)
     out << '/' << x.myDenominator;

   return out;
}

istream & operator>>(istream & in, Rational & x)
{
   in >> x.myNumerator;

   if (in.peek() == '/')
   {
     in.get();
     in >> x.myDenominator;
   }
   else
     x.myDenominator = 1;

   return in;
}
```

13. **Types:** `complex<T>` **where** T **is** `float`, `double`, **or** `long double`

    Declaration:
        `complex c(re, im);`   `re` **and** `im` **of type** T, 0, 0 **if omitted**

Operations:	Types of operands	Type of result	Comment
+, -, *, /,	complex<T> or T	complex<T>	
unary +, -	complex<T> or T	complex<T>	
==, !=	complex<T> or T	complex<T>	
>>, <<	a stream and complex<T>	stream	
=, +=, -=, *=, /=	complex<T> and complex<T> or T	complex<T>	assignment
real(c)	complex<T>	T	real part
imag(c)	complex<T>	T	imaginary part
abs(c)	complex<T>	T	magnitude
arg(c)	complex<T>	T	argument
norm(c)	complex<T>	T	magnitude
conj(c)	complex<T>	complex<T>	conjugate
polar(r, t)	T, T	complex<T>	convert from polar form
cos(c)	complex<T>	complex<T>	cosine
cosh(c)	complex<T>	complex<T>	hyperbolic cosine

`log(c)`	`complex<T>`	`complex<T>`	**natural logarithm**
`log10(c)`	`complex<T>`	`complex<T>`	**base-10 logarithm**

`pow(c, n)`	`complex<T>` **and** `int`, `T`, **or** `complex<T>`
	or
	`T` **and** `complex<T>`
		`complex<T>`	**power**

`sin(c)`	`complex<T>`	`complex<T>`	**sine**
`sinh(c)`	`complex<T>`	`complex<T>`	**hyperbolic sine**
`sqrt(c)`	`complex<T>`	`complex<T>`	**square root**
`tan(c)`	`complex<T>`	`complex<T>`	**tangent**
`tanh(c)`	`complex<T>`	`complex<T>`	**hyperbolic tangent**

Chapter 11: Enumerations

Exercises 11.2

1. enum MonthAbbrev { MonthAbbrevUnderflow = -1,
                       Jan, Feb, Mar, Apr, May, Jun,
                       Jul, Aug, Sep, Oct, Nov, Dec,
                       NumberOfMonthAbbrev, MonthAbbrevOverflow = 12};

2. true	3. true	4. Oct **(10)**	
5. Mar **(2)**	6. Oct **(10)**	7. Jun **(6)**	

8-12.
//MonthAbbrev.doc

```
/* This file contains the documentation for library MonthAbbrev.
 *
 * Names Declared:
 *    MonthAbbrev, an enumeration of the first three letters
 *                of each of the 12 months
 *    IntToMonth(), a function that converts a month number to a MonthAbbrev
 *    Next(), a function that finds the successor of a MonthAbbrev
 *    Successor(), a function that finds the n-th successor of a MonthAbbrev
 *    <<, >>, I/O operators
 ************************************************************************/

#ifndef MONTHABBREV
#define MONTHABBREV

#include <iostream.h>

/*----- the enumeration type -----*/

enum MonthAbbrev { MONTH_ABBREV_UNDERFLOW= -1,
              JAN, FEB, MAR, APR, MAY, JUN,
              JUL, AUG, SEP, OCT, NOV, DEC,
              NUMBER_OF_MONTH_ABBREV,
              MONTH_ABBREV_OVERFLOW = 12 };

/* IntToMonth converts an integer into a MonthAbbrev.
 *
 * Receive:  monthNum, a numeric month (1=JANuary, etc.)
 * Return:   a MonthAbbrev corresponding to monthNum,
 *           or MONTH_ABBREV_OVERFLOW on error
 ***********************************************************/

MonthAbbrev IntToMonth(int monthNum);

/* operator<< outputs a MonthAbbrev to an output stream.
 *
 * Receive: out, an ostream reference
 *          monthVal, a MonthAbbrev
 * Output:  a string corresponding to MonthVal
 * Return:  out
 ***********************************************************/

ostream & operator<<(ostream & Out, MonthAbbrev MonthVal);
```

```
/* operator>> inputs a MonthAbbrev from an input stream.
 *
 * Receive:    in, an istream reference and a reference
 *             to a MonthAbbrev monthVal
 * Input:      a string (at least three characters of
 *             a valid month)
 * Pass back: monthVal, with the proper value,
 *             or MONTH_ABBREV_OVERFLOW on error
 * Return:     in
 ************************************************************/

istream & operator>>(istream& In, MonthAbbrev & monthVal);

/* Next returns the successor of abbrev.
 *
 * Receive:  abbrev, a MonthAbbrev
 *           num, a nonnegative integer
 * Return:   the MonthAbbrev after abbrev
 ************************************************************/

MonthAbbrev Next(MonthAbbrev abbrev);


/* Successor returns the num'th successor of abbrev.
 *
 * Receive:  abbrev, a MonthAbbrev
 *           num, a nonnegative integer
 * Return:   the MonthAbbrev num months after abbrev
 ************************************************************/

MonthAbbrev Successor(MonthAbbrev abbrev, unsigned num);

#endif
```

//MonthAbbrev.h

```
/* This file contains the interface for library MonthAbbrev.
 *
 ****************************************************************************/

#ifndef MONTHABBREV
#define MONTHABBREV

#include <iostream.h>

enum MonthAbbrev { MONTH_ABBREV_UNDERFLOW= -1,
                   JAN, FEB, MAR, APR, MAY, JUN, JUL, AUG, SEP,
                   OCT, NOV, DEC, NUMBER_OF_MONTH_ABBREV, MONTH_ABBREV_OVERFLOW= 12 };

MonthAbbrev IntToMonth(int monthNum);

ostream & operator<<(ostream & Out, MonthAbbrev MonthVal);

istream & operator>>(istream& In, MonthAbbrev & monthVal);

MonthAbbrev Next(MonthAbbrev abbrev);

MonthAbbrev Successor(MonthAbbrev abbrev, unsigned num);

#endif
```

```
//MonthAbbrev.cpp
/* This file contains the implementation for library MonthAbbrev.
 *
 ********************************************************************/

#include "MonthAbbrev.h"

#include <string>
#include <ctype.h>

//--------------------------------------------------------

MonthAbbrev IntToMonth(int monthNum)
{
    switch (monthNum)
    {
       case 1:  return JAN;
       case 2:  return FEB;
       case 3:  return MAR;
       case 4:  return APR;
       case 5:  return MAY;
       case 6:  return JUN;
       case 7:  return JUL;
       case 8:  return AUG;
       case 9:  return SEP;
       case 10: return OCT;
       case 11: return NOV;
       case 12: return DEC;
       default: return MONTH_ABBREV_OVERFLOW ;
    }
}

//--------------------------------------------------------

ostream & operator<<(ostream & out, MonthAbbrev monthVal)
{
    switch (monthVal)
    {
       case JAN:  out << "Jan"; break;
       case FEB:  out << "Feb"; break;
       case MAR:  out << "Mar"; break;
       case APR:  out << "Apr"; break;
       case MAY:  out << "May"; break;
       case JUN:  out << "Jun"; break;
       case JUL:  out << "Jul"; break;
       case AUG:  out << "Aug"; break;
       case SEP:  out << "Sep"; break;
       case OCT:  out << "Oct"; break;
       case NOV:  out << "Nov"; break;
       case DEC:  out << "Dec"; break;

       case MONTH_ABBREV_UNDERFLOW : out << "Underflow"; break;
       case MONTH_ABBREV_OVERFLOW :  out << "Overflow"; break;
       default:                      out << "ERROR"; break;
    }

    return out ;
}

//--------------------------------------------------------
```

```
istream & operator>>(istream & in, MonthAbbrev & monthVal)
{
    string inputString;

    in >> inputString;                    // read a string

    int inputLength = inputString.length();

    if (inputLength < 3)                  // need at least 3 chars
    {
        monthVal = MONTH_ABBREV_OVERFLOW;
        return in;
    }

    string abbr = inputString.substr(0,3); // get first 3 chars

    for (int i = 0; i < 3; i++)           // change to lowercase
        if (islower(abbr[i]))
            abbr[i] = toupper(abbr[i]);

    if (abbr == "JAN")                    // compare to constants
        monthVal = JAN;
    else if (abbr == "FEB")
        monthVal = FEB;
    else if (abbr == "MAR")
        monthVal = MAR;
    else if (abbr == "APR")
        monthVal = APR;
    else if (abbr == "MAY")
        monthVal = MAY;
    else if (abbr == "JUN")
        monthVal = JUN;
    else if (abbr == "JUL")
        monthVal = JUL;
    else if (abbr == "AUG")
        monthVal = AUG;
    else if (abbr == "SEP")
        monthVal = SEP;
    else if (abbr == "OCT")
        monthVal = OCT;
    else if (abbr == "NOV")
        monthVal = NOV;
    else if (abbr == "DEC")
        monthVal = DEC;
    else
        monthVal = MONTH_ABBREV_OVERFLOW;

    return in;
}

MonthAbbrev Next(MonthAbbrev abbrev)
{
    switch (abbrev)
    {
        case JAN: return FEB;
        case FEB: return MAR;
        case MAR: return APR;
        case APR: return MAY;
        case MAY: return JUN;
        case JUN: return JUL;
        case JUL: return AUG;
```

```
      case AUG: return SEP;
      case SEP: return OCT;
      case OCT: return NOV;
      case NOV: return DEC;
      case DEC: return MONTH_ABBREV_OVERFLOW;

      default:  return MONTH_ABBREV_OVERFLOW;
   }

   return abbrev;
}

MonthAbbrev Successor(MonthAbbrev abbrev, unsigned num)
{
   while (num--)
   {
      switch (abbrev)
      {
         case JAN: return FEB;
         case FEB: return MAR;
         case MAR: return APR;
         case APR: return MAY;
         case MAY: return JUN;
         case JUN: return JUL;
         case JUL: return AUG;
         case AUG: return SEP;
         case SEP: return OCT;
         case OCT: return NOV;
         case NOV: return DEC;
         case DEC: return JAN;

         default:  return MONTH_ABBREV_OVERFLOW;
      }
   }

   return abbrev;
}
```

13.
```
/*------------------------------------------------------
Successor returns the num'th successor of abbrev.

   Receive:  abbrev, a MonthAbbrev
             num, a nonnegative integer
   Return:   the MonthAbbrev num months after abbrev
------------------------------------------------------*/

MonthAbbrev Successor(MonthAbbrev abbrev, unsigned num)
{
   switch (abbrev)
   {
      case JAN: abbrev = FEB; break;
      case FEB: abbrev = MAR; break;
      case MAR: abbrev = APR; break;
      case APR: abbrev = MAY; break;
      case MAY: abbrev = JUN; break;
      case JUN: abbrev = JUL; break;
      case JUL: abbrev = AUG; break;
      case AUG: abbrev = SEP; break;
      case SEP: abbrev = OCT; break;
      case OCT: abbrev = NOV; break;
```

```
      case NOV: abbrev = DEC; break;
      case DEC: abbrev = JAN; break;

      default:  return MONTH_ABBREV_OVERFLOW;
   }

   if (num == 1)
      return abbrev;
   else
      return Successor(abbrev, num-1);
}
```

14-16.
//Day.doc
```
/* This file contains the interface for library Day.
*
*  Names Declared:
*     Day, an enumeration of the values Sunday through Saturday
*     operator<<, a function to output a Day value
*     operator>>, a function to input a Day value
******************************************************************/

#include <iostream.h>
#include <fstream.h>

/********** the enumeration type **********/

enum Day {DAY_UNDERFLOW = -1, SUNDAY, MONDAY, TUESDAY, WEDNESDAY,
          THURSDAY, FRIDAY, SATURDAY, NUMBER_OF_DAY, DAY_OVERFLOW = 7};


/* operator<< outputs a Day to an output stream.
*
*  Receive:  out, an ostream reference
*            dayVal, a Day value
*  Output:   the character string corresponding to dayVal onto out
*  Return:   out
******************************************************************/

ostream & operator<< (ostream & out, Day dayVal);


/* operator>> inputs a MonthAbbrev from an input stream.
 *
 * Receive:   in, an istream reference and a reference
 *            to a Day dayVal
 * Input:     a string, from in
 * Pass back: dayVal, with the proper value,
 *            or DAY_OVERFLOW on error
 * Return:    in
 ****************************************************************/

istream& operator>> (istream & In, Day & dayVal);
```

```
/* Next returns the successor of abbrev.
 *
 * Receive: dayVal, a Day value
 * Return:  The following Day value, with Saturday followed
 *          by Sunday.
 ******************************************************************/

Day Next (Day dayVal);
```

//Day.h
```
/* This file contains the interface for library Day.
 *
 ******************************************************************/
#include <iostream.h>
#include <fstream.h>

enum Day {DAY_UNDERFLOW = -1, SUNDAY, MONDAY, TUESDAY, WEDNESDAY,
          THURSDAY, FRIDAY, SATURDAY, NUMBER_OF_DAY, DAY_OVERFLOW = 7};

ostream & operator<< (ostream & out, Day dayVal);

istream& operator>> (istream & In, Day & dayVal);

Day Next (Day dayVal);
```

//Day.cpp
```
/* This file contains the implementation for library Day.
 *
 ******************************************************************/

#include "Day.h"

#include <iostream.h>
const char ERROR_MSG[] = "\n*** <<: invalid Day value received!\n";

//----------------------------------------------------------------

ostream & operator<< (ostream & out, Day dayVal)
{
   switch (dayVal)
   {
      case SUNDAY:         out << "SUNDAY";
                           break;
      case MONDAY:         out << "MONDAY";
                           break;
      case TUESDAY:        out << "TUESDAY";
                           break;
      case WEDNESDAY:      out << "WEDNESDAY";
                           break;
      case THURSDAY:       out << "THURSDAY";
                           break;
      case FRIDAY:         out << "FRIDAY";
                           break;
      case SATURDAY:       out << "SATURDAY";
                           break;
      case DAY_OVERFLOW:    out << "Day Overflow";
                           break;
      case DAY_UNDERFLOW:   out << "Day Underflow";
                           break;
```

```
            default:
                                cerr << ERROR_MSG;
    }

    return out;
}

#include <ctype.h>
#include <string>

istream& operator>> (istream & in, Day & dayVal)
{
    string str;
    const char
        ErrorMsg[] = "\n*** >>: invalid Day value received!\n";

    in >> str;

    for (int i = 0; i < str.length(); i++)
        if (islower(str[i]))
            str[i] = toupper(str[i]);

    if (str == "SUNDAY")
        dayVal = SUNDAY;
    else if (str == "MONDAY")
        dayVal = MONDAY;
    else if (str == "TUESDAY")
        dayVal = TUESDAY;
    else if (str == "WEDNESDAY")
        dayVal = WEDNESDAY;
    else if (str == "THURSDAY")
        dayVal = THURSDAY;
    else if (str == "FRIDAY")
        dayVal = FRIDAY;
    else if (str == "SATURDAY")
        dayVal  = SATURDAY;
    else
    {
        dayVal = DAY_OVERFLOW;
        cerr << ERROR_MSG;
    }

    return in;
}

Day Next(Day dayVal)
{
    switch (dayVal)
    {
        case SUNDAY:        return MONDAY;
        case MONDAY:        return TUESDAY;
        case TUESDAY:       return WEDNESDAY;
        case WEDNESDAY:     return THURSDAY;
        case THURSDAY:      return FRIDAY;
        case FRIDAY:        return SATURDAY;
        case SATURDAY:      return DAY_OVERFLOW;
        case DAY_OVERFLOW:  return DAY_OVERFLOW;
        case DAY_UNDERFLOW: return SUNDAY;
        default:            return DAY_OVERFLOW;
    }
}
```

Exercises 11.3

1.

```
//Month.h
/* Month.h presents the declaration of class Month.
 *   ...
 **************************************************************/

#ifndef MONTH
#define MONTH

#include <iostream.h>

enum MonthAbbrev { MONTH_UNDERFLOW = -1,
                   JAN, FEB, MAR, APR, MAY, JUN,
                   JUL, AUG, SEP, OCT, NOV, DEC,
                   MONTH_OVERFLOW, NUMBER_OF_MONTHS = 12 };

class Month
{
 public:
                                         // constructors
   Month();                              //    default
   Month(MonthAbbrev initialMonthValue); //    explicit value

   void Read(istream & in);              // I/O
   void Print(ostream & out) const;

                                         // relationals
   friend bool operator==(const Month & left, const Month & right);
   friend bool operator!=(const Month & left, const Month & right);
   friend bool operator<(const Month & left, const Month & right);
   friend bool operator>(const Month & left, const Month & right);
   friend bool operator<=(const Month & left, const Month & right);
   friend bool operator>=(const Month & left, const Month & right);

   Month operator++();                   // prefix ++
   Month operator++(int);                // postfix ++
   Month Successor(unsigned num);        // num-th successor

   Month operator--();                   // prefix --
   Month operator--(int);                // postfix --

   unsigned Days();                      // days in month -- Prog. Problem 5

 private:
   MonthAbbrev myMonthValue;
};

// inline definitions

// ------- Default Value Constructor ------------------------------------

inline Month::Month()
{
   myMonthValue = JAN;
}
```

```
// ------- Explicit Value Constructor ------------------------------------

#include <assert.h>                                      // assert()

inline Month::Month(MonthAbbrev initialMonthValue)
{
    assert(JAN <= initialMonthValue && initialMonthValue <= DEC);
    myMonthValue = initialMonthValue;
}


// -------- Non-member Input -------------------------------------

inline istream & operator>>(istream & in, Month & theMonth)
{
    theMonth.Read(in);
    return in;
 }


// -------- Non-member Output -----------------------------------

inline ostream & operator<<(ostream & out, const Month & theMonth)
{
    theMonth.Print(out);
    return out;
 }


// -------- Equality --------------------------------------------

inline bool operator==(const Month & left, const Month & right)
{
    return left.myMonthValue == right.myMonthValue;
}


// -------- Less-than -------------------------------------------

inline bool operator<(const Month & left, const Month & right)
{
    return left.myMonthValue < right.myMonthValue;
}


// -------- Less-than-or-equal ----------------------------------

inline bool operator<=(const Month & left, const Month & right)
{
    return left.myMonthValue <= right.myMonthValue;
}

// ... remaining relational operators omitted

#endif
```

//Month.cpp

```
/* Month.cpp provides the implementation of class Month operations
 *
 ********************************************************************/

#include "Month.h"                                  // class Month

// ------- Input Function Member -------------------------------------

#include <string>                        // string
#include <stdlib.h>                       // exit()
void Month::Read(istream & in)
{
   string inputString;

   in >> inputString;                     // read a string

   int inputLength = inputString.length();

   if (inputLength < 3)                   // need at least 3 chars
   {
      cerr << "\n*** Read: invalid month received!\n";
      exit(1);
   }

   string abbr = inputString.substr(0,3); // get first 3 chars

   for (int i = 0; i < 3; i++)            // change to lowercase
      if (islower(abbr[i]))
         abbr[i] = toupper(abbr[i]);

   if (abbr == "JAN")                     // compare to constants
      myMonthValue = JAN;
   else if (abbr == "FEB")
      myMonthValue = FEB;
   else if (abbr == "MAR")
      myMonthValue = MAR;
   else if (abbr == "APR")
      myMonthValue = APR;
   else if (abbr == "MAY")
      myMonthValue = MAY;
   else if (abbr == "JUN")
      myMonthValue = JUN;
   else if (abbr == "JUL")
      myMonthValue = JUL;
   else if (abbr == "AUG")
      myMonthValue = AUG;
   else if (abbr == "SEP")
      myMonthValue = SEP;
   else if (abbr == "OCT")
      myMonthValue = OCT;
   else if (abbr == "NOV")
      myMonthValue = NOV;
   else if (abbr == "DEC")
      myMonthValue = DEC;
   else
   {
      cerr << "\n*** Read: invalid month received!\n";
      exit(1);
   }
}
```

```
// ------- output function member --------------------------------------
void Month::Print(ostream & out) const
{
    switch (myMonthValue)
    {
        case JAN: out << "Jan"; break;
        case FEB: out << "Feb"; break;
        case MAR: out << "Mar"; break;
        case APR: out << "Apr"; break;
        case MAY: out << "May"; break;
        case JUN: out << "Jun"; break;
        case JUL: out << "Jul"; break;
        case AUG: out << "Aug"; break;
        case SEP: out << "Sep"; break;
        case OCT: out << "Oct"; break;
        case NOV: out << "Nov"; break;
        case DEC: out << "Dec"; break;
    }
}


// -------- Prefix Increment ---------------------------------------

Month Month::operator++()
{
    switch(myMonthValue)
    {
        case JAN:  myMonthValue = FEB; break;
        case FEB:  myMonthValue = MAR; break;
        case MAR:  myMonthValue = APR; break;
        case APR:  myMonthValue = MAY; break;
        case MAY:  myMonthValue = JUN; break;
        case JUN:  myMonthValue = JUL; break;
        case JUL:  myMonthValue = AUG; break;
        case AUG:  myMonthValue = SEP; break;
        case SEP:  myMonthValue = OCT; break;
        case OCT:  myMonthValue = NOV; break;
        case NOV:  myMonthValue = DEC; break;
        case DEC:  myMonthValue = MONTH_OVERFLOW; break;
    }

    return Month(myMonthValue);
}

// -------- Postfix Increment ---------------------------------------

Month Month::operator++(int)
{
    Month myOriginalMonth(myMonthValue);

    switch(myMonthValue)
    {
        case JAN:  myMonthValue = FEB; break;
        case FEB:  myMonthValue = MAR; break;
        case MAR:  myMonthValue = APR; break;
        case APR:  myMonthValue = MAY; break;
        case MAY:  myMonthValue = JUN; break;
        case JUN:  myMonthValue = JUL; break;
        case JUL:  myMonthValue = AUG; break;
        case AUG:  myMonthValue = SEP; break;
        case SEP:  myMonthValue = OCT; break;
        case OCT:  myMonthValue = NOV; break;
```

```
         case NOV:   myMonthValue = DEC; break;
         case DEC:   myMonthValue = MONTH_OVERFLOW; break;
      }

   return myOriginalMonth;
}

Month Month::Successor(unsigned num)
{
   assert(num >= 0);

   MonthAbbrev abb = myMonthValue;
   while (num > 0)
   {
      switch (abb)
      {
         case JAN: abb = FEB; break;
         case FEB: abb = MAR; break;
         case MAR: abb = APR; break;
         case APR: abb = MAY; break;
         case MAY: abb = JUN; break;
         case JUN: abb = JUL; break;
         case JUL: abb = AUG; break;
         case AUG: abb = SEP; break;
         case SEP: abb = OCT; break;
         case OCT: abb = NOV; break;
         case NOV: abb = DEC; break;
         case DEC: abb = JAN;
      }
      num--;
   }
   return abb;
}

/* IsLeapYear determines if a year is a leap year.
 *
 * Receive: year, an int
 * Return:  true if year is a leap year, false otherwise
 ************************************************************/

bool IsLeapYear(int year)
{
   return (year % 4 == 0) &&
          (!(year % 100 == 0) || (year % 400 == 0));
}

unsigned Month::Days(int year)            // days in month -- Prog. Problem 5
{
   assert(1538 <= year && year <= 1999);
   if (*this == FEB)
      if (IsLeapYear(year))
         return 29;
      else
         return 28;
   else if ( (*this == APR) || (*this == JUN) ||
             (*this == SEP) || (*this == NOV) )
      return 30;
   else
      return 31;
}

// ... remaining operators omitted
```

2.
//Day.h
```
/* Day.h presents the declaration of class Day.
 *
 **************************************************/

#ifndef DAY
#define DAY

#include <iostream.h>

enum DayName { DAY_UNDERFLOW = -1,
               SUNDAY, MONDAY, TUESDAY, WEDNESDAY, THURSDAY, FRIDAY,
               SATURDAY, DAY_OVERFLOW, NUMBER_OF_DAYS = 7 };

class Day
{
 public:
                                              // constructors
   Day();                                     //   default
   Day(DayName initialDayValue);              //   explicit value

   void Read(istream & in);                   // I/O
   void Print(ostream & out) const;

                                              // relationals
   friend bool operator==(const Day & left, const Day & right);
   friend bool operator!=(const Day & left, const Day & right);
   friend bool operator<(const Day & left, const Day & right);
   friend bool operator>(const Day & left, const Day & right);
   friend bool operator<=(const Day & left, const Day & right);
   friend bool operator>=(const Day & left, const Day & right);

   Day operator++();                          // prefix ++
   Day operator++(int);                       // postfix ++
   Day Successor(unsigned num);               // num-th successor

   Day operator--();                          // prefix --
   Day operator--(int);                       // postfix --

   private:
   DayName myDayValue;
                                  };

// inline definitions

// ------- Default Value Constructor -------------------------------------

inline Day::Day()
{
   myDayValue = SUNDAY;
 }


// ------- Explicit Value Constructor ------------------------------------

#include <assert.h>                                   // assert()
```

```cpp
inline Day::Day(DayName initialDayValue)
{
   assert(SUNDAY <= initialDayValue && initialDayValue <= SATURDAY);
   myDayValue = initialDayValue;
}


// -------- Non-member Input -------------------------------------

inline istream & operator>>(istream & in, Day & theDay)
{
   theDay.Read(in);
   return in;
}


// -------- Non-member Output ------------------------------------

inline ostream & operator<<(ostream & out, const Day & theDay)
{
   theDay.Print(out);
   return out;
}


// -------- Equality ---------------------------------------------

inline bool operator==(const Day & left, const Day & right)
{
   return left.myDayValue == right.myDayValue;
}


// -------- Less-than --------------------------------------------

inline bool operator<(const Day & left, const Day & right)
{
   return left.myDayValue < right.myDayValue;
}


// -------- Less-than-or-equal -----------------------------------

inline bool operator<=(const Day & left, const Day & right)
{
   return left.myDayValue <= right.myDayValue;
}

// ... remaining relational operators omitted

#endif
```

```
//Day.cpp
/* Day.cpp provides the implementation of class Day operations
 *
 ********************************************************************/

#include "Day.h"                                    // class Day

// ------- Input Function Member -----------------------------------

#include <string>                                   // string
#include <stdlib.h>                                 // exit()
void Day::Read(istream & in)
{
   string inputString;
   cin >> inputString;

   for (int i = 0; i < inputString.length(); i++)  // change to lowercase
      if (islower(inputString[i]))
         inputString[i] = toupper(inputString[i]);

   if (inputString == "SUNDAY")                     // compare to constants
      myDayValue = SUNDAY;
   else if (inputString == "MONDAY")
      myDayValue = MONDAY;
   else if (inputString == "TUESDAY")
      myDayValue = TUESDAY;
   else if (inputString == "WEDNESDAY")
      myDayValue = WEDNESDAY;
   else if (inputString == "THURSDAY")
      myDayValue = THURSDAY;
   else if (inputString == "FRIDAY")
      myDayValue = FRIDAY;
   else if (inputString == "SATURDAY")
      myDayValue = SATURDAY;
   else
   {
      cerr << "\n*** Read: invalid day received!\n";
      exit(1);
   }
}

// ------- output function member ----------------------------------
void Day::Print(ostream & out) const
{
   switch (myDayValue)
   {
      case SUNDAY:    out << "Sunday"; break;
      case MONDAY:    out << "Monday"; break;
      case TUESDAY:   out << "Tuesday"; break;
      case WEDNESDAY: out << "Wednesday"; break;
      case THURSDAY:  out << "Thursday"; break;
      case FRIDAY:    out << "Friday"; break;
      case SATURDAY:  out << "Saturday";
   }
}
```

```
// -------- Prefix Increment --------------------------------------

Day Day::operator++()
{
   switch(myDayValue)
   {
      case SUNDAY:    myDayValue = MONDAY;    break;
      case MONDAY:    myDayValue = TUESDAY;   break;
      case TUESDAY:   myDayValue = WEDNESDAY; break;
      case WEDNESDAY: myDayValue = THURSDAY;  break;
      case THURSDAY:  myDayValue = FRIDAY;    break;
      case FRIDAY:    myDayValue = SATURDAY;  break;
      case SATURDAY:  myDayValue = SUNDAY;    break;
    }

   return Day(myDayValue);
}

// -------- Postfix Increment -------------------------------------

Day Day::operator++(int)
{
   Day myOriginalDay(myDayValue);

   switch(myDayValue)
   {
      case SUNDAY:    myDayValue = MONDAY;    break;
      case MONDAY:    myDayValue = TUESDAY;   break;
      case TUESDAY:   myDayValue = WEDNESDAY; break;
      case WEDNESDAY: myDayValue = THURSDAY;  break;
      case THURSDAY:  myDayValue = FRIDAY;    break;
      case FRIDAY:    myDayValue = SATURDAY;  break;
      case SATURDAY:  myDayValue = SUNDAY;
   }

   return myOriginalDay;
}

Day Day::Successor(unsigned num)
{
   assert(num >= 0);

   DayName name = myDayValue;
   while (num > 0)
   {
      switch (name)
      {
         case SUNDAY:    name = MONDAY;    break;
         case MONDAY:    name = TUESDAY;   break;
         case TUESDAY:   name = WEDNESDAY; break;
         case WEDNESDAY: name = THURSDAY;  break;
         case THURSDAY:  name = FRIDAY;    break;
         case FRIDAY:    name = SATURDAY;  break;
         case SATURDAY:  name = SUNDAY;    break;
      }
      num--;
   }
   return name;
}

// ... remaining operators omitted
```

3.
```
// Date.h
/* Date.h provides the interface for the class Date
 *
 ********************************************************************/
#include <iostream.h>
#include <string>

class Date
{
 public:
    Date();                                 // default constructor
    Date(string m, unsigned d, unsigned y); // explicit-value constructor

    string Month() const;                   // extractor functions
    unsigned Day() const;
    unsigned Year() const;

    void Read(istream & in);                // I/O
    void Print(ostream & out) const;

                                            // rel. ops
    friend bool operator==(const Date & date1, const & Date date2);
    friend bool operator<(const Date & date1, const & Date date2);

    int MonthNumber() const;                // utility functions
    bool IsLeapYear() const;

 private:
    string myMonth;
    unsigned myDay,
             myYear;
};

inline Date::Date()
{   myMonth = "January";
    myDay = 1;
    myYear = 1900;
}

inline Date::Date(string m, unsigned d, unsigned y)
{   myMonth = m;
    myDay = d;
    myYear = y;
}

inline string Date::Month() const
{ return myMonth; }

inline unsigned Date::Day() const
{ return myDay; }

inline unsigned Date::Year() const
{ return myYear; }


inline void Date::Print(ostream & out) const
{
    out << myMonth << ' ' << myDay << ", " << myYear;
}
```

```
inline istream & operator>>(istream & in, Date & d)
{
   d.Read(in);
   return in;
}

inline ostream & operator<<(ostream & out, Date d)
{
   d.Print(out);
   return out;
}

inline bool operator==(const Date & date1, const & Date date2);
{
   return (date1.myMonth == date2.myMonth &&
           date1.myDay == date2.myDay &&
           date1.myYear == date2.myYear );
}
```

```
//Date.cpp
/* Date.cpp provides the implementation of class Date operations
 *
 ******************************************************************/

#include "Date.h"

const string MONTH_NAME[12] =
     {"JANUARY", "FEBRUARY", "MARCH", "APRIL", "MAY", "JUNE",
      "JULY", "AUGUST", "SEPTEMBER", "OCTOBER", "NOVEMBER", "DECEMBER"};

int Date::MonthNumber() const
{
    for (int i = 0; i < 12; i++)
       if (myMonth == MONTH_NAME[i])
           return i + 1;

    cerr << "\nMonthNumber:  illegal month name: "
         << myMonth << endl;

    return 0;

}

bool Date::IsLeapYear() const
{
   return (myYear % 4 == 0) &&
          (!(myYear % 100 == 0) || (myYear % 400 == 0));
}


//-- Member input function ---------------------------------
#include <ctype.h>              // islower(), toupper()

void Date::Read(istream & in)
{
   char comma;

   in >> myMonth >> myDay;
   in.get(comma);
   in >> myYear;
```

```
   for (int i = 0; i < myMonth.length(); i++)  // change to lowercase
       if (islower(myMonth[i]))
          myMonth[i] = toupper(myMonth[i]);

   bool OK = false;
   for (int i = 0; i < 12; i++)
       if(myMonth == MONTH_NAME[i])
       {
          OK = true;
          break;
       }

   if (!OK)
   {
       cerr << "Illegal month -- " << myMonth << endl;
       exit(1);
   }
   if (myMonth == "SEPTEMBER" || myMonth == "APRIL" ||
       myMonth == "JUNE" || myMonth == "NOVEMBER")
       assert(myDay <= 30);
   else if (myMonth == "FEBRUARY")
       if (IsLeapYear())
          assert(myDay <= 29);
       else
          assert(myDay <= 28);
    else
       assert(myDay <= 31);
}

bool operator<(const Date & date1, const & Date date2);
{
   if (date1.myYear < date2.myYear) return true;
   if (date1.myYear > date2.myYear) return false;

   // years are the same
   if (date1.MonthNumber() < date2.MonthNumber()) return true;
   if (date1.MonthNumber() > date2.MonthNumber()) return false;

   // years and months are the same

   if (date1.myDay < date2.myYear)
      return true;
   else
      return false;
}
```

4.
//Numeral.h
```
/* Numeral.h presents the declaration of class Numeral.
 *
 ******************************************************/

#ifndef NUMERAL
#define NUMERAL

#include <iostream.h>
#include <string>
```

```
enum NumeralName { NUMERAL_UNDERFLOW = -1,
                   ZERO, ONE, TWO, THREE, FOUR, FIVE, SIX, SEVEN,
                   EIGHT, NINE, TEN, NUMERAL_OVERFLOW,
                   NUMBER_OF_NUMERALS = 11 };

const string NAMESTR[NUMBER_OF_NUMERALS + 1] =
          {"ZERO", "ONE", "TWO", "THREE", "FOUR", "FIVE", "SIX",
           "SEVEN", "EIGHT", "NINE", "TEN", "NUMERAL_OVERFLOW"};

class Numeral
{
 public:
                                              // constructors
   Numeral();                                 //    default
   Numeral(int intValue);                     //    explicit value

   void Read(istream & in);                   // I/O
   void Print(ostream & out) const;

                                              // relationals
   friend bool operator==(const Numeral & left, const Numeral & right);
   friend bool operator<(const Numeral & left, const Numeral & right);
   // other relational operations are similar

                                              // addition
   friend Numeral operator+(const Numeral & left, const Numeral & right);
   // other arithmetic operations are similar

 private:
   NumeralName myName;
};

// inline definitions

// ------- Default Value Constructor -------------------------- ---------

inline Numeral::Numeral()
{
   myName = ZERO;
 }


// ------- Explicit Value Constructor ------------------------------------

#include <assert.h>                           // assert()

inline Numeral::Numeral(int intValue)
{
   assert(0 <= intValue && intValue <= 10);

   myName = NumeralName(intValue);
 }

// ------- output function member ---------------------------------------
inline void Numeral::Print(ostream & out) const
{
   out << NAMESTR[myName];
 }
```

```
// -------- Non-member Input --------------------------------------

inline istream & operator>>(istream & in, Numeral & theNumeral)
{
   theNumeral.Read(in);
   return in;
 }


// -------- Non-member Output -------------------------------------

inline ostream & operator<<(ostream & out, const Numeral& theNumeral)
{
   theNumeral.Print(out);
   return out;
 }


// -------- Equality ----------------------------------------------

inline bool operator==(const Numeral & left, const Numeral & right)
{
   return left.myName == right.myName;
}


// -------- Less Than ---------------------------------------------

inline bool operator<(const Numeral & left, const Numeral & right)
{
   return left.myName < right.myName;
 }

#endif
```

//Numeral.cpp
```
/* Numeral.cpp provides the implementation of class Numeral operations
 *
 ********************************************************************/

#include "Numeral.h"                            // class Numeral

// ------- Input Function Member ---------------------------------

#include <string>                               // string
#include <stdlib.h>                             // exit()

void Numeral::Read(istream & in)
{
   string inputStr;
   cin >> inputStr;

   for (int i = 0; i < inputStr.length(); i++)  // change to lowercase
      if (islower(inputStr[i]))
         inputStr[i] = toupper(inputStr[i]);
```

```
    for (int i = 0; i < NUMBER_OF_NUMERALS; i++) // compare to constants
        if (NAMESTR[i] == inputStr)
        {
            myName = NumeralName(i);
            return;
        }

    cerr << "\n*** Read: invalid numeral received!\n";
    exit(1);
}


// -------- Addition ---------------------------------------------------

Numeral operator+(const Numeral & left, const Numeral & right)
{
  Numeral sum;

  sum.myName = NumeralName(left.myName + right.myName);
      if (sum.myName > NUMBER_OF_NUMERALS)
        sum.myName = NUMERAL_OVERFLOW;
  return sum;
}
```

5. The solution to Exercises 9-17 of Section 10.5 can be easily transformed into a `PlayingCard` class.

Programming Problems
Section 11.2

1.
```
/* prog11-1.cpp is a driver program to test the library MonthAbbrev
 * from Exercises 8-12.
 *
 * Input:  abbreviations and numbers of months
 * Output: names of months
 ********************************************************************/

#include <iostream.h>                    // cin, cout, >>, <<
#include "MonthAbbrev.h"

int main()
{
    MonthAbbrev month;
    char response;
    int num;
    do
    {
        cout << "Enter a 3-letter month abbreviation: ";
        cin >> month;
        cout << "Month is " << month <<
              "\nIt's successor is " << Next(month) << endl;
        cout << "Enter a number: ";
        cin >> num;
        cout << "It's " << num << "-th successor is "
              << Successor(month, num) << endl;
```

```
        cout << "\nMore (Y or N)? ";
        cin >> response;
    }
    while (response == 'Y' || response == 'y');

    for (;;)
    {
        cout << "\nEnter a month number (negative to stop): ";
        cin >> num;
        if (num < 0) break;

        cout << "Month is " << IntToMonth(num) << endl;
    }
    return 0;
}
```

2.
```
/* prog11-2.cpp is a driver program to test the library Day from
 * Exercises 14-16.
 *
 * Input:  names of days
 * Output: names of days
 ********************************************************************/

#include <iostream.h>                    // cin, cout, >>, <<
#include "Day.h"

int main()
{
    Day dayValue;
    char response;
    do
    {
        cout << "Enter a day name: ";
        cin >> dayValue;
        cout << "This day is " << dayValue<<
             "\nIt's successor is " << Next(dayValue) << endl;

        cout << "\nMore (Y or N)? ";
        cin >> response;
    }
    while (response == 'Y' || response == 'y');
}
```

Section 11.3

3. See the solution to Problem 5.

4.
```
/* prog11-4.cpp reads monthly rainfalls and then calculates and
 * displays the average monthly rainfall.
 *
 * Input:  rainfall amounts
 * Output: month abbreviations
 ********************************************************************/

#include <iostream.h>                    // cin, cout, >>, <<
#include "Month.h"
```

```
int main()
{
   double rain,
          totalRain = 0;
   Month mon;
   for (mon = JAN; mon <= DEC; mon++)
   {
      cout << "Enter the rainfall for " << mon << ": ";
      cin >> rain;
      totalRain += rain;
   }

   cout << "Average rainfall for this year is "
        << totalRain / 12.0 << endl;

   return 0;
}
```

5.
```
/* prog11-5.cpp is a driver program to test the class Month from
 * Problem 5.
 *
 * Input:  abbreviations of months, integers. amd years
 * Output: names of months, days in months
 *********************************************************************/

#include <iostream.h>                      // cin, cout, >>, <<
#include "Month.h"

int main()
{
   Month month1,            // default constructor
         month2(MAR);       // explicit-value constructor

   cout << "Months constructed: \nmonth1 = " << month1
        << "\nmonth2 = " << month2 << endl;

   month1 = ++month2;
   cout << "After month1 = ++month2;\nmonth2 = " << month2
        << "\nmonth1 = " << month1 << endl;

   month1 = month2++;
   cout << "\nAfter month1 = month2++;\nmonth2 = " << month2
        << "\nmonth1 = " << month1 << endl;

   char response;
   Month month;
   int num,
       aYear;
   do
   {
      cout << "\nEnter a 3-letter month abbreviation: ";
      cin >> month;
      cout << "Enter a number: ";
      cin >> num;
```

```
        cout << "Month is " << month
                << "\nIt's " << num << "-th successor is "
                << month.Successor(num) << endl;
        cout << "\nEnter a year (1538 - 1999): ";
        cin >> aYear;
        cout << month << ", " << aYear << " has/had "
                << month.Days(aYear) << " days\n";

        cout << "\nMore (Y or N)? ";
        cin >> response;
    }
    while (response == 'Y' || response == 'y');

    return 0;
}
```


6.

```
/* prog11-6.cpp finds the number of days between two dates in the
 * same year.
 *
 * Input:  two dates in the same year
 * Output: number of days between.
 ************************************************************************/

#include <iostream.h>                      // cin, cout, >>, <<
#include "Month.h"

int DaysBetween(Month fromMonth, int fromDay, int year,
         Month toMonth, int toDay);

int main()
{
    Month month1, month2;
    int day1, day2, year;

    cout << "Enter a 3-letter month abbreviation, day in that month, and the"
            "\ncurrent year: ";
    cin >> month1 >> day1 >> year;
    cout << "Enter a 3-letter abbreviation for a later month"
            "\nand a day in that month: ";
    cin >> month2 >> day2;

    cout << "There are " << DaysBetween(month1, day1, year, month2, day2)
        << " days between these two dates.\n";

    return 0;
}

/* DaysBetween returns the number of days between two dates
 * in the same year.
 *
 * Receive:  fromMonth, fromDay, toMonth, toDay, and year
 * Return:   The number of days between the "from" date
 *           and the "to" date
 ************************************************************************/

int DaysBetween(Month fromMonth, int fromDay, int year,
             Month toMonth, int toDay)
```

```
{
    int days = fromMonth.Days(year) - fromDay + 1;

    fromMonth++;
    while (fromMonth < toMonth)
    {
        days += fromMonth.Days(year);
        fromMonth++;
    }

    days += toDay;

    return days;
}
```

7.
```
/* prog11-7.cpp is a driver program to test the class Day from
 * Exercise 2.
 *
 * Input:  names of days
 * Output: names of days
 ************************************************************************/
#include <iostream.h>                    // cin, cout, >>, <<
#include "Day.h"

int main()
{
    Day day1,            // default constructor
        day2(MONDAY);    // explicit-value constructor

    cout << "Days constructed: \nday1 = " << day1
         << "\nday2 = " << day2 << endl;

    day1 = ++day2;
    cout << "After day1 = ++day2;\nday2 = " << day2
         << "\nday1 = " << day1 << endl;

    day1 = day2++;
    cout << "\nAfter day1 = day2++;\nday2 = " << day2
         << "\nday1 = " << day1 << endl;

    char response;
    Day d;
    int num;
    do
    {
        cout << "\nEnter a day name: ";
        cin >> d;
        cout << "Enter a number: ";
        cin >> num;
        cout << "Day is " << d
             << "\nIt's " << num << "-th successor is "
             << d.Successor(num) << endl;

        cout << "\nMore (Y or N)? ";
        cin >> response;
    }
    while (response == 'Y' || response == 'y');

    return 0;
}
```

8.
```cpp
/* prog11-8.cpp reads an employee's name, hourly pay rate, number of hours
 * worked for each weekday and then calculates and displays his or her
 * total hours and wages.
 *
 * Input:  empNum, hourlyRate, hoursWorked
 * Output: names of weekdays, total hours worked, and wages
 ***********************************************************************/

#include <iostream.h>                 // cin, cout, >>, <<
#include <iomanip.h>                  // setprecision(), setiosflags()
#include "Day.h"                      // class Day
#include <string>                     // string

double Wages(double hours, double rate);

int main()
{
   string empName;                    // employee name
   double hourlyRate,                 // hourly rate
          hoursWorked;                // hours worked

   cout << "Enter employee's name: ";
   getline(cin, empName);
   cout << "Enter employee's hourly rate: ";
   cin >> hourlyRate;

   Day workday;
   double totalHours = 0;
   cout << "Enter hours worked on ";
   for (workday = MONDAY; workday <= FRIDAY; workday++)
   {
      cout << workday << ": ";
      cin >> hoursWorked;
      totalHours += hoursWorked;
   }

   cout << endl << empName << " worked " << totalHours
        << " hours. \nWages = "
        << setprecision(2) << setiosflags(ios::fixed | ios::showpoint)
        << ": $" << Wages(totalHours, hourlyRate) << endl;

   return 0;
}

/* Wages computes an employee's wages.   Hours over 40 are paid
 * at 1.5 times the regular hourly rate.
 *
 * Receive: hours worked and hourly rate
 * Output:  wages.
 ***********************************************************/

double Wages(double hours, double rate)
{
   if (hours <= 40.0)
      return hours * rate;
   else
      return hours * rate + ((hours - 40) * (rate * 0.5));
}
```

9.

```
/* prog11-9.cpp reads a customer's account number and current balance,
 * transactions (deposits and withdrawals) for each weekday and updates
 * the balance.
 *
 * Input:  accountNumber, balance, kind of transaction (D or W), amount
 * Output: accountNumber, names of weekdays, updated balance
 ***********************************************************************/

#include <iostream.h>            // cin, cout, >>, <<
#include <iomanip.h>             // setprecision(), setiosflags()
#include "Day.h"                 // class Day

int main()
{
   long int accountNumber;       // employee name
   char transCode;               // D(eposit), W(ithdrawal)
   double balance,               // current balance
          amount;    // amount of transaction

   cout << "Enter customer's account number and current balance: ";
   cin >> accountNumber >> balance;

   cout << "\nWeek's transactions for " << accountNumber << ": \n\n"
           "    Day   Code  Amount    Balance\n"
           "========= ====  ======   =======\n";
   cout << setprecision(2) << setiosflags(ios::fixed | ios::showpoint)
        << setw(32) << balance << endl;

   Day weekday;
   for (weekday = MONDAY; weekday <= FRIDAY; weekday++)
   {
      cout << setw(9) << weekday;
      cin >> transCode >> amount;
      if (transCode == 'D')
         balance += amount;
      else if (transCode == 'W')
         balance -= amount;
      else
         cout << "*** Illegal transaction";
      cout << setw(32) << balance << endl;
   }

   return 0;
}
```

10.

```
/* prog11-10.cpp is a driver program to test the class Date from
 * Exercise 3.
 *
 * Input:  dates
 * Output: dates
 *********************************************************************/

#include <iostream.h>                  // cin, cout, >>, <<
#include "Date.h"

int main()
{
   Date date1,                         // default constructor
        date2("December", 25, 1997);   // explicit-value constructor
```

```
      cout << "Dates constructed: \ndate1 = " << date1
           << "\ndate2 = " << date2 << endl;

      char response;
      do
      {
         cout << "\nEnter a date:  ";
         cin >> date1;
         cout << "Date is " << date1 << endl;

         cout << "\nMore (Y or N)? ";
         cin >> response;
      }
      while (response == 'Y' || response == 'y');

      return 0;
   }



11.
/* prog11-11.cpp finds the number of days between two dates=.
 *
 * Input:  two dates
 * Output: number of days between.
 ************************************************************************/

#include <iostream.h>                    // cin, cout, >>, <<
#include "Date.h"

int DaysBetween(Date fromDate, Date toDate);

int main()
{
   Date date1, date2;

   cout << "Enter a date and then a later date:\n";
   cin >> date1 >> date2;

   cout << "There are " << DaysBetween(date1, date2)
        << " days between " << date1 << " and " << date2 << endl;

   return 0;
}

/* DaysIn finds the numbef of days in a month.
 *
 * Receive: a month number and a year
 * Return:  number of days in month
 ********************************************************/
unsigned DaysIn(int month, int year)
{
   assert(1538 <= year && year <= 1999);
   if (month == 2)
   {
      Date d("February", 1, year);
      if (d.IsLeapYear())
         return 29;
      else
         return 28;
   }
```

```
      else if ( (month == 4) || (month == 6) ||
                (month == 9) || (month == 11) )
         return 30;
      else
         return 31;
}

/* Daysbetween returns the number of days between two dates.
 *
 * Receive:  fromDate and toDate
 * Return:   The number of days between the "from" date
 *           and the "to" date
 ****************************************************************/

#include <string>

int DaysBetween(Date fromDate, Date toDate)
{

   int fromYear = fromDate.Year(),
       fromMonth = fromDate.MonthNumber(),
       fromDay = fromDate.Day(),
       toYear = toDate.Year(),
       toMonth = toDate.MonthNumber(),
       toDay = toDate.Day(),
       days = 0;

   while ( (fromYear != toYear) ||
           (fromMonth != toMonth) ||
           (fromDay != toDay) )
   {
      fromDay++;

      if (fromDay > DaysIn(fromMonth, fromYear))
      {
         fromDay = 1;
         fromMonth++;

         if (fromMonth > 12)
         {
            fromMonth = 1;
            fromYear++;
         }
      }

      days++;
   }
   return days;
}


12.
// Event.h
/* Event.h provides the interface for the class Event
 *
 ****************************************************************/
#include <iostream.h>
#include <string>

#include "Date.h"
```

```
class Event
{
 public:

    string TheEvent() const;                    // extractor functions
    Date EventDate() const;

    void Read(istream & in);                    // I/O
    void Print(ostream & out) const;

    friend bool operator<(const Event & event1, const Event & event2);

 private:
    string myEvent;
    Date myDate;
};

inline string Event::TheEvent() const
{ return myEvent; }

inline Date Event::EventDate() const
{ return myDate; }

inline void Event::Read(istream & in)
{
   in >> myEvent >> myDate;
}

inline void Event::Print(ostream & out) const
{
   out << myDate << " -- " << myEvent;
}

inline istream & operator>>(istream & in, Event & anEvent)
{
   anEvent.Read(in);
   return in;
}

inline ostream & operator<<(ostream & out, Event & anEvent)
{
   anEvent.Print(out);
   return out;
}

inline bool operator<(const Event & event1, const Event & event2)
{
   return (event1.myDate < event2.myDate);
}


/* Prog11-12.cpp reads Events, stores them in a vector<Event>, sorts
 * into chronological order, and displays the sorted list. *
 * Input:  Events
 * Output: Sorted Events
 ********************************************************************/

#include <iostream.h>              // cin, cout, >>, <<
#include "Event.h"                 // class Event
#include <vector>                  // vector<Event>
#include <algorithm>               // sort()
```

```
int main()
{
   vector<Event> Events;
   char response;
   Event ev;
   do
   {
      cout << "\nEnter en event:  ";
      cin >> ev;
      Events.push_back(ev);

      cout << "\nMore events (Y or N)? ";
      cin >> response;
   }
   while (response == 'Y' || response == 'y');

   sort(Events.begin(), Events.end());

   cout << "Schedule of events in chronological order:\n";
   for (int i = 0; i < Events.size(); i++)
      cout << Events[i] << endl;

   return 0;
}
```

13 & 14.

```
/* prog11-13+14.cpp is a driver program to test the class Numeral from
 * Exercise 4.
 *
 * Input:  numerals
 * Output: numerals
 ***********************************************************************/

#include <iostream.h>                      // cin, cout, >>, <<
#include <string>

#include "Numeral.h"

int main()
{
   Numeral num1,            // default constructor
           num2(ONE);   // explicit-value constructor

   cout << "Numerals constructed: \nnum1 = " << num1
        << "\nnum2 = " << num2 << endl;

   string op;
   do
   {
      cout << "\nEnter two numerals:  ";
      cin >> num1 >> num2;

      for (;;)
      {
         cout << "Enter operation (==, +, QUIT: ";
         cin >> op;
         if (op == "QUIT") break);
```

```
            cout << num1 << ' ' << op << ' ' << num2 << " = ";
            if (op == "==")
               cout << (num1 == num2 ? "true" : "false") << endl;
            else if (op == "+")
            {
               Numeral num3 = num1 + num2;
               cout << num3 << endl;
            }
            else
               cout << "Illegal operator\n"
         }

      cout << "\nMore (Y or N)? ";
      cin >> response;
   }
   while (response == 'Y' || response == 'y');

   return 0;
}
```

15. This is an easy adaptation of the solution to Exercises 9-17 of Section 10.5.

17-19. These are larger projects.

Section 11.4

20.
```
// RockTexture.h
/* RockTexture.h declares class RockTexture.
 *
 *     The value of myRockTextureName is one of the following:
 *        COARSE, INTERMEDIATE, FINE,
 ***************************************************************/

#ifndef ROCK_TEXTURE
#define ROCK_TEXTURE

enum RockTextureName {TEXTURE_UNDERFLOW = -1,
                      COARSE, INTERMEDIATE, FINE,
                      NUMBER_OF_TEXTURES,
                      TEXTURE_OVERFLOW = NUMBER_OF_TEXTURES};

#include <iostream.h>                     // istream, ostream

class RockTexture
{
 public:                                 // constructors:
   RockTexture();                              //   default value
   RockTexture(RockTextureName initialRock); //  explicit value

   void Read(istream & in);              // input
   void Print(ostream & out) const;      // output

   RockTexture operator++();             // prefix ++
   RockTexture operator++(int);          // postfix ++
   RockTexture operator--();             // prefix --
   RockTexture operator--(int);          // postfix --
```

```
      friend bool operator==(const RockTexture & left, const RockTexture & right);
      friend bool operator!=(const RockTexture & left, const RockTexture & right);
      friend bool operator<(const RockTexture & left, const RockTexture & right);
      friend bool operator>(const RockTexture & left, const RockTexture & right);
      friend bool operator<=(const RockTexture & left, const RockTexture & right);
      friend bool operator>=(const RockTexture & left, const RockTexture & right);

  private:
     RockTextureName myRockTextureName;
};

// -------- Non-member input --------------------------------------
inline istream & operator>>(istream & in, RockTexture & theRockTexture)
{
     theRockTexture.Read(in);
     return in;
}

// -------- Non-member output -------------------------------------
inline ostream & operator<<(ostream & out, const RockTexture & theRockTexture)
{
     theRockTexture.Print(out);
     return out;
}

// -------- Initialize me (default-value) -------------------------
inline RockTexture::RockTexture()
{
     myRockTextureName = COARSE;
}

// -------- Initialize me (explicit-value) ------------------------
#include <cassert>
inline RockTexture::RockTexture(RockTextureName initialRockTextureName)
{
     assert(COARSE <= initialRockTextureName &&
            initialRockTextureName < NUMBER_OF_TEXTURES);
     myRockTextureName = initialRockTextureName;
}

// --------- Compare me and anotherRockTexture using == --------------
inline bool operator==(const RockTexture & left, const RockTexture & right)
{
     return left.myRockTextureName == right.myRockTextureName;
}

// ---   Inline definitions for operators !=, <, >, <=, and >= are
// ---   essentially the same and are omitted here to save space.

#endif


// RockTexture.cpp
/* RockTexture.cpp defines the nontrivial members of class RockTexture.
 ****************************************************************/

#include <string>
#include <ctype.h>

#include "RockTexture.h"
```

```
// -------- Read a value into me from in ---------------------------
void RockTexture::Read(istream & in)
{
    string rockKindString;
    in >> rockKindString;

    for (int i = 0; i < rockKindString.size(); i++)
        if (islower(rockKindString[i]))
            rockKindString[i] = toupper(rockKindString[i]);

    if (rockKindString== "COARSE")
        myRockTextureName = COARSE;
    else if (rockKindString== "INTERMEDIATE")
        myRockTextureName = INTERMEDIATE;
    else if (rockKindString== "FINE")
        myRockTextureName = FINE;
    else
    {
        cerr << "\n*** Read: Rock texture is unknown\n"
             << endl;
        in.setstate(ios::failbit);
    }
}


// -------- Display me via out -------------------------
void RockTexture::Print(ostream & out) const
{
    switch(myRockTextureName)
    {
        case COARSE:        out << "COARSE";
                            break;
        case INTERMEDIATE:  out << "INTERMEDIATE";
                            break;
        case FINE:          out << "FINE";
                            break;
    }
}


// -------- Increment me (prefix) ------------------------
RockTexture RockTexture::operator++()
{
    switch(myRockTextureName)
    {
        case COARSE:        myRockTextureName = INTERMEDIATE;
                            break;
        case INTERMEDIATE:  myRockTextureName = FINE;
                            break;
        case FINE:          myRockTextureName = TEXTURE_OVERFLOW;
                            break;
    }
    return RockTexture(myRockTextureName);
}
```

```
// -------- Increment me (postfix) -------------------------
RockTexture RockTexture::operator++(int)
{
   RockTextureName savedRockTextureName = myRockTextureName;
   switch(myRockTextureName)
   {
      case COARSE:        myRockTextureName = INTERMEDIATE;
                          break;
      case INTERMEDIATE:  myRockTextureName = FINE;
                          break;
      case FINE:          myRockTextureName = TEXTURE_OVERFLOW;
                          break;
   }
   return RockTexture(savedRockTextureName);
}

// -------- Decrement me (prefix) --------------------------------
// -------- Decrement me (postfix) -------------------------------

// Definitions of operator--() and operator--(int) are similar to those
// of operator++() and perator++(int) and are omitted to save space.
```

21.

```
// -------- My texture (coarse, fine, ...) ------------------
RockTexture Rock::Texture() const
{
   switch (myRockName)                    // if the rock is...
   {
      case GRANITE:  case SANDSTONE:   // texture is coarse
      case DOLOMITE: case LIMESTONE:
                             return RockTexture(COARSE);
      case BASALT: case SHALE:          // texture is intermediate
      case SLATE:
                             return RockTexture(INTERMEDIATE);
      case OBSIDIAN: case MARBLE:       // texture is find
                             return RockTexture(FINE);
   }
}
```

Chapter 12: Multidimensional Arrays

Exercises 12.2

1. 5000
2. 676
3. 4
4. 16
5. 1200
6. 5

7.
```
0   1   2
1   2   3
2   3   4
```

8.
```
0   1   1
1   0   1
1   1   0
```

9.
```
0   -1   -1
1    0   -1
1    1    0
```

10.
```
2   2   2        Note:  There is a semicolon missing after the last line in the 1st printing of the text.
0   2   2
0   0   2
```

11. ```
Computers
and More!
```

12. ```
Ca
on
md
p
uM
to
er
re
s!
```

13. Since C++ does not perform run-time checking of array access, this code segment produces a logical error because more than two rows are accessed. The question marks will appear as garbage on your screen.
```
Ca?????
on?????
```

14. ```
sretupmoC
!eroM dna
```
```

15.
```
void AverageTemps(TemperatureTable temp,
                  double & out1, double & out2, double & out3)
{
    out1 = (Temp[MIDNIGHT][outlet1] + Temp[SIX_AM][outlet1] +
            Temp[NOON][outlet1] + Temp[SixPM][outlet1]) / 4.0;
    out2 = (Temp[MIDNIGHT][outlet2] + Temp[SIX_AM][outlet2] +
            Temp[NOON][outlet2] + Temp[SixPM][outlet2]) / 4.0;
    out3 = (Temp[MIDNIGHT][outlet3] + Temp[SIX_AM][outlet3] +
            Temp[NOON][outlet3] + Temp[SixPM][outlet3]) / 4.0;
}
```

16. Enumeration declarations:

```
/* AutoModel enumeration */

enum AutoModel { BUICK, CHEVY, DODGE, FORD, HONDA,
                 ISUZU, JEEP, MAZDA, OLDS, VOLVO, NUM_MODELS };

ostream& operator<<(ostream& out, AutoModel model);

/* EmployeeName enumeration */

enum EmployeeName { BILL, DAN, ED, JON,
                    LIZ, MIKE, SAM, TOM , NUM_EMPLOYEES};

ostream& operator<<(ostream& out, EmployeeName name);

typedef int SalesTable[NUM_MODELS][NUM_EMPLOYEES];
```

Enumeration output functions:

```
/* AutoModel enumeration */

ostream& operator<<(ostream& out, AutoModel model)
{
  switch (model)
  {
    case BUICK:  out << "BUICK"; break;
    case CHEVY:  out << "CHEVY"; break;
    case DODGE:  out << "DODGE"; break;
    case FORD:   out << "FORD "; break;
    case HONDA:  out << "HONDA"; break;
    case ISUZU:  out << "ISUZU"; break;
    case JEEP:   out << "JEEP "; break;
    case MAZDA:  out << "MAZDA"; break;
    case OLDS:   out << "OLDS "; break;
    case VOLVO:  out << "VOLVO"; break;
  }

  return out;
}
```

```
/* EmployeeName enumeration */

ostream& operator<<(ostream& out, EmployeeName name)
{
  switch (name)
  {
    case BILL:  out << "BILL"; break;
    case DAN:   out << "DAN "; break;
    case ED:    out << "ED  "; break;
    case JON:   out << "JON "; break;
    case LIZ:   out << "LIZ "; break;
    case MIKE:  out << "MIKE"; break;
    case SAM:   out << "SAM "; break;
    case TOM:   out << "TOM "; break;
  }

  return out;
}

istream operator>>(istream & in, SalesTable & sales)
{
    for (int i = 0; i < NUM_MODELS; i++)
       for (int j = 0; j < NUM_EMPLOYEES; j++)
          in >> sales[i][j];
}

ostream operator<<(ostream & out, const SalesTable & sales)
{
    cout << "        |";
    for (int emp = 0; emp < NUM_EMPLOYEES; emp++)
       out << EmployeeName(emp) << ' ';
    cout << endl;

    cout << "        |";
    for (int emp = 0; emp < NUM_EMPLOYEES; emp++)
       cout << "-------";
    cout << endl;

    for (int model = 0; model < NUM_MODELS; model++)
    {
       cout  << ModelName(model) <' |';
       for (int j = 0; j < NUM_EMPLOYEES; j++)
          out << setw(7) << sales[i][j];
       cout << endl;
    }
}
```

17.

(a)

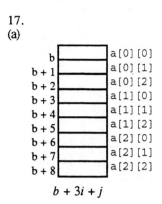

$$b + 3i + j$$

(b)

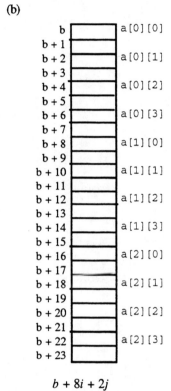

$$b + 8i + 2j$$

Exercises 12.3

1.

```
/* SetEkem sets the element at a given row & column in a Table.
 *
 * Receive:    row, a row index,    col, a column index,
 *             element, a double,    aTable, a Table object
 * Pass back: aTable with element in the specified row and column
 *             set to element
 ********************************************************************/
#include <assert.h>

void SetElem(unsigned row, unsigned col, double element, const Table & aTable)
{
   assert(row < ROWS && col < COLUMNS);
   aTable[row][col] = element;
}
```

2.

```
/* RowSum sums the elements of a given row in a Table object.
 *
 * Receive: row, a row index and aTable, a Table object
 * Return:  the sum of the elements in the row-th row of aTable
 ********************************************************************/
#include <assert.h>
double RowSum(unsigned row, const Table & aTable)
{
   assert(row < aTable.size());

   double sum = 0.0;
   for (int col = 0; col < aTable[row].size(); col++)
      sum += aTable[row][col];

   return sum;
}
```

3.

```
/* ColumnSum sums the elements of a given column in a Table object.
 *
 * Receive: col, a column index and aTable, a Table object
 * Return:  the sum of the elements in the col-th column of aTable
 ********************************************************************/
#include <assert.h>
double ColumnSum(unsigned col, const Table & aTable)
{
   assert(col < aTable[0].size());

   double sum = 0.0;
   for (int row = 0; row < aTable.size(); row++)
      sum += aTable[row][col];

   return sum;
}
```

4.

```
/* RowAverage averages the elements of a given row in a Table object.
 *
 * Receive: row, a row index and aTable, a Table object
 * Return:  the average of the elements in the row-th row of aTable
 ********************************************************************/
```

```
#include <assert.h>
double RowAverage(unsigned row, const Table & aTable)
{
   assert(row < aTable.size());

   return RowSum(row, aTable) / aTable[row].size();
}
```

5.
```
/* RowStdDeviation finds the standard deviation of the elements of a
 * given row in a Table object.
 *
 * Receive: row, a row index and aTable, a Table object
 * Return:  the standard deviation of the elements in the row-th row
 *          of aTable
 ******************************************************************/
#include <assert.h>
#include <math.h>
double RowStdDeviation(unsigned row, const Table & aTable)
{
   assert(row < aTable.size());

   double mean = RowAverage(row, aTable),
          sum = 0.0;
   int numValues = aTable[row].size();

   for (int j = 0; j < numValues; j++)
      sum += pow(aTable[row][j] - mean, 2);

   return sqrt(sum / numValues);
}
```

6
```
/* ColumnAverage averages the elements of a given column in a Table object.
 *
 * Receive: col, a column index and aTable, a Table object
 * Return:  the average of the elements in the col-th column of aTable
 ******************************************************************/
double ColumnAverage(unsigned col, const Table & aTable)
{
   assert(col < aTable[0].size());

   return ColumnSum(col, aTable) / aTable.size();
}
```

7.
```
/* ColumnStdDeviation finds the standard deviation of the elements of a
 * given column in a Table object.
 *
 * Receive: row, a row index and aTable, a Table object
 * Receive: col, a column index and aTable, a Table object
 * Return:  the standard deviation of the elements in the col-th
 *          column of aTable
 ******************************************************************/
#include <assert.h>
#include <math.h>
```

```
double ColumnStdDeviation(unsigned col, const Table & aTable)
{
    assert(col < aTable[0].size());

    double mean = ColumnAverage(col, aTable),
           sum = 0.0;
    int numValues = aTable.size();

    for (int i = 0; i < numValues; i++)
       sum += pow(aTable[i][col] - mean, 2);

    return sqrt(sum / numValues);
}
```

Exercises 12.4

1.
```
Matrix::Matrix(OneDimVector aVector, int oneRow)
{
  myRows = 1;
  myColumns = aVector.size();
  (*this)[0] = aVector;
}
```

2.
```
Matrix::Matrix(int oneCol, OneDimVector aVector)
{
  myRows = aVector.size();
  myColumns = 1;

  for (int i = 0; i < myRows; i++)
     (*this)[i][0] = aVector[i];
}
```

3.
```
#include <assert.h>
Matrix Matrix::operator+(const Matrix & mat2)
{
  assert(myRows == mat2.Rows() &&
         myColumns == mat2.Columns());          // check dimensions

  Matrix mat3 (myRows, myColumns);              // build result Matrix

  for (int i = 0; i < myRows; i++)              // for each of my rows:
    for (int j = 0; j < mat2.Columns(); j++)    //   for each col in mat2:
       mat3[i][j] = (*this)[i][j] + mat2[i][j]; //   put sum in result Matrix

  return mat3;                                  // return result matrix
}
```

4.
```
#include <assert.h>
Matrix Matrix::operator-(const Matrix & mat2)
{
  assert(myRows == mat2.Rows() &&
         myColumns == mat2.Columns());          // check dimensions

  Matrix mat3 (myRows, myColumns);              // build result Matrix
```

```
  for (int i = 0; i < myRows; i++)              // for each of my rows:
    for (int j = 0; j < mat2.Columns(); j++)    // for each col in mat2:
      mat3[i][j] = (*this)[i][j] - mat2[i][j];// put diff. in result Matrix

  return mat3;                                  // return result matrix
}
```

5.
```
Matrix Matrix::Transpose()
{
  Matrix trans(myColumns, myRows);        // build result Matrix

  for (int i = 0; i < myColumns; i++)        // for each of my rows:
    for (int j = 0; j < myRows; j++) //  for each col in mat2:
      trans[i][j] = (*this)[j][i];      //   put value in trans

  return trans;                              // return transpose matrix
}
```

Programming Problems
Section 12.1 - 12.3

1.
```
/* prog12-1.cpp calculates and displays a specified number of rows
 * of Pascal's triangle.
 *
 * Input:  number of rows
 * Output: rows of Pascal's triangle
 ********************************************************************/

#include <iostream.h>            // cin, cout, >>, <<
#include <iomanip.h>             // setw()

int main()
{
  int Pascal[10][10],
      row,
      col;

  // fill Pascal's Triangle

  Pascal[0][0] = 1;

  for (row = 1; row < 10; row++)
  {
    for (col = 0; col <= row; col++)
    {
      Pascal[row][col] = ( (col > 0)   ? Pascal[row-1][col-1] : 0) +
                         ( (col < row) ? Pascal[row-1][col]   : 0);
    }
  }
```

```
  // display Pascal's Triangle

  for (row = 0; row < 10; row++)
  {
    for (col = 0; col < 9-row; col++)
      cout << "   ";

    for (col = 0; col <= row; col++)
    {
      cout << setw(5) << Pascal[row][col] << ' ';
    }

    cout << endl;
  }

  return 0;
}
```

2.
```
/* prog12-2.cpp finds populatons of varous regions based on
 * given population shifts.
 *
 * Input:  number of regions, migration percentages, and # of years
 * Output: population of each region
 **************************************************************/

#include <iostream.h>          // cin, cout, >>, <<
#include <iomanip.h>           // setprecison(), setiosflags(), setw()

enum RegionType { URBAN, SUBURBAN, EXURBAN, NUMBER_REGIONS };

ostream& operator<<(ostream& out, RegionType region);
RegionType Next(RegionType region);

int main()
{
  const int WIDTH = 10;

  double migration[NUMBER_REGIONS][NUMBER_REGIONS],
         before[NUMBER_REGIONS],
         after[NUMBER_REGIONS];

  RegionType region,
             from,
             to;

  cout << setprecision(1)
       << setiosflags(ios::showpoint | ios::fixed);

  cout << endl;
  for (from = URBAN; from != NUMBER_REGIONS; from = Next(from))
  {
    for (to = URBAN; to != NUMBER_REGIONS; to = Next(to))
    {
      cout << "Annual migration percentage from " << from
           << " to " << to << ": ";
      cin >> migration[from][to];
    }
  }
```

```
    cout << endl;
    for (region = URBAN; region != NUMBER_REGIONS; region = Next(region))
    {
      cout << "Current population in " << region << " (in millions): ";
      cin >> before[region];
    }

    cout << endl << setw(WIDTH) << "";
    for (region = URBAN; region != NUMBER_REGIONS; region = Next(region))
      cout << setw(WIDTH) << region;
    cout << endl;

    for (int i = 0; i <= 50; i++)
    {
      for (region = URBAN; region != NUMBER_REGIONS; region = Next(region))
        after[region] = before[region];

      for (from = URBAN; from != NUMBER_REGIONS; from = Next(from))
        for (to = URBAN; to != NUMBER_REGIONS; to = Next(to))
          after[to] += before[from] * (migration[from][to] / 100.0);

      if (i % 10 == 0)
      {
        cout << setw(WIDTH - 7) << i << " years ";
        for (region = URBAN; region != NUMBER_REGIONS; region = Next(region))
          cout << setw(WIDTH) << after[region];
        cout << endl;
      }

      for (region = URBAN; region != NUMBER_REGIONS; region = Next(region))
        before[region] = after[region];
    }

    return 0;
}

ostream& operator<<(ostream& out, RegionType region)
{
    switch (region)
    {
      case URBAN:     out << "Urban";    break;
      case SUBURBAN:  out << "Suburban"; break;
      case EXURBAN:   out << "Exurban";  break;
    }

    return out;
}

RegionType Next(RegionType region)
{
    switch (region)
    {
      case URBAN:     return SUBURBAN;
      case SUBURBAN:  return EXURBAN;
      case EXURBAN:   return NUMBER_REGIONS;
      default:        return NUMBER_REGIONS;
    }
}
```

3.

```cpp
/* prog12-3.cpp solves the G.H. Hardy taxicab problem.
 *
 * Output: least positive integer that can be written as the sum of
 *         two cubes in two different ways
 **********************************************************************/

#include <iostream.h>          // cout, <<
#include <iomanip.h>           // setw()

int main()
{
  const int MAX_XY = 15;

  int table[MAX_XY][MAX_XY];

  table[0][0] = 1;
  cout << setw(5) << table[0][0] << endl;

  for (int row = 1, done = 0; row < MAX_XY && !done; row++)
  {
    // compute values for this row and display
    for (int col = 0; col <= row; col++)
    {
      table[row][col] = (row+1) * (row+1) * (row+1) +
                        (col+1) * (col+1) * (col+1);
      cout << setw(5) << table[row][col];
    }
    cout << endl;

    // search for duplicates
    bool done = false;
    for (int col = 0; col <= row && !done; col++)
    {
      for (int y = 0; y < row && !done; y++)
      {
        for (int x = 0; x <= y && !done; x++)
        {
          if (table[row][col] == table[y][x])
          {
            cout << endl
                 << (row+1) << "^3 * " << (col+1) << "^3 == "
                 << (y+1) << "^3 * " << (x+1) << "^3 == "
                 << table[row][col] << "\n\n";
            done = 1;
          }
        }
      }
    }
  }

  return 0;
}
```

4.
```
/* prog12-4.cpp reads a table of scores from a file and calculates
 * the overall percentage for each student and the average for
 * each student.
 *
 * Input (keyboard): name of file
 * Input (inFile):   number of students and number of scores in first
 *                   line of file; scores for each student
 * Output (screen):  overall percentage for each student and the
 *                   average for each student
 *******************************************************************/

#include <iostream.h>        // cin, cout, >>, <<
#include <iomanip.h>         // setprecison(), setiosflags(), setw()
#include <string>            // string
#include "Table.h"

double RowAverage(unsigned row, const Table & aTable);
double ColumnAverage(unsigned col, const Table & aTable);

int main()
{
   string fileName;
   cout << "Enter name of file: ";
   getline(cin, fileName);

   Table scoresTable;
   Fill(fileName, scoresTable);

   cout << setprecision(1) << setiosflags(ios::fixed | ios::showpoint);
   for (int row = 0; row < scoresTable.size(); row++)
      cout << "\nOverall percentage for student " << row << ": "
           << RowAverage(row, scoresTable);

   cout << "\n\n";
   int numScores = scoresTable[0].size();
   for (int col = 0; col < numScores; col++)
      cout << "Average on test #" << col << ": "
           << ColumnAverage(col, scoresTable) << endl;
}

/* Insert functions RowSum, ColumnSum, RowAverage and
   ColumnAverage from Exercises 2-4 & 6 of Section 12.3 here.
```

5.
```
/* prog12-5.cpp reads a table of noise levels from a file, displays
 * the table, and calculates the average noice level for each
 * car model, the average noice level for each speed, and the
 * overall average noise level.
 *
 * Input (keyboard): name of file
 * Input (inFile):   number of care models and number of speeds in
 *                   first line of file; noise levels for each model
 * Output (screen):  average noise level for each car model and the
 *                   average for each speed and overall average
 *******************************************************************/

#include <iostream.h>        // cin, cout, >>, <<
#include <iomanip.h>         // setprecison(), setiosflags(), setw()
#include <string>            // string
#include "Table.h"
```

```
void DisplayReport(ostream& out, Table noiseTable);
double RowSum(unsigned row, const Table & aTable);
double RowAverage(unsigned row, const Table & aTable);
double ColumnSum(unsigned col, const Table & aTable);
double ColumnAverage(unsigned col, const Table & aTable);

int main()
{
    cout << "This program generates a noise level report, given"
            "\na file of noise levels organized as a table, whose"
            "\nrows are the auto models and whose columns are speeds.\n";

    string fileName;
    cout << "\nEnter name of file: ";
    getline(cin, fileName);

    Table noiseTable;
    Fill(fileName, noiseTable);

    DisplayReport(cout, noiseTable);

    cout << setprecision(1) << setiosflags(ios::fixed | ios::showpoint);
    for (int row = 0; row <noiseTable.size(); row++)
        cout << "\nOverall percentage for car model " << row << ": "
            << RowAverage(row, noiseTable);

    cout << "\n\n";
    int numSpeeds = noiseTable[0].size();
    for (int col = 0; col < numSpeeds; col++)
        cout << "Average on test #" << col << ": "
            << ColumnAverage(col, noiseTable) << endl;
}

/* Insert functions RowSum, ColumnSum, RowAverage and
   ColumnAverage from Exercises 2-4 & 6 of Section 12.3 here.

/* DisplayReport displays a table of noise levels.
 *
 * Receive:  an ostream
 * Output:   table of noise levels
 ************************************************************/

void DisplayReport(ostream& out, Table noiseTable)
{
    const int WIDTH = 5;

    out << setprecision(0);

    out << "\n                      Speed (mi/hr)"
        << "\n  Car :    20   30   40   50   60   70   80"
        << "\n----------------------------------------------------\n";

    for (int row = 0; row < noiseTable.size(); row++)
    {
        out << setw(WIDTH) << (row + 1) << " : ";

        for (int col = 0; col < noiseTable[0].size(); col++)
            out << setw(WIDTH) << noiseTable[row][col];

        cout << endl;
    }
}
```

6.
```
/* prog12-6.cpp provides a monthly sales report, given a sales table.
 *
 * Input (keyboard): name of file containing sales table
 * Input (file):     the dimensions and entries of the sales table
 * Output (screen):  User prompts and a monthly sales report
 ********************************************************************/


#include <iostream.h>          // cin, cout, >>, <<
#include <iomanip.h>           // setprecison(), setiosflags(), setw()
#include <string>              // string
#include "Table.h"

double RowSum(unsigned row, const Table & aTable);
double ColumnSum(unsigned col, const Table & aTable);
void DisplaySalesReport(const Table& salesTab);

int main()
{
   cout << "\nThis program generates a monthly sales report,\n"
        << "given a file of the month's sales figures,\n"
        << "organized as a table whose rows are the auto models\n"
        << "and whose columns are the salespersons.\n";

   string fileName;
   cout << "\nEnter name of file: ";
   getline(cin, fileName);

   Table salesTable;

   Fill(fileName, salesTable);
   DisplaySalesReport(salesTable);

   return 0;
}

/* Insert functions RowSum and ColumnSum from
   Exercises 2 & 3 of Section 12.3 here.

/* DisplaySalesReport displays a salestable as a summary report.
 *
 * Receive:         a Table named salesTable
 * Output (screen): salesTable, in easy-to-read format,
 *                  with column and row headings, and
 *                  with column and row summaries
 ********************************************************************/

void DisplaySalesReport(const Table & salesTable)
{
   const int WIDTH = 5;

   cout << "\n                          Salesperson\n";
   cout << " Models :    1    2    3    4    5    6    "
        << "7    8   : Totals\n";
   cout << "-------------------------------------------"
        << "---------------\n";

   cout << setprecision(0) << setiosflags(ios::showpoint | ios:fixed);
```

```
   for (int row = 0; row < salesTable.size(); row++):
   {
      cout << setw(Width) << row + 1 << "    : ";


      for (int col = 0; col < salesTable[0].size(); col++)
         cout << setw(WIDTH) << salesTable[row][col];
       cout << "    :" << setw(WIDTH)
            << RowSum(row, salesTable) << endl;
   }

   cout << "----------------------------------------"
        << "----------------------\n";
   cout << " Totals : ";

   for (int col = 0; col < salesTable[0].size(); col++)
      cout << setw(Width) << ColumnSum(col, salesTable);

   cout << "\n\n";
}
```

Listing of sample `file12-6.dat`:

```
10 8
0   0   2   0   5   6   3   0
5   1   9   0   0   2   3   2
0   0   0   1   0   0   0   0
1   1   1   0   2   2   2   1
5   3   2   0   0   2   5   5
2   2   1   0   1   1   0   0
3   2   5   0   1   2   0   4
3   0   7   1   3   5   2   4
0   2   6   1   0   5   2   1
4   0   2   0   3   2   1   0
```

```
7.
/* prog12-7.cpp provides a list of dollar sales by salespersons.
 *
 * Input (keyboard): name of file containing sales table
 *                   list of prices of automobile models
 * Input (file):     the dimensions and entries of the sales table
 * Output (screen):  user prompts and total dollar sales for
 *                   each salesperson.
 **********************************************************************/

#include <iostream.h>          // cin, cout, >>, <<
#include <iomanip.h>           // setprecison(), setiosflags()
#include <string>              // string
#include <vector>              // vector<T>
#include "Table.h"

int main()
{
   string fileName;
   cout << "\nEnter name of file containing sales table: ";
   getline(cin, fileName);

   Table salesTable;

   Fill(fileName, salesTable);

   vector<double> price(salesTable.size());
   cout << "Enter the price of\n";
```

```
      for (int model = 0; model < price.size(); model++)
      {
         cout << "model #" << model + 1 << ": ";
         cin >> price[model];
      }

      cout << "\nTotal dollar sales for salesperson\n";
      cout << setprecision(0) << setiosflags(ios::showpoint | ios::fixed);
      for (int emp = 0; emp < salesTable[0].size(); emp++)
      {
         double total = 0;
         for (int model = 0; model < salesTable.size(); model++)
            total += price[model] * salesTable[model][emp];
         cout << emp + 1 << ": $" << total << endl;
      }

      return 0;
   }


8.
/* prog12-8.cpp provides a total sales, commmission, and income for
 * salespersons.
 *
 * Input (keyboard): name of file containing sales table
 *                   list of prices of items
 * Input (file):     the dimensions and entries of the sales table
 * Output (screen):  user prompts and total total sales, commmission,
 *                   and income for each salesperson.
 ****************************************************************************/

#include <iostream.h>          // cin, cout, >>, <<
#include <iomanip.h>           // setprecison(), setiosflags()
#include <string>              // string
#include <vector>              // vector<T>
#include "Table.h"

int main()
{
   const double COMMISSION_RATE = 0.10,
                SALARY = 200.00;

   string fileName;
   cout << "\nEnter name of file containing sales table: ";
   getline(cin, fileName);

   Table salesTable;

   Fill(fileName, salesTable);

   vector<double> price(salesTable.size());
   cout << "Enter the price of\n";
   for (int item = 0; item < price.size(); item++)
   {
      cout << "item #" << item + 1 << ": ";
      cin >> price[item ];
   }

   double totalSales,
          commision;
```

```
   cout << "\nSalesperson Total Sales  Commission  Income"
           "\n=========================================="\n;
   cout << setprecision(0) << setiosflags(ios::showpoint | ios::fixed);
   for (int emp = 0; emp < salesTable[0].size(); emp++)
   {
      double totalSales = 0;
      for (int item = 0; item < salesTable.size(); item++)
         totalSales += price[item] * salesTable[emp][item];
      commission = COMMISION_RATE * totalSales;

      cout << setw(6) << emp + 1 << setw(14) << totalSales
           << setw(13) << commission
           << setw(10) << SALARY + commision << endl;
   }

   return 0;
}
```

9.
```
/* prog12-9.cpp process data collected by several engineering sections in
 * an experiment to determine the tensile strength of two  different
 * alloys.
 *
 * Input:  number of alloys, number of sectoins, section numbers,
 *         tensile strength
 * Output: user prompts average tensile strengths for each alloy, number
 *         in a given section who recorded strength measures of a certain
 *         value or higher, and average of strengths recorded for alloy 2
 *         by students who recorded a strength lower than 3 for alloy 1.
 **********************************************************************/

#include <iostream.h>          // cin, cout, >>, <<
#include <vector>

typedef vector<double> Readings;
typedef vector<Readings> RowVector;
typedef vector<RowVector> Measurements;

double Average(Readings x);

int main()
{
   const double LOW_MEASURE = 3.0,
                HIGH_MEASURE = 5.00;

   int numAlloys,
       numSections;

   cout << "Enter the number of alloys and the number of sections: ";
   cin >> numAlloys >> numSections;

   Measurements measure(numSections, RowVector(numAlloys));

   cout << "Enter section number (0 to stop)  and then the tensile\n"
     "strengths for the " << numAlloys << " alloys.\n";

   int sectionNumber;
   double tensileStrength;
```

```
for (;;)
{
   cout << "->";
   cin >> sectionNumber;
   if (sectionNumber == 0) break;

   for (int i = 0; i < numAlloys; i++)
   {
      cin >> tensileStrength;
      measure[sectionNumber-1][i].push_back(tensileStrength);
   }
}

// Find average tensile strengths for each alloy and for each section
for (int sect = 0; sect < numSections; sect++)
{
   cout << "For section " << sect+1
        << " average tensile strength for:\n";
   for (int alloy =  0; alloy < numAlloys; alloy++)
      cout << "\tAlloy " << alloy+1 << ": "
           << Average(measure[sect][alloy]) << endl;
}

// Count measurements in a section >= to HIGH_MEASURE
int numHigh = 0;
cout << "\nEnter number of section for which to count measurements >= "
     << HIGH_MEASURE << ": ";
cin >> sectionNumber;
for (int alloy = 0; alloy < numAlloys; alloy++)
{
   int count = 0;
   for (int i = 0; i < measure[sectionNumber-1][alloy].size(); i++)
      if (measure[sectionNumber-1][alloy][i] >= HIGH_MEASURE)
         count++;
   cout << "For alloy " << alloy+1 << ": " << count << " high readings\n";
   numHigh += count;
}
cout << "A total of " << numHigh << " high readings\n";

// Count and average measurements for alloy 2 by those who recorded
// a reading lower than LOW_MEASURE for alloy 1
double lowSum = 0;
int lowCount = 0;
for (int sect = 0; sect < numSections; sect++)
{
  for (int i = 0; i < measure[sect][0].size(); i++)
     if (measure[sect][0][i] < LOW_MEASURE)
     {
        lowCount++;
        lowSum += measure[sect][1][i];
     }
}
```

10.
MagicSquare.h
```
/* MagicSquare.h contaisn the interface for class MagicSquare.
 *
 ****************************************************************/

#include <vector>              // vector<T>

typedef vector<int> IntRow;
typedef vector<IntRow> IntTable;

class MagicSquare
{
 public:
   MagicSquare(unsigned size);
   friend ostream & operator<< (ostream & out, const MagicSquare & t);
 private:
   unsigned mySize;
   IntTable myGrid;
};

// Documentation
/* The constructor constructs a magic square of odd size.
 *
 * Receive:        size of square, an integer
 * Precondition:   size of square is odd positive integer
 * Postcondition:  myGrid stores a magic square of this size
 ****************************************************************/

/* The output operator displays a magic square.
 *
 * Receive: output stream out and a magic square
 * Output:  the magic square to out
 * Return:  out with elements of magic square inserted
 ****************************************************************/
```

MagicSquare.cpp
```
/* MagicSquare.cppimplements the operations for class MagicSquare.
 *
 ****************************************************************/

#include <stdlib.h>

//------ Constructor -----
MagicSquare::MagicSquare(unsigned n
{
   if (squareSize % 2 == 0)
   {
     cerr << "Size of magic square must be odd.\n";
     exit(1);
    }


   myGrid.reserve(n);
   int row,
       col;

   for (row = 0; row < n; row++)
      for (col = 0; col < n; col++)
         myGrid[row][col] = 0;

   row = 0;
   col = n / 2;
```

```
   for (int k = 1; k <= n * n; k++)
   {
      myGrid[row][col] = k;

      row--;
      col++;

      if (row < 0 && col >= n)
      {
         row += 2;
         col--;
      }

      if (row < 0)
         row = n - 1;

      if (col >= n)
         col = 0;

      if (myGrid[row][col] != 0)
      {
         row += 2;
         col--;
      }
   }
}

//------ Output operator -----

ostream & operator<<(ostream & out, IntTable t)
{
   const int WIDTH = 4;
   for (int i = 0; i < t.size(); i++)
   {
      for(int j = 0; j < t.size(); j++)
         out << setw(WIDTH) << t.myGrid[i][j];
      out << endl << endl;
   }
   return out;
}


/* prog12-10.cpp constructs magic squares of odd size.
 *
 * Input:  size of square (odd #)
 * Output: magic square
 ************************************************************/

#include <iostream.h>          // cin, cout, >>, <<
#include "MagicSquare.h"

typedef vector<int> IntRow;
typedef vector<IntRow> IntTable;

void MakeMagic(IntTable & square);
ostream & operator<< (ostream & out, IntTable t);
```

```
int main()
{
   unsigned sizeOfSquare;

   cout << "\nEnter size of magic square (odd number): ";
   cin >> sizeOfSquare;

   MagicSquare square(sizeOfSquare);

   cout << "constructed\n";

   cout << "\nMagic square is:\n\n" << square << endl;

   return 0;
}
```

11.
BlobGrid.h
```
/* BlobGrid.h contaisn the interface for class BlobGrid.
 *
 ********************************************************/


#include <iostream.h>          // istream, ostream
#include <vector>              // vector<T>

typedef vector<char> CharRow;
typedef vector<CharRow> CharTable;

class BlobGrid
{
 public:
   BlobGrid(unsigned rows, unsigned columns);
   friend istream & operator>>(istream & in, BlobGrid & b);
   friend ostream & operator<<(ostream & out, const BlobGrid & b);
   unsigned EatAllBlobs();
   void EatOneBlob(unsigned row, unsigned col);

 private:
   unsigned myRows,
            myColumns;
   CharTable myGrid;
};

// Documentation
/* The constructor constructs an empty BlobGrid with specified rows
 * and columns.
 *
 * Receive:        number of rows and columns (integers)
 * Postcondition:  myGrid is a CharArray of this size
 ****************************************************************/

/* The input operator displays a BlobGrid.
 *
 * Receive: input stream in and a BlobGrid
 * Input:   in BlobGrid from in
 * Return:  out with BlobGrid removed
 ************************************************************/

/* The output operator displays a BlobGrid.
 *
 * Receive: output stream out and a BlobGrid
 * Output:  the BlobGrid to out
 * Return:  out with a BlobGric inserted
 ************************************************************/
```

```
/* EatAllBlobs removes all blobs and returns the number removed.
 *
 * Postcondition: all blobs have been removed
 * Returns:        number of blobs found
 ******************************************************************/

/* EatOneBlob is a recursive function used internally by EatBlobs().
 *
 * Receive:         a row and column number
 * Postcondition: the blob at this position has been removed
 ******************************************************************/
```

BlobGrid.cpp
```
//BlobGrid.cpp
/* BlobGrid.cpp implements the operations for class BlobGrid.
 *
 ******************************************************************/

#include "BlobGrid.h"

//------ Constructor --------

BlobGrid::BlobGrid(unsigned rows, unsigned columns)
{
  CharTable temp(rows, CharRow(columns, '.'));
  myRows = rows;
  myColumns = columns;
  myGrid = temp;
}

//------ Input operator -----

istream & operator>>(istream & in, BlobGrid & b)
{
   char ch;

   for (int row = 0; row < b.myRows; row++)
      for (int col = 0; col < b.myColumns; col++)
         in >> b.myGrid[row][col];

   return in;
}

//------ Output operator -----

ostream& operator<<(ostream& out, const BlobGrid & b)
{
   for (int row = 0; row < b.myRows; row++)
   {
      for (int col = 0; col < b.myColumns; col++)
         out << b.myGrid[row][col] << ' ';

      out << endl;
   }

   return out;
}
```

```cpp
unsigned BlobGrid::EatAllBlobs()
{
    unsigned number = 0;

    for (int row = 0; row < myRows; row++)
    {
        for (int col = 0; col < myColumns; col++)
        {
            if (myGrid[row][col] == '*')
            {
                EatOneBlob(row, col);
                number++;
            }
        }
    }

    return number;
}

void BlobGrid::EatOneBlob(unsigned row, unsigned col)
{
    if ( (row >= myRows) || (col >= myColumns) )
        return;

    if (myGrid[row][col] != '*')
        return;

    myGrid[row][col] = '.';

    EatOneBlob(row-1, col);
    EatOneBlob(row+1, col);
    EatOneBlob(row, col-1);
    EatOneBlob(row, col+1);
}

/* prog12-11.cpp finds "blobs" in a BlobGrid.
 *
 * Input:  size of grid and locations of *'s
 * Output: number of blobs in the grid
 **********************************************/

#include <iostream.h>          // cin, cout, >>, <<
#include "BlobGrid.h"

int main()
{
    unsigned numRows, numColumns;

    cout << "Enter number of rows and number of columsn in grid: ";
    cin >> numRows >> numColumns;

    BlobGrid blobs(numRows, numColumns);

    cout << "\nEnter " << numRows << " x " << numColumns
         << " grid of *'s and .'s:\n";
    cin >> blobs;

    cout << "\nYou entered:\n" << blobs << endl;

    cout << "\nThere are " << blobs.EatAllBlobs()
         << " blobs in there...\n";

    return 0;
}
```

12.

Life.h:

```
/* Life.h contains the interface for the class Life.
 *
 ************************************************************/

#ifndef LIFE
#define LIFE

#include <iostream.h>
#include <vector>

typedef vector<char> CharRow;
typedef vector<CharRow> CharTable;

class Life
{

public:

  // constructor - specify height and width of Life board
  Life(unsigned height = 0, unsigned width = 0);

  // Set - place organism at specified location
  void Set(int row, int col);

  // Clear - remove organism from specified locatino
  void Clear(int row, int col);

  // Display - output board to stream
  void Display(ostream & out) const;

  // Generate - advance board one generation
  void Generate();

private:


  CharTable myBoard;
  int myHeight,
      myWidth;
  bool IsSet(int row, int col) const;

};

#endif
```

Life.cpp:

```
/* Life.cpp contains the implementation for the class Life.
 *
 ************************************************************/

#include "Life.h"
#include "assert.h"

Life::Life(unsigned height, unsigned width)
{
  CharTable temp(height, CharRow(width, '.'));

  myHeight = height;
  myWidth = width;
  myBoard = temp;
}
```

```
void Life::Set(int row, int col)
{
  if (row >= 0 && row < myHeight &&
      col >= 0 && col < myWidth)
    myBoard[row][col] = '0';
}

void Life::Clear(int row, int col)
{
  if (row >= 0 && row < myHeight &&
      col >= 0 && col < myWidth)
    myBoard[row][col] = '.';
}

void Life::Display(ostream& out) const
{
  int row, col;

  out << '+';
  for (col = 0; col < myWidth; col++)
    out << '-';
  out << '+' << endl;

  for (row = 0; row < myHeight; row++)
  {
    out << '|';
    for (col = 0; col < myWidth; col++)
      out << myBoard[row][col];
    out << '|' << endl;
  }

  out << '+';
  for (col = 0; col < myWidth; col++)
    out << '-';
  out << '+' << endl;
}

bool Life::IsSet(int row, int col) const
{
  if (row >= 0 && row < myHeight &&
      col >= 0 && col < myWidth)
    return myBoard[row][col] == '0';
  else
    return false;
}

void Life::Generate()
{
  int row, col,
      neighbors;

  CharTable newBoard(myHeight, CharRow(myWidth, '.') );

  for (row = 0; row < myHeight; row++)
  {
    for (col = 0; col < myWidth; col++)
    {
      neighbors = IsSet(row-1,col-1) +
                  IsSet(row,col-1) +
                  IsSet(row+1,col-1) +
                  IsSet(row+1,col) +
                  IsSet(row+1,col+1) +
                  IsSet(row,col+1) +
```

```
                          IsSet(row-1,col+1) +
                          IsSet(row-1,col);

       if (myBoard[row][col] == '0')
       {
         if (neighbors == 2 || neighbors == 3)
           newBoard[row][col] = '0';
       }
       else  // empty cell
         if (neighbors == 3)
           newBoard[row][col] = '0';
    }
  }

  for (int i = 0; i < myHeight; i++)
    for (int j = 0; j < myWidth; j++)
      myBoard[i][j] = newBoard[i][j];
}

/* prog12-12.cpp plays the game of Life.
 *
 * Input:  commands
 * Output: menu of commands, Life configurations
 ********************************************************/
#include <iostream.h>
#include <ctype.h>
#include "Life.h"


int main()
{
  const char HELP_TEXT[] =
                "\nCommands:\n"
                "  s <row> <col> - set organism at given coordinates\n"
                "  c <row> <col> - clear organism at given coordinates\n"
                "  g <num> - display given number of generations\n"
                "  n - display one generation\n"
                "  d - display board again\n"
                "  q - quit program\n";

  int row, col;

  cout << "This program plays the game of Life by John H. Conway.\n";

  cout << "Height and width of grid? ";
  int h, w;
  cin >> h >> w;
  Life board(h, w);

  for (;;)
  {
    char command;
    cout << "Command (h=help): ";
    cin >> command;
    if (isupper(command))
      command = tolower(command);

    if (command == 'q')  break;

    switch (command)
    {
      case 'h':  cout << HELP_TEXT << endl;
                 break;
```

```
        case 's':  cin >> row >> col;
                   board.Set(row, col);
                   board.Display(cout);
                   break;

        case 'c':  cin >> row >> col;
                   board.Clear(row, col);
                   board.Display(cout);
                   break;

        case 'g':  cin >> col;
                   for (int i = 0; i < col; i++)
                   {
                      board.Generate();
                      board.Display(cout);
                   }
                   break;

        case 'n':  board.Generate();
                   board.Display(cout);
                   break;

        case 'd':  board.Display(cout);
                   break;

      }
   }

   return 0;
}
```

13. **This is a challenging project.**

14. **This project is fairly straightforward once you decide what strategies the computer will use in playing.**

Section 12.4

15-19.
```
/* prog12-15-19.cpp tests the Matrix operations in Exercises 1-5.
 *
 * Input:  vectors and matrices
 * Output: matrices
 *******************************************************************/

#include <iostream.h>                 // cin, cout, >>, <<
#include "Matrix.h"

int main()
{
   OneDimVector x(3);
   x[0] = 0; x[1] = 1; x[2] = 2;

   // Test constructor in Exercise 1.
   Matrix m1(x, 0);
   cout << "Matrix constructed by Exer-1 constructor is m1 =\n";
   cout << m1 << endl;
```

```cpp
   // Test constructor in Exercise 2.
   Matrix m2(0, x);
   cout << "\nMatrix constructed by Exer-2 constructor is m2 =\n";
   cout << m2 << endl;

   // Test operations in Exercise 3 = 5.
   Matrix a(2,3), b(2,3);
   cout << "Enter 2 x 3 matrix a:\n";
   cin >> a;
   cout << "Enter 2 x 3 matrix b:\n";
   cin >> b;

   cout << "\na + b =\n"
        << a + b << endl;

   cout << "\na - b =\n"
        << a - b << endl;

   cout << "\nTranspose of a is:\n"
        << a.Transpose() << endl;
}
```

20.
(a)
```cpp
/* prog12-20a.cpp calculates the cost of manufacturing electronic
 * devices.
 *
 * Input:  matrix whose i,j entry is for the i-th device, the
 *         number of component j needed; price per component
 * Output: total cost of each device
 ********************************************************************/

#include <iostream.h>

#include "Matrix.h"    // the 2nd version -- derived from vector<double>

int main()
{
   int numDevices,
       numComponents;

   cout << "Enter number of devices and number of different components: ";
   cin >> numDevices >> numComponents;

   Matrix compsNeeded(numDevices, numComponents);

   cout << "Enter the device-component matrix in which the i-th row consists\n"
           "of the number of each component needed for the i-th device:\n";
   cin >> compsNeeded;

   Matrix price(numComponents, 1);
   cout << "Enter the prices of the components:\n";
   cin >> price;

   cout << "\n- Number of Components (Device # by Component #) -\n";
   cout << compsNeeded;

   cout << "\n- Price (by Component #) -\n";
   cout << price;

   Matrix product(numDevices, 1);
   product.Copy(compsNeeded * price);
```

```
    cout << "\n- Total Cost (by Device #) -\n";
    cout <<product << endl;

  return 0;
}
```

Here, `Copy()` is the following member function added to the class `Matrix`:

```
// Copy operation
void Matrix::Copy(const Matrix & mat2)
{
  myRows = mat2.Rows();
  myColumns = mat2.Columns();

  for (int i = 0; i < myRows; i++)
    for (int j = 0; j < myColumns; j++)
      (*this)[i][j] = mat2[i][j];
}
```

(b) Simply add statements to multiply each element of `product` by 0.1, and use the + operation to add
     this matrix to `product`.

21. This problem is similar to the previous problem. The main work is reading the values from the keyboard and
     constructing the desired matrices with those values. Multiplying the matrices is simply a matter of using the *
     operator.

22.
```
/* prog12-22.cpp reads a transition matrix and calculates an
 * arbitrary power of that matrix.
 *
 * Input (keyboard): name of file containing matrix
 *                   the integral power n
 * Input (files):    a matrix, with number of rows and columns
 *                       listed first
 * Output (screen):  the matrix and the matrix to the nth power
 ******************************************************************/

#include <iostream.h>

#include "Matrix.h"    // the 2nd version -- derived from vector<double>

int main()
{
  cout << "This program reads a transition matrix and\n"
       << "calculates an arbitrary power of that matrix.\n";

  int matSize;

  cout << "\nEnter the size of the matrix: ";
  cin >> matSize;

  Matrix matrix1(matSize, matSize);
  cout << "\nEnter the matrix row by row: ";
  cin >> matrix1;

  cout << "\n- matrix1 -------------------------------------\n";
  cout << matrix1 << endl;

  int n;
  cout << "\nEnter n (>0) to calculate matrix1 to the nth power: ";
  cin >> n;
```

```
.

    Matrix matrix2(matSize, matSize);
    matrix2.Copy(matrix1);

    for (int i = 2; i <= n; i++)
      matrix2.Copy(matrix2 * matrix1);

    cout << "\n- matrix1 ^ " << n << " -------------------------\n";
    cout << matrix2 << endl;

    return 0;
}
```

23. **This exercise is similar to the previous exercise, as the main work is done by calculating a power of a matrix.**

24.
```
/* prog12-24.cpp calculates the manufacturing costs.
 *
 * Input:  matrix whose i,j entry is for the i-th product,
 *           the number of hours needed in Department j;
 *           cost per hour of operation in each department
 * Output: total cost of each product
 ***************************************************************/

#include <iostream.h>

#include "Matrix.h"    // the 2nd version -- derived from vector<double>

int main()
{
    int numProducts,
        numDepartments;

    cout << "Enter number of products and number of departments: ";
    cin >> numProducts >> numDepartments;

    Matrix hoursNeeded(numProducts, numDepartments);

    cout << "Enter the product-department matrix in which the i-th row consists\n"
            "of the number of hours in each department needed for the i-th product:\n";
    cin >> hoursNeeded;

    Matrix hourlyCost(numDepartments, 1);
    cout << "Enter the hourly costs for the departments:\n";
    cin >> hourlyCost;

    cout << "\n- Number of Hours (Product # by Department #) -\n";
    cout << hoursNeeded;

    cout << "\n- Hourly cost (by Department #) -\n";
    cout << hourlyCost;

    Matrix totalCost(numProducts, 1);
    totalCost.Copy(hoursNeeded * hourlyCost);
    cout << "\n- Total Cost (by Product #) -\n";
    cout << totalCost << endl;

    return 0;
}
```

25.

```cpp
/* prog12-25.cpp finds the inverse of a matrix.
 *
 * Input:  size (n) of the matrix A and the matrix
 * Output: inverse of A or a message that matrix is (nearly) singular
 ********************************************************************/

#include <iostream.h>
#include <stdlib.h>          // exit()

#include "Matrix.h"          // the 2nd version -- derived from vector<double>

void GaussElim(Matrix A, Matrix & soln);

int main()
{
   int n;                    // size of matrix

   cout << "Enter size of matrix: ";
   cin >> n;

   Matrix A(n, n),           // the matrix
          A_Inverse(n, n);   // its inverse

   cout << "Enter coefficient matrix rowwise:\n";
   cin >> A;

   for (int k = 0; k < n; k ++)
   {
      Matrix augmentedMatrix(n, n+1);
      for (int i = 0; i < n; i++)
      {
         for (int j = 0; j < n; j++)
            augmentedMatrix[i][j] = A[i][j];
         augmentedMatrix[i][n] = 0;
      }
      augmentedMatrix[k][n] = 1.0;

      Matrix solutionVector(n, 1);
      GaussElim(augmentedMatrix, solutionVector);

      for (int i = 0; i < n; i++)
         A_Inverse[i][k] = solutionVector[i][0];
   }

   cout << "Inverse matrix is:\n" << A_Inverse << endl;
}

inline double Abs(double val)
{
  return (val < 0) ? -(val) : val;
}

inline void Swap(double & a, double & b)
{
  double t = a; a = b; b = t;
}

bool Reduce(Matrix & augMat)
{
  const double EPSILON = 1.0E-6;
  bool isSingular = false;
```

```
    int i = 0,
        j,
        k,
        numRows = augMat.Rows(),
        pivotRow;
    double quotient,
           absolutePivot;

    while ((!isSingular) && (i < numRows))
    {
      absolutePivot = Abs(augMat[i][i]);
      pivotRow = i;
      for (k = i+1; k < numRows; k++)
        if (Abs(augMat[k][i]) > absolutePivot)
        {
          absolutePivot = Abs(augMat[k][i]);
          pivotRow = k;
        }
      isSingular = absolutePivot < EPSILON;
      if (!isSingular)
      {
        if (i != pivotRow)
          for (j = 0; j <= numRows; j++)
            Swap(augMat[i][j], augMat[pivotRow][j]);

        for (j = i+1; j < numRows; j++)
        {
          quotient = -augMat[j][i] / augMat[i][i];
          for (k = i; k <= numRows; k++)
            augMat[j][k] = augMat[j][k] + quotient * augMat[i][k];
        }
      }
      i++;
    }
    return isSingular;
}

void Solve(Matrix & augMat, Matrix & solutionVector)
{
  int n = augMat.Rows()-1;

  solutionVector[n][0] = augMat[n][n+1] / augMat[n][n];

  for (int i = n-1; i >= 0; i--)
  {
    solutionVector[i][0] = augMat[i][n+1];

    for (int j = i+1; j <= n; j++)
      solutionVector[i][0] -= augMat[i][j] * solutionVector[j][0];

    solutionVector[i][0] /= augMat[i][i];
  }
}
```

```
void GaussElim(Matrix augmentedMatrix, Matrix & soln)
{

   bool isSingular = Reduce(augmentedMatrix);

   if (isSingular)
   {
      cerr << "\n*** GaussElim: Matrix is (nearly) singular!\n";
      exit (0);
   }

   Solve(augmentedMatrix, soln);
}
```

26. Create a member function `GraphParametric()`. It must accept as parameters two functions `X(t)` and `Y(t)`, the values `a` and `b` from `a<= t <= b`, a `Points` value to determine the number of points to plot in the graph, and the `Color`.

27. Create a member function `ScatterPlot()`. It must accept as parameters the `fileName` and the `color`.

28-29. These exercises are standard programs reading data into an array and performing a conversion on the values stored in the array.

Chapter 13: Pointers and Run-Time Allocation

Exercises 13.1

1. `double * ptr1,`
    `        * ptr2;`

2. `p1 = &d1;`

3. Not possible; `p2` may store only the address of a location where a `double` is stored.

4. `Point * q;`

5. `int * ptr1 = &l1,`
    `      ptr2 = &l2;`

6. `p2 = p1;`

7. `*ptr1 = *ptr2;`

8. `cout << q->x() << "   " << q->y() << endl;`
    or
    `cout << (*q).x() << "   " << (*q)y() << endl;`

9. `double temp = *p1;`
    `   *p1 = *p2;`
    `   *p2 = temp;`

10-16.
```
#include <iostream.h>
#include <string>

int main()
{
  string str1 = "Bye!",
         str2 = "Auf WIedersehen!";
  string * ptr1  = &str1,
         * ptr2 = &str2;

  cout << "\n sizeof:  \ttype\tpointer"
       << "\n int      \t " << sizeof(int)   << "\t "
                            << sizeof(int *)
       << "\n float    \t " << sizeof(float) << "\t "
                            << sizeof(float *)
       << "\n double   \t " << sizeof(double) << "\t  "
                            << sizeof(double *)
       << "\n short int\t " << sizeof(long double) << "\t  "
                            << sizeof(long double *)
       << "\n str1     \t " << sizeof str1 << "\t  "
                            << sizeof(ptr1)
       << "\n str2     \t " << sizeof str2 << "\t  "
                            << sizeof(ptr2)
       << endl;
  return 0;
}
```

Sample run in gnu C++:

```
sizeof:       type    pointer
int            4        4
float          4        4
double         8        4
short int     16        4
str1           4        4
str2           4        4
```

17-18.
```cpp
#include <iostream.h>

int main()
{
  const int SIZE = 10;
  char charArray[SIZE];
  int intArray[SIZE];
  double doubleArray[SIZE];
  char charVar;

  cout << "\n              \taddress of    size of"
       << "\n charArray   \t" << (void*)(&charArray)   << "\t"
                              << sizeof(char[SIZE])
       << "\n intArray    \t" << (void*)(&intArray)    << "\t"
                              << sizeof(int[SIZE])
       << "\n doubleArray \t" << (void*)(&doubleArray) << "\t"
                              << sizeof(double[SIZE])
       << "\n char        \t" << (void*)(&charVar)     << "\t"
                              << sizeof(char)

       << endl;
  return 0;
}
```

Sample run in gnu C++:

```
             address of    size of
charArray    0xeffff768      10
intArray     0xeffff740      40
doubleArray  0xeffff6f0      80
char         0xeffff6ef       1
```

19. For an array a of type T with base address b, a[i] is stored at location $b + (i - 1)*sizeof(T)$.

20. typedef char * CharPointer;

21-22.
```cpp
#include <iostream.h>

int main()
{
  double anArray[10];

  cout << "Address of anArray[0]: " << (void*)(&(anArray[0])) << endl
       << "Value of anArray:      " << anArray << endl;

  return 0;
}
```

.

```
Address of anArray[0]: 0xeffff730
Value of anArray:      0xeffff730
```

23. The value associated with an array variable is the base address of the array (the address of its first element).

Exercises 13.2

1.  ```
    char * charPtr;
    ```

2.  ```
    charPtr = new char;
    ```

3.  ```
    cin >> *charPtr;
    ```

4.  ```
    cout << *charPtr;
    ```

5.  ```
    if (isupper(*charPtr))
        *charPtr = tolower(*charPtr);
    ```

6.  ```
    double *( doublePtr;
    ```

7.  ```
    cin >> n;
    doublePtr = new double[n];
    ```

8.  ```
    for (int i = 0; i < n; i++)
        cin >> doublePtr[i];
    ```

9.  ```
    double sum = 0;
    for (int i = 0; i < n; i++)
        sum +_ doublePtr[i];
    cout << "Average = " << sum / n << endl;
    ```

10. ```
    delete [] doublePtr;
    ```

11. Simply output the value of `doublePtr`.

    If this value is *b* and `doubles` take 8 bytes, the memory map might appear as follows:

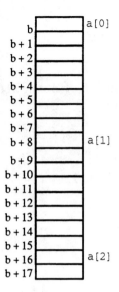

12. 1
    13
    63
    55
    77
    99

Exercises 13.3

1. 123   456

2. 34   34

3. 34   34

4. Error — `p2->next` is null, so `p2->next->data` is undefined.

5. 12   34
    34   34
    34
    34

6. 111   222
    222
    111

7. 34   34
    34   34

Programming Problems
Section 13.1 - 13.3

1.

BigInt.h

```
/* This file contains the interface for the class BigInt.
   ***************************************************************/

#ifndef BIGINT_H
#define BIGINT_H


#include <iostream.h>          .   // cin, cout, >>, <<
#include <iomanip.h>               // setfill()
#include <list>                    // list<T>
#include <algorithm>               // reverse()

class BigInt
{
 public:
   BigInt();
   BigInt(int n);
   void ReadBig(istream & in);
   void PrintBig(ostream & out);
   BigInt operator=(const BigInt & int2);
   friend bool operator<(BigInt int1, BigInt int2);
   friend BigInt operator+(BigInt int1, BigInt int2);
   friend BigInt operator-(BigInt int1, BigInt int2);
 private:
   char mySign;
   list<short int> myList;
};

inline BigInt::BigInt()
{
   mySign = '+';
}

inline BigInt::BigInt(int n)
{
   myList.push_back(n);
   mySign = '+';
}


inline BigInt BigInt::operator=(const BigInt & int2)
{
   mySign = int2.mySign;
   myList = int2.myList;

   return *this;
}

inline istream & operator>>(istream & in, BigInt & x)
{
   x.ReadBig(in);
   return in;
}
```

```
inline ostream & operator<<(ostream & out, BigInt x)
{
   x.PrintBig(out);
   return out;
}

#endif
```

BigInt.cpp
```
/* This file contains the implementation for class BigInt.
 ****************************************************************/

#include "BigInt.h"

/* ReadBig reads a BigInt.
 *
 * Receive:    istream in
 * Pass back: istream with a BigInt value removed from
 *            it and x with this value assigned to it
 ********************************************************/

void BigInt::ReadBig(istream & in)
{
   short int block;
   for (;;)
   {
      in >> block;
      if (block < 0) return;
      myList.push_back(block);
   }
}

/* PrintBig displays a BigInt.
 *
 * Receive:    ostream out
 * Pass back: ostream with a BigInt value inserted
 * Output:     x
 ********************************************************/

#include <iomanip.h>              // setfill, setw
void BigInt::PrintBig(ostream & out)
{
   out << mySign << setfill('0');
   int count = 1;
   for (list<short int>::iterator it = myList.begin();
                            it != myList.end(); it++)
   {
      out << setw(3) << *it << ' ';
      if (count % 20 == 0) out << endl;
      count ++;
   }
   out << endl;
}

/* operator< comparess two BigInts.
 *
 * Receive:    BigInts int1 and int2
 * Pass back: truth or falsity of int1 < int2
 ********************************************************/
```

```
bool operator<(BigInt int1, BigInt int2)
{
  if (int1.mySign != int2.mySign)
    return (int1.mySign == '-') && (int2.mySign == '+');  // neg. < pos

  // they have the same sign
  list<short int> :: iterator it1 = int1.myList.begin(),
                                it2 = int2.myList.begin();
  while (it1!= int1.myList.end() && *it1 == *it2)
  {
    it1++;
    it2++;
  }
  if (it1 == int1.myList.end())     // they're equal
    return false;

  if (*it1 < *it2)
    return int1.mySign == '+';
  // else
  return int1.mySign == '-';
}


BigInt operator+(BigInt int1, BigInt int2);

/* operator+ adds two BigInts.
 *
 * Receive:    BigInts int1 and int2
 * Pass back : int1 + int2
 ********************************************************/

BigInt operator+(BigInt int1, BigInt int2)
{
    short int first,        // a block of int1
              second,       // a block of int2
              result,       // a block in their sum
              carry = 0;    // the carry in adding two blocks
    BigInt answer;          // the sum

    reverse(int1.myList.begin(), int1.myList.end());
    reverse(int2.myList.begin(), int2.myList.end());

    list<short int>::iterator it1 = int1.myList.begin();
    list<short int>::iterator it2 = int2.myList.begin();

    for(;;)
    {
        if (it1 == int1.myList.end() && it2 == int2.myList.end()) break;

        if (it1 != int1.myList.end())
        {
            first = *it1;
            it1++;
        }
        else
            first = 0;

        if (it2 != int2.myList.end())
        {
            second = *it2;
            it2++;
        }
```

```
        else
            second = 0;

        short int temp = first + second + carry;
        result = temp % 1000;
        carry = temp / 1000;
        answer.myList.push_back(result);
    }

    if (carry > 0)
        answer.myList.push_back(carry);

    reverse(answer.myList.begin(), answer.myList.end());
    return answer;
}


/* operator- subtracts two BigInts.
 *
 * Receive:    BigInts int1 and int2
 * Pass back : int1 - int2
 ********************************************/

BigInt operator-(BigInt int1, BigInt int2)
{
    short int first,          // a block of int1
              second,         // a block of int2
              result,         // a block in their difference
              borrow = 0;     // the carry in subtracting two blocks
    BigInt temp,              // used to swap int1 and int2
           answer;            // the difference

    if (int1 < int2)
    {
      temp = int1;
      int1 = int2;
      int2 = temp;
      answer.mySign = '-';
    }

    reverse(int1.myList.begin(), int1.myList.end());
    reverse(int2.myList.begin(), int2.myList.end());

    list<short int>::iterator it1 = int1.myList.begin(),
                              it2 = int2.myList.begin();
    for(;;)
    {
        if (it1 == int1.myList.end() && it2 == int2.myList.end()) break;

        if (it1 != int1.myList.end())
        {
            first = *it1;
            it1++;
        }
        else
            first = 0;

        if (it2 != int2.myList.end())
        {
            second = *it2;
            it2++;
        }
```

```
         else
            second = 0;

         result = first - second - borrow;
         if (result < 0)
         {
            result += 1000;
            borrow = 1;
         }
         else
            borrow = 0;
         answer.myList.push_back(result);
      }

   if (borrow > 0)
      answer.mySign = '-';

   reverse(answer.myList.begin(), answer.myList.end());
   return answer;
}


/* prog13-1.cpp is a driver program to test class BigInt.
 *
 * Input:  operation (+, -, Q) and two BigInts
 * Output: The sum or difference of the BigInts
 *************************************************************/

#include <iostream.h>

#include "BigInt.h"

int main()
{
   cout << "Enter BigInts in blocks of 3 digits (-1 to stop).\n";

   char option;
   for (;;)
   {
      cout << "\nEnter +, -, or Q (to quit): ";
      cin >> option;

      if (option == 'Q' || option == 'q') break;

      BigInt int1, int2, answer;
      cout << "Enter first BigInt:  ";
      cin >> int1;
      cout << "Enter second BigInt: ";
      cin >> int2;

      switch (option)
      {
         case '+' : cout << int1 + int2 << endl;
                    break;
         case '-' : cout << int1 - int2 << endl;
                    break;
         default  : cerr << "Illegal operation\n";
      }
   }
}
```

2. Overloading * and / are considerably more difficult than + and -. What follows is a *complete* BigInt class from the first edition of this text prepared by Ed Ball. It is a working class that contains all of the basic arithmetic operators, relational operators, increment, decrement, and ahortcut assignment operators. Modifying it to use the standard string library instead of the Strings library we defined in the first edition is straightforward.

BigInt.h

```
/* This file contains the interface for the class BigInt,
   a class written by Ed Ball for the first edition
   of this course.
   ------------------------------------------------------*/
#ifndef BIGINT_H
#define BIGINT_H

#include <iostream.h>

#include "Strings.h"

class BigInt
{
public:

    // constructor -- constructs zero
    BigInt()
    { Zero(); }

    // constructor -- constructs from a standard integer
    BigInt(long Int)
    { *this = Int; }

    // constructor -- constructs from a string
    BigInt(const Strings& String)
    { *this = String; }

    // copy constructor
    BigInt(const BigInt& Int)
    { *this = Int; }

    // operator= -- assignment
    BigInt& operator=(long Long);
    BigInt& operator=(const BigInt& Int);
    BigInt& operator=(const Strings& String);

    // Zero() -- set to zero
    void Zero();

    // Digits -- number of digits
    int Digits() const;

    // Sign -- 1 if positive, -1 if negative, 0 if zero
    int Sign() const
    { return Sign_; }

    // ToString -- copy to a string
    void ToString(Strings& String) const;

    // equality/inequality operators
    friend int operator==(const BigInt& Int1, const BigInt& Int2);
    friend int operator!=(const BigInt& Int1, const BigInt& Int2);
    friend int operator< (const BigInt& Int1, const BigInt& Int2);
    friend int operator<=(const BigInt& Int1, const BigInt& Int2);
```

```
    friend int operator> (const BigInt& Int1, const BigInt& Int2);
    friend int operator>=(const BigInt& Int1, const BigInt& Int2);

    // operator+, operator- -- unary positive, negative
    BigInt operator+() const;
    BigInt operator-() const;

    // operator++, operator-- -- increment, decrement
    void operator++(int);
    BigInt& operator++();
    void operator--(int);
    BigInt& operator--();

    // operator+=, operator+ -- addition
    BigInt& operator+=(const BigInt& Int);
    friend BigInt operator+(const BigInt& Int1, const BigInt& Int2);

    // operator-=, operator- -- subtraction
    BigInt& operator-=(const BigInt& Int);
    friend BigInt operator-(const BigInt& Int1, const BigInt& Int2);

    // operator*=, operator* -- multiplication
    BigInt& operator*=(const BigInt& Int);
    friend BigInt operator*(const BigInt& Int1, const BigInt& Int2);

    // operator/=, operator/ -- division
    BigInt& operator/=(const BigInt& Int);
    friend BigInt operator/(const BigInt& Int1, const BigInt& Int2);

    // operator%=, operator% -- modulus
    BigInt& operator%=(const BigInt& Int);
    friend BigInt operator%(const BigInt& Int1, const BigInt& Int2);

    // Divide - division and modulus
    friend void Divide(const BigInt& Int1, const BigInt& Int2,
                       BigInt& Quotient, BigInt& Remainder);

    // operator>> -- vector stream input
    friend istream& operator>>(istream& In, BigInt& Int);

    // operator<< -- vector stream output
    friend ostream& operator<<(ostream& Out, const BigInt& Int);

private:

    // digits per unsigned short int
    enum { DigitsPerInt = 4 };
    enum { IntModulus = 10000 };

    // size of array of unsigned short ints needed
    enum { ArraySize = 75 };

    // EqualFunc -- equality disregarding sign
    friend int EqualFunc(const BigInt& Int1, const BigInt& Int2);

    // LessFunc -- less than disregarding sign
    friend int LessFunc(const BigInt& Int1, const BigInt& Int2);

    // AddFunc -- addition disregarding sign
    friend void AddFunc(const BigInt& Int1,
                        const BigInt& Int2, BigInt& Answer);
```

```
    // SubtractFunc -- subtraction disregarding sign, Int1 < Int2
    friend void SubtractFunc(const BigInt& Int1,
                             const BigInt& Int2, BigInt& Answer);

    // IncFunc, DecFunc -- increment/decrement disregarding sign
    void IncFunc();
    void DecFunc();

    short
        Array_[ArraySize];
    int
        Sign_;

public:

    // the maximum number of digits in a BigInt
    enum { MaxDigits = DigitsPerInt * ArraySize };
};

#endif
```

BigInt.cpp

```
/* This file contains the implementation of the class BigInt,
   a class written by Ed Ball for the first edition
   of this course.
----------------------------------------------------------*/
#include "BigInt.h"

#include <ctype.h>

BigInt& BigInt::operator=(long Int)
{
    Zero();

    if (Int == 0)
        return *this;

    Sign_ = 1;

    if (Int < 0)
    {
        Sign_ = -1;
        Int = -Int;
    }

    int
        Loc = 0;

    while (Int > 0)
    {
        Array_[Loc] = Int % IntModulus;
        Int /= IntModulus;
        Loc++;
    }

    return *this;
}

BigInt& BigInt::operator=(const BigInt& Int)
{
    Sign_ = Int.Sign_;
```

```
      for (int i = 0; i < ArraySize; i++)
         Array_[i] = Int.Array_[i];

      return *this;
}

BigInt& BigInt::operator=(const Strings& String)
{
   Sign_ = 1;

   int
      Length = String.Length(),
      Pos = Length - 1,
      First = 0,
      Digits = -1;
   short
      Value;

   // if no string, set to zero and return
   if (Length == 0)
   {
      Zero();
      return *this;
   }

   // read sign, if there
   if (String[First] == '-')
   {
      Sign_ = -1;
      First++;
   }
   else if (String[First] == '+')
      First++;

   // read all opening zero's
   while (First < Length && String[First] == '0')
      First++;

   // if only sign and/or zero's, set to zero and return
   if (First == Length)
   {
      Zero();
      return *this;
   }

   // read all numbers, starting at end
   do
   {
      Digits++;

      // if non-digit found, set to zero and return
      if (!isdigit(String[Pos]))
      {
         Zero();
         return *this;
      }

      // get value of digit
      Value = short(String[Pos] - '0');
```

```
      // set appropriate array value accordingly
      if (Digits % DigitsPerInt == 0)
         Array_[Digits / DigitsPerInt] = Value;
      else
      {
         for (int i = 0; i < Digits % DigitsPerInt; i++)
            Value *= 10;
         Array_[Digits / DigitsPerInt] += Value;
      }

      Pos--;
   }
   while (Pos >= First);

   // zero remaining digits
   for (int i = Digits / DigitsPerInt + 1; i < ArraySize; i++)
      Array_[i] = 0;

   return *this;
}

void BigInt::Zero()
{
   for (int i = 0; i < ArraySize; i++)
      Array_[i] = 0;

   Sign_ = 0;
}

int BigInt::Digits() const
{
   // zero has one digit
   if (Sign_ == 0)
      return 1;

   int
      Dig = MaxDigits,
      Loc = ArraySize - 1;

   // subtract opening zero's from maximum digits
   while (Loc >= 0 && Array_[Loc] == 0)
   {
      Dig -= DigitsPerInt;
      Loc--;
   }

   // figure out final answer
   if (Loc >= 0)
   {
      Dig -= DigitsPerInt;

      short
         Value = Array_[Loc];

      while (Value > 0)
      {
         Dig++;
         Value /= 10;
      }
   }

   return Dig;
}

void BigInt::ToString(Strings& String) const
```

```
{
   short
      Value;
   int
      Digits = BigInt::Digits(),
      Length = (Sign_ == -1) ? Digits+1 : Digits;

   // set string of given length
   String = Strings(' ',Length);

   // start with minus if integer is negative
   if (Sign_ == -1)
      String[0] = '-';

   // each digit
   for (int i = 0; i < Digits; i++)
   {
      Value = Array_[i/4];

      for (int j = 0; j < i%4; j++)
         Value /= 10;

      String[Length-1-i] = char(Value % 10) + '0';
   }
}

int operator==(const BigInt& Int1, const BigInt& Int2)
{
   return Int1.Sign_ == Int2.Sign_ &&
          EqualFunc(Int1,Int2);
}

int operator!=(const BigInt& Int1, const BigInt& Int2)
{
   return Int1.Sign_ != Int2.Sign_ ||
          !EqualFunc(Int1,Int2);
}

int operator< (const BigInt& Int1, const BigInt& Int2)
{
   if (Int1.Sign_ < Int2.Sign_)
      return 1;

   else if (Int1.Sign_ > Int2.Sign_)
      return 0;

   else if (Int1.Sign_ == 1)
      return LessFunc(Int1,Int2);
   else if (Int1.Sign_ == -1)
      return !LessFunc(Int1,Int2);
   else
      return 0;
}

int operator<=(const BigInt& Int1, const BigInt& Int2)
{
   return Int1 < Int2 || Int1 == Int2;
}
```

```
int operator> (const BigInt& Int1, const BigInt& Int2)
{
   return !(Int1 < Int2) && Int1 != Int2;
}

int operator>=(const BigInt& Int1, const BigInt& Int2)
{
   return !(Int1 < Int2);
}

BigInt BigInt::operator+() const
{
   return *this;
}

BigInt BigInt::operator-() const
{
   BigInt Negation = *this;
   Negation.Sign_ = -Negation.Sign_;
   return Negation;
}

void BigInt::operator++(int)
{
   if (Sign_ == 0)
      *this = 1;
   else if (Sign_ > 0)
      IncFunc();
   else
      DecFunc();
}

BigInt& BigInt::operator++()
{
   (*this)++;
   return *this;
}

void BigInt::operator--(int)
{
   if (Sign_ == 0)
      *this = -1;
   else if (Sign_ > 0)
      DecFunc();
   else
      IncFunc();
}

BigInt& BigInt::operator--()
{
   (*this)--;
   return *this;
}

BigInt operator+(const BigInt& Int1, const BigInt& Int2)
{
   // if Int1 is zero, answer is Int2
   if (Int1.Sign_ == 0)
      return Int2;
```

```
   // if Int2 is zero, answer is Int1
   if (Int2.Sign_ == 0)
      return Int1;

   BigInt Answer;

   // if signs are the same, do the addition
   if (Int1.Sign_ == Int2.Sign_)
   {
      Answer.Sign_ = Int1.Sign_;
      AddFunc(Int1,Int2,Answer);
   }

   // if signs and digits are different
   else if (!EqualFunc(Int1,Int2))
   {
      if (Int1.Sign_ == 1)
      {
         if (LessFunc(Int1,Int2))  // +4 + -7 == -(7 - 4)
         {
            Answer.Sign_ = -1;
            SubtractFunc(Int2,Int1,Answer);
         }
         else                      // +7 + -4 == +(7 - 4)
         {
            Answer.Sign_ = 1;
            SubtractFunc(Int1,Int2,Answer);
         }
      }
      else
      {
         if (LessFunc(Int1,Int2))  // -4 + +7 == +(7 - 4)
         {
            Answer.Sign_ = 1;
            SubtractFunc(Int2,Int1,Answer);
         }
         else                      // -7 + +4 == -(7 - 4)
         {
            Answer.Sign_ = -1;
            SubtractFunc(Int1,Int2,Answer);
         }
      }
   }

   // (if signs are different but digits are same, leave as zero)

   return Answer;
}

BigInt& BigInt::operator+=(const BigInt& Int)
{
   *this = *this + Int;

   return *this;
}

BigInt operator-(const BigInt& Int1, const BigInt& Int2)
{
   return Int1 + -Int2;
}
```

```
BigInt& BigInt::operator-=(const BigInt& Int)
{
    *this = *this - Int;

    return *this;
}

BigInt operator*(const BigInt& Int1, const BigInt& Int2)
{
    BigInt
        FinalResult,
        AResult;
    short
        First,
        Second,
        Result,
        Carry,
        Overflow = 0;

    if (Int1.Sign_ == 0 || Int2.Sign_ == 0)
        return FinalResult;

    for (int i = 0; i < BigInt::ArraySize; i++)
    {
        AResult.Zero();
        AResult.Sign_ = 1;

        Second = Int2.Array_[i];
        Carry = 0;

        for (int j = 0; j < BigInt::ArraySize; j++)
        {
            First = Int1.Array_[j];

            long Temp = (long(First) * Second) + Carry;
            Result = short(Temp % BigInt::IntModulus);
            Carry = short(Temp / BigInt::IntModulus);

            if (j + i < BigInt::ArraySize)
                AResult.Array_[j+i] = Result;
            else if (Result != 0)
                Overflow = 1;
        }

        FinalResult += AResult;
    }

    FinalResult.Sign_ = Int1.Sign_ * Int2.Sign_;

    if (Overflow)
        cerr << "\nBigInt multiplication overflow\n";

    return FinalResult;
}

BigInt& BigInt::operator*=(const BigInt& Int)
{
    *this = *this * Int;

    return *this;
}
```

```
BigInt operator/(const BigInt& Int1, const BigInt& Int2)
{
   BigInt
      Quotient,
      Remainder;

   Divide(Int1,Int2,Quotient,Remainder);

   return Quotient;
}

BigInt& BigInt::operator/=(const BigInt& Int)
{
   *this = *this / Int;

   return *this;
}

BigInt operator%(const BigInt& Int1, const BigInt& Int2)
{
   BigInt
      Quotient,
      Remainder;

   Divide(Int1,Int2,Quotient,Remainder);

   return Remainder;
}

BigInt& BigInt::operator%=(const BigInt& Int)
{
   *this = *this % Int;

   return *this;
}

void Divide(const BigInt& Int1, const BigInt& Int2,
            BigInt& Quotient, BigInt& Remainder)
{
   BigInt
      One = 1;

   Quotient.Zero();
   Remainder.Zero();

   if (Int2.Sign_ == 0)           // x/0 == ?, x%0 == ?
   {
      cerr << "\nBigInt division by zero\n";
      return;
   }

   if (Int1.Sign_ == 0)           // 0/x == 0, 0%x == 0
      return;

   if (EqualFunc(Int1,One))       // 1/1 == 1, 1/x == 0, 1%x == 1
   {
      if (EqualFunc(Int2,One))
      {
         Quotient = One;
         Quotient.Sign_ = Int1.Sign_ * Int2.Sign_;
      }
```

```
      Remainder = One;
      Remainder.Sign_ = Int1.Sign_;
      return;
   }

   if (EqualFunc(Int2,One))        // x/1 == x, x%1 == 0
   {
      Quotient = Int1;
      Quotient.Sign_ = Int1.Sign_ * Int2.Sign_;
      return;
   }

   if (EqualFunc(Int1,Int2))       // x/x == 1, x%x == 0
   {
      Quotient = One;
      Quotient.Sign_ = Int1.Sign_ * Int2.Sign_;
      return;
   }

   if (LessFunc(Int1,Int2))        // (x<y): x/y == 0, x%y == x
   {
      Remainder = Int1;
      Remainder.Sign_ = Int1.Sign_;
      return;
   }

   // (1 < y < x): x/y == ...

   for (int Int1Start = BigInt::ArraySize - 1; Int1Start >= 0; Int1Start--)
      if (Int1.Array_[Int1Start] != 0)
         break;

   for (int Int2Start = BigInt::ArraySize - 1; Int2Start >= 0; Int2Start--)
      if (Int2.Array_[Int2Start] != 0)
         break;

   Remainder = Int1;
   Remainder.Sign_ = 1;

   for (int j = Int1Start - Int2Start; j >= 0; j--)
   {
      BigInt
         Temp;
      for (int i = Int2Start; i >= 0; i--)
         Temp.Array_[Int1Start - Int2Start + i] = Int2.Array_[i];
      Temp.Sign_ = 1;

      short
         Digit = 0;

      for (;;)
      {
         Remainder -= Temp;
         if (Remainder.Sign() < 0)
            break;
         else
            Digit++;
      }
      Remainder += Temp;
```

```
        Quotient.Array_[j] = Digit;
        Int1Start--;
    }

    Quotient.Sign_ = Int1.Sign_ * Int2.Sign_;
    Remainder.Sign_ *= Int1.Sign_;
}

istream& operator>>(istream& In, BigInt& Int)
{
    Strings Input;

    In >> Input;

    Int = Input;

    return In;
}

ostream& operator<<(ostream& Out, const BigInt& Int)
{
    Strings Output;

    Int.ToString(Output);

    Out << Output;

    return Out;
}

int EqualFunc(const BigInt& Int1, const BigInt& Int2)
{
    for (int i = 0; i < BigInt::ArraySize; i++)
        if (Int1.Array_[i] != Int2.Array_[i])
            return 0;

    return 1;
}

int LessFunc(const BigInt& Int1, const BigInt& Int2)
{
    int i = BigInt::ArraySize - 1;

    while (i > 0 && Int1.Array_[i] == Int2.Array_[i])
        i--;

    return Int1.Array_[i] < Int2.Array_[i];
}

void AddFunc(const BigInt& Int1, const BigInt& Int2, BigInt& Answer)
{
    short
        First,          // each array element of Int1
        Second,         // each array element of Int2
        Result,         // the array element result of their addition
        Carry = 0;      // the array element carry of their addition
```

```
    for (int i = 0; i < BigInt::ArraySize; i++)
    {
        First = Int1.Array_[i];
        Second = Int2.Array_[i];

        short Temp = First + Second + Carry;
        Result = Temp % BigInt::IntModulus;
        Carry = Temp / BigInt::IntModulus;

        Answer.Array_[i] = Result;
    }

    if (Carry > 0)
        cerr << "\nBigInt overflow\n";
}

void SubtractFunc(const BigInt& Int1, const BigInt& Int2, BigInt& Answer)
{
    short
        First,        // each array element of Int1
        Second,       // each array element of Int2
        Result,       // the array element result of their subtraction
        Borrow = 0;   // 1 if borrow needed, 0 if not

    for (int i = 0; i < BigInt::ArraySize; i++)
    {
        First = Int1.Array_[i];
        Second = Int2.Array_[i];
        Result = First - Second - Borrow;
        if (Result < 0)
        {
            Result += BigInt::IntModulus;
            Borrow = 1;
        }
        else
            Borrow = 0;

        Answer.Array_[i] = Result;
    }
}

void BigInt::IncFunc()
{
    short
        Result,
        Carry;
    int
        Loc = 0;

    do
    {
        Result = Array_[Loc] + 1;
        Array_[Loc] = Result % BigInt::IntModulus;
        Carry = Result / BigInt::IntModulus;
        Loc++;
    }
    while (Carry > 0 && Loc < BigInt::ArraySize);
}
```

```
void BigInt::DecFunc()
{
   short
      Result,
      Borrow;
   int
      Loc = 0;

   do
   {
      Result = Array_[Loc] - 1;
      Borrow = Result < 0;
      Array_[Loc] = Borrow ? 999 : Result % BigInt::IntModulus;
      Loc++;
   }
   while (Borrow > 0 && Loc < BigInt::ArraySize);
}
```

Calculator program to test BigInt:

```
#include "BigInt.h"

#include <iostream.h>

int main(void)
{
   BigInt x, y;
   char ch;

   do
   {
      cout << "\nEnter calculation (e.g. 12 * 13): ";

      cin >> x >> ch >> y;

      cout << endl << x << ' ' << ch << ' ' << y << " = ";

      switch (ch)
      {
         case '+':  cout << (x + y); break;
         case '-':  cout << (x - y); break;
         case '*':  cout << (x * y); break;
         case '/':  cout << (x / y); break;
         case '%':  cout << (x % y); break;
         default:   cout << "INVALID OPERATION!"; break;
      }

      cout << "\n\nAnother? ";
      cin >> ch;
   }
   while (ch == 'y' || ch == 'Y');

   return 0;
}
```

3.
```
/*prog 13-3.cpp is the Hoops basketball-ticket program.
 *
 * Input (keyboard): number of tickets available,
 * Input (file):     names, addresses of people ordering tickets,
 *                   and number of tickets requested
 * Output:           mailing labels for ticket orders that can be filled.
 * Condition:        no person receives more than MAX_TICKETS tickets and
 *                   multiple requests are not allowed.
 ***********************************************************************/

#include <fstream.h>
#include <string>
#include <list>
#include <algorithm>

const MAX_TICKETS = 4;

class TicketOrder
{
 public:
    void Read(ifstream & in);
    void PrintLabel(ostream & out) const;
    short int NumRequested() const;
    void SetRequest(short int num);
    bool DupOrder(TicketOrder order2) const;

 private:
    string myName,
           myStreetAddress,
           myCity_and_Street;
    unsigned myZip;
    short int myRequest;
};


// Read a ticket order from a file
void TicketOrder::Read(ifstream & in)
{
    char ch;
    getline(in, myName);
    getline(in, myStreetAddress);
    getline(in, myCity_and_Street);
    in >> myZip >> myRequest;
    if (myRequest > MAX_TICKETS)
       myRequest = 4;
    ch = in.get();   // chew up end-of-line mark
 }

// Display a mailing label
void TicketOrder::PrintLabel(ostream & out) const
{
    cout << endl << myName << endl
         << myStreetAddress << endl
         << myCity_and_Street << myZip << endl
         << "------------------------ " << myRequest << " tickets\n\n";
}
```

```
// Retrieve # of tickets ordered
inline short int TicketOrder::NumRequested() const
{
  return myRequest;
}

// Change the # of tickets ordered
inline void TicketOrder::SetRequest(short int num)
{
   myRequest = num;
}
// Function to check if two ticket orders are from the same person

bool TicketOrder::DupOrder(TicketOrder order2) const
{
   return myName == order2.myName &&
          myStreetAddress == order2.myStreetAddress &&
          myCity_and_Street == order2.myCity_and_Street &&
          myZip == order2.myZip;
 }

// Operation ==
inline bool operator==(TicketOrder order1, TicketOrder order2)
{
  return order1.DupOrder(order2);
}


// Operation !=
inline bool operator!=(TicketOrder order1, TicketOrder order2)
{
   return !order1.DupOrder(order2);
}

// End of file for class TicketOrder


// Function to output a list of ticket orders to the screen

ostream & operator<<(ostream & out, list<TicketOrder> orders)
{
   for (list<TicketOrder>::iterator it = orders.begin();
                                    it != orders.end(); it++)
      (*it).PrintLabel(out);

   return out;
}


int main()
{
   int ticketsAvailable;

   cout << "How many tickets are available? ";
   cin >> ticketsAvailable;

   string fileName;
   cout << "Enter name of file containing orders: ";
   cin >> fileName;
   ifstream inStream (fileName.data());
```

```
    if (!inStream.is_open())
    {
        cerr << "Error in opening file " << fileName << endl;
        exit(1);
    }

    list<TicketOrder> orders;
    TicketOrder anOrder;
    for (;;)
    {
        anOrder.Read(inStream);
        if (anOrder.NumRequested() < 0) break;   // end of data

        if (find(orders.begin(), orders.end(), anOrder) != orders.end())
        {
            anOrder.PrintLabel(cerr);
            cerr << "The above order was processed earlier\n";
        }
        else
        {
            if (anOrder.NumRequested() > ticketsAvailable)
                anOrder.SetRequest(ticketsAvailable);
            orders.push_back(anOrder);
            ticketsAvailable -= anOrder.NumRequested();
        }

        if (ticketsAvailable <= 0)
        {
            cout << "\n\n\n*** NO MORE TICKETS ***\n";
            break;
        }

    }

    cout << "Mailing labels for the valid orders: \n" << orders;

    return 0;
}
```

// Sample data file to use with program

```
John Doe
123 Alpha Drive
Someplace, USA
99999
6
Mary Smith
111 Beta Road
Anyplace, USA
11111
2
John Doe
444 Gamma St.
AnotherPlace, USA
22222
3
Mary Smith
111 Beta Road
Anyplace, USA
11111
4
```

.

```
Pete Jones
222 Delta Ave.
Nowhere, USA
00000
1
THIS IS A DUMMY ORDER
WITH A NEGATIVE NUMBER
OF TICKETS ORDERE TO SIGNAL END OF ORDERS
0
-1
```

4-6.
// Polynomial.h
```cpp
// Polynomial.h
/* This file is the interface for class Polynomial.
   *****************************************************/

#ifndef POLYNOMIAL
#define POLYNOMIAL

#include <iostream.h>
#include <list>

class Polynomial
{
 public:

  // SetCoefficient -- set a coefficient of the polynomial
  void SetCoefficient(double coeff, int expo);

  // GetCoefficient -- get a coefficient of the polynomial
  double GetCoefficient(int expo);

  // Evaluate -- evaluate a polynomial
  double Evaluate(double value);

  // operator+ -- add two polynomials
  Polynomial operator+(Polynomial p);

  // operator* -- multiply two polynomials
  Polynomial operator*(Polynomial p);

  // Print -- output a polynomial to an ostream
  void Print(ostream & out);

  // Input -- input a polynomial from an istream
  void Input(istream & in);

private:

  struct PolyTerm
  {
    double myCoeff;
    int myExp;
    // constructor

    PolyTerm(double coef = 0.0, int expo = 0)
    { myCoeff = coef;  myExp = expo; }
  };
```

```
  // Define == to mean have the same exponent
  friend bool operator==(PolyTerm term1, PolyTerm term2)
  { return term1.myExp == term2.myExp;}

  friend bool operator!=(PolyTerm term1, PolyTerm term2)
  { return term1.myExp != term2.myExp;}

  // Define < to mean has a smaller exponent
  friend bool operator<(PolyTerm term1, PolyTerm term2)
  { return term1.myExp < term2.myExp;}

  list<PolyTerm> myList;

};

inline ostream & operator<<(ostream & out, Polynomial poly)
{
  poly.Print(out);
  return out;
}

inline istream & operator>>(istream & in, Polynomial & poly)
{
  poly.Input(in);
  return in;
}

#endif
```

//Polynomial.cpp:
```
/* This file is the implementation for class Polynomial.
 *********************************************************/

#include "Polynomial.h"
#include <math.h>
#include <algorithm>

void Polynomial::SetCoefficient(double coeff, int expo)
{
  // search for a term with this exponent
  Polynomial::PolyTerm term(coeff, expo);
  list<PolyTerm>::iterator it = find(myList.begin(), myList.end(), term);

  if (it != myList.end())
  // term found
  {
    if (coeff == 0.0)              // term to be removed
      myList.erase(it);
    else                          // change coefficient in term
      (*it).myCoeff = coeff;
    return;
  }

  // no term with this exponent found -- have to insert one

  myList.push_back(term);
  myList.sort();                   // keep terms in order}
}
```

```
double Polynomial::GetCoefficient(int expo)
{
  // search for a term with this exponent
  Polynomial::PolyTerm term(0.0, expo);
  list<Polynomial::PolyTerm>::iterator it =
                    find(myList.begin(), myList.end(), term);

  if (it != myList.end())           // term found, return its coefficient
    return (*it).myCoeff;

  return 0.0;                        // no term found, return 0
}

double Polynomial::Evaluate(double value)
{

  double answer = 0.0;

  for (list<Polynomial::PolyTerm>::iterator it = myList.begin();
                                    it != myList.end(); it++)
    if ((*it) != 0)
      answer += (*it).myCoeff * pow(value, (*it).myExp);
    else
      answer += (*it).myCoeff;

  return answer;
}

Polynomial Polynomial::operator+(Polynomial p)
{
  Polynomial answer = p;

  for (list<Polynomial::PolyTerm>::iterator it = myList.begin();
                                    it != myList.end(); it++)
  {
    double coeff = (*it).myCoeff + p.GetCoefficient((*it).myExp);
    answer.SetCoefficient(coeff, (*it).myExp);
  }

  return answer;
}

Polynomial Polynomial::operator*(Polynomial p)
{
  Polynomial answer;

  int expo;
  double coeff;
  for (list<Polynomial::PolyTerm>::iterator it1 = myList.begin();
                                    it1 != myList.end(); it1++)
    for (list<Polynomial::PolyTerm>::iterator it2 = p.myList.begin();
                                    it2 != p.myList.end(); it2++)
    {
      expo = (*it1).myExp + (*it2).myExp;
      coeff = answer.GetCoefficient(expo) +
              (*it1).myCoeff * (*it2).myCoeff;
      answer.SetCoefficient(coeff, expo);
    }

  return answer;
}
```

```cpp
void Polynomial::Print(ostream & out)
{
  list<Polynomial::PolyTerm>::iterator it = myList.begin();
  if(!myList.empty())
  {
    if ((*it).myExp == 0 ||  ((*it).myCoeff != 1.0 && (*it).myCoeff != -1.0))
      out << (*it).myCoeff;
    if ((*it).myExp >= 1)
      out << 'x';
    if ((*it).myExp >= 2)
      out << '^' << (*it).myExp;
    it++;
  }
  else
  {
    out << '0';
    return;
  }

  while (it != myList.end() )
  {
    out << (((*it).myCoeff < 0.0) ? " - " : " + ");
    if ((*it).myExp == 0 || ((*it).myCoeff != 1 && (*it).myCoeff != -1))
      out << (((*it).myCoeff < 0.0) ? -(*it).myCoeff : (*it).myCoeff);
    if ((*it).myExp >= 1)
      out << 'x';
    if ((*it).myExp >= 2)
      out << '^' << (*it).myExp;
    it++;
  }
}

void Polynomial::Input(istream & in)
{
  int expo;
  double coeff;

  for (;;)
  {
    cout << "\n  Exponent (-1 to stop): ";
    cin >> expo;

    if (expo< 0) break;

    cout << "  Coefficient for x^" << expo<< ": ";
    cin >> coeff;

    (*this).SetCoefficient(coeff, expo);
  }
}


/* prog13-4-6.cpp tests the class Polynomial.
 *
 * Input:  polynomials
 * Output: polynomials
 **************************************************/

#include <iostream.h>
#include "Polynomial.h"
```

```cpp
int main()
{
  Polynomial poly;

  cout << "\nInput the polynomial:";
  cin >> poly;

  cout << "\nThe polynomial you entered is:\n"
       << poly << endl;


  double value;
  char answer;

  do
  {
    cout << "\nValue at which to evaulate the polynomial: ";
    cin >> value;

    cout << "Answer: " << poly.Evaluate(value) << endl;

    cout << "\nEvaluate again (y/n)? ";
    cin >> answer;
  }
  while (answer == 'y' || answer == 'Y');

  cout << "\n\n Now test polynomial operations:\n";

  Polynomial poly1, poly2;

  cout << "\nInput the first polynomial:";
  cin >> poly1;

  cout << "\nInput the second polynomial:";
  cin >> poly2;

  cout << "\nThe first polynomial you entered is:\n" << poly1
       << "\nThe second polynomial you entered is:\n" << poly2
       << "\nThe sum of the two polynomials is:\n" << poly1 + poly2
       << "\nThe product of the two is:\n" << poly1 * poly2
       << endl;

  return 0;
}
```

7. This is a straightforward, albeit lengthy, project. Essentially all that is needed is to overload all the operations from `list<T>` in `OrderedList<T>` that modify the list (except `sort()`) by having each of them call the `sort()` function. For example,

```cpp
#include <list>

template <class T>
class OrderedList : public list<T>
{
 public:
   // . . .
     void push_back(T value);
   // . . .
};
```

```
template<class T>
inline void OrderedList<T>:: push_back(T value)
{
    list<T>::push_back(value);
    sort();
} // . . .
```

8.

// PQueue.h
```
/* This is the file for class template PQueue.
 ***************************************************/

#ifndef PQUEUE
#define PQUEUE

#include <iostream.h>
#include <list>

template <class T>
class PQueue
{
public:

    // Add -- add an element to the queue
    void Add(T item, int priority);

    // Remove -- remove the next element from the queue
    bool Remove(T & data);

    // Print -- output elements to stream
    void Print(ostream & out);

private:

    struct PQElement
    {
        T myData;
        int myPriority;

        PQElement()
        {}

        PQElement(T data, int priority)
        { myData = data; myPriority = priority; }
    };

    list<PQElement> myList;
};


template <class T>
void PQueue<T>::Add(T item, int priority)
{
    PQueue<T>::PQElement value(item, priority);

    if (myList.empty())
    {
        myList.push_back(value);
        return;
    }
```

```
   if (priority > myList.front().myPriority)
   {
     myList.push_front(value);
     return;
   }

  // Search list for place to insert item
    list<PQueue<T>::PQElement>::iterator it = myList.begin();

    for (;;)
    {
       if (it == myList.end())                // end of list
       {
         myList.push_back(value);
         return;
       }

       if (priority > (*it).myPriority)
       {
         myList.insert(it, value);
         return;
       }
       it++;
    }
}

template <class T>
bool PQueue<T>::Remove(T & data)
{
  if (myList.empty())
    return false;

  PQElement item  = myList.front();
  data = item.myData;
  myList.pop_front();
  return true;
}
template <class T>
void PQueue<T>::Print(ostream& out)
{
  for (list<PQueue<T>::PQElement>::iterator it = myList.begin();
                            it != myList.end(); it++)
    out << (*it).myData << endl;
}

#endif


/* prog16-8.cpp tests the class PQueue.
 *
 * Input:  codes for operations to perform and items to add to priority queue
 * Output: results of operation.
 **************************************************************************/

#include <iostream.h>
#include "PQueue.h"

const char HELP_TEXT[] =
  "\nValid Commands:\n"
  "A <entry> <priority> - add an entry\n"
  "R - remove the next item in the queue\n"
  "P - display the items in the queue\n"
```

```
      "H - this help text\n"
      "Q - quit the program\n";

int main()
{
   cout << "This program demonstrates a priority queue.\n";

   PQueue<unsigned> pq;

   unsigned job;
   int priority;

   for (;;)
   {
      char command;

      cout << "\nCommand (H = help): ";
      cin >> command;

      if (command == 'q' || command == 'Q') break;

      switch (command)
      {
         case 'a': case 'A':
                           cin >> job >> priority;
                           pq.Add(job, priority);
                           cout << "Job " << job << " added.\n";
                           break;

         case 'r': case 'R':
                           if (pq.Remove(job))
                              cout << "Job " << job << " removed.\n";
                           else
                              cout << "Priority queue is empty!\n";
                           break;

         case 'p': case 'P':
                           cout << "List of jobs in priority queue:\n";
                           pq.Print(cout);
                           break;

         case 'h': case 'H':
                           cout << HELP_TEXT;
                           break;
         default:
                           cout << "Illegal command -- select one of"
                                << HELP_TEXT;
      }
   }

   return 0;
}
```

9. This is similar to Problem 2. Simply read questions and answers from the file; ask the user each question and
    input an answer; use push_back() to add those that are answered incorrectly to a list of structs containing a
    question and its answer; and when all the questions have been asked, simply traverse this list and ask these
    questions again.

10.
```
/* prog13-10.cpp reads student records, stores them in a vector of sorted
 * lists, one for each class, then displays each list.
 *
 * input(keyboard): name of student file
 * input(file):     the student records
 * output(screen):  lists of student records
 **************************************************************************/

#include <iostream.h>
#include <fstream.h>
#include <string>
#include <list>
#include <vector>

struct StudentRecord
{
    int myNumber;
    string myFirstName, myLastName;
    char myMiddleInit;
    string myCity, myState;
    string myPhoneNumber;
    char myGender;
    int myYear;
    string myMajor;
    int myCredits;
    double myGPA;

    void Print(ostream & out);
    void Read(istream & in);
};

void StudentRecord::Print(ostream & out)
{
    out << "\n#" << myNumber << ' ' << myLastName << ' '
        << myFirstName << ' ' << myMiddleInit << ".\n"
        << myCity << ' ' << myState
        << "\nPhone: " << myPhoneNumber
        << (myGender == 'F' ? "   Female" : "   Male")
        << "   Year: " << myYear
        << "\nMajor: " << myMajor << "   Credits:" << myCredits
        << "   GPA: " << myGPA << endl;
}

void StudentRecord::Read(istream & in)
{
    in >> myNumber >> myLastName >> myFirstName >> myMiddleInit
       >> myCity >> myState
       >> myPhoneNumber >> myGender >> myYear >> myCredits >> myGPA
       >> myMajor;
}

bool operator<(StudentRecord one, StudentRecord two)
{
  return one.myNumber < two.myNumber;
}

int main()
{
    string fileName;
    cout << "Enter name of file containing student records: ";
    cin >> fileName;
```

```
   ifstream inStream (fileName.data());
   if (!inStream.is_open())
   {
      cerr << "Error in opening student file " << fileName << endl;
      exit(1);
   }

   vector< list<StudentRecord> > stuList(5);
   StudentRecord stuRec;
   for (;;)
   {
      stuRec.Read(inStream);
      if (inStream.eof()) break;

      if (stuRec.myYear < 1 || stuRec.myYear > 5)
         cerr << "*** Bad Student Record for " << stuRec.myNumber
              << " ***\n";
      else
         stuList[stuRec.myYear - 1].push_back(stuRec);
   }

   for (int i = 0; i < 5; i++)
   {
      stuList[i].sort();
      cout << "\nList of students for year " << i + 1 << endl;
      for (list<StudentRecord>::iterator it = stuList[i].begin();
                                    it != stuList[i].end(); it++)
        (*it).Print(cout);
      cout << endl << endl;
   }
   return 0;
}
```

11-12.

```
/* prog13-11-12.cpp lists the words and their frequencies of a file.
 *
 * input(keyboard): name of file
 * input(file):     text from the file
 * output(screen):  lists of words and their frequencies
 ************************************************************************/

#include <iostream.h>
#include <fstream.h>
#include <ctype.h>
#include <string>
#include <list>
#include <algorithm>

struct WordInfo
{
  string myWord;
  int myTimes;

  WordInfo(string w = "", int t = 0)
  { myWord = w; myTimes = t; }

};
```

```
bool operator<(WordInfo one, WordInfo two)
{
   return one.myWord < two.myWord;
}

bool operator==(WordInfo one, WordInfo two)
{
   return one.myWord == two.myWord;
}

bool operator!=(WordInfo one, WordInfo two)
{
   return !(one.myWord == two.myWord);
 }

ostream & operator<<(ostream & out, list<WordInfo> l)
{
   for (list<WordInfo>::iterator it = l.begin();
                           it != l.end(); it++)
     out << (*it).myWord << " (" << (*it).myTimes << ")\n";
}


class Concordance
{
public:
   Concordance(int n);
   void Insert(string word);
   friend ostream & operator<<(ostream & out, const Concordance & c);

private:
   list<WordInfo> myWords[27];
};


// Implementations of Concordance operations

Concordance::Concordance(int n)
{ }

void Concordance::Insert(string word)
{
   char firstChar = word[0];
   int index;

   if (isalpha(word[0]))
     index = int(firstChar - 'A' + 1);
   else
     index = 0;

   list<WordInfo>::iterator it =
               find(myWords[index].begin(),
                   myWords[index].end(),
                   WordInfo(word, 0));

   if (it != myWords[index].end())  // word already in concordance
     (*it).myTimes++;
```

```
else
  {
    myWords[index].push_back(WordInfo(word, 1));

    if (myWords[index].size() > 1)
      myWords[index].sort();
  }
}

ostream & operator<<(ostream & out, const Concordance & c)
{
  for (int i = 0; i < 27; i++)
    if (!c.myWords[i].empty())
    {
      if (i == 0)
        out << endl << "Words not beginning with a letter:\n";
      else
        out << endl << char('A' + i - 1) << "-words:\n";

      out << c.myWords[i];
    }

  return out;
}

int main()
{
  string fileName;
  cout << "Enter name of file containing text: ";
  cin >> fileName;
  ifstream inStream (fileName.data());
  if (!inStream.is_open())
  {
    cerr << "Error in opening file " << fileName << endl;
    exit(1);
  }

  Concordance words(27);
  string aWord;

  while (!inStream.eof())
  {
    inStream >> aWord;
    // remove trailing punctuation
    int i = aWord.length() - 1;
    while (!isalpha(aWord[i]))
    {
      aWord = aWord.substr(0, i);
      i--;
    }

    words.Insert(aWord);
  }

  cout << "\nConcordance:\n" << words << endl;

  return 0;
}
```